W9-AYH-183

JOSEPH R. MANCUSO

How to Prepare and Present a Business Plan

Prentice-Hall, Inc., Englewood Cliffs, N.J. 07632

Library of Congress Cataloging in Publication Data

Mancuso, Joseph.
 How to prepare and present a business plan.

 Includes index.
  1. Small business—Finance. 2. Venture capital.
3. Corporate planning. I. Title. II. Title: Business
plan.
HG 4027.7.M35   1983   658.1'522   82-18064
ISBN 0-13-430629-5
ISBN 0-13-430611-2 (pbk.)

Production/editorial supervision: Suse L. Cioffi
Cover design by Jeannette Jacobs
Manufacturing buyer: Cathie Lenard

ISBN 0-13-430611-2 {PBK.}

ISBN 0-13-430629-5

10   9

Printed in the United States of America

CONTENTS

CHAPTER ONE

A BUSINESS PLAN

A document written to raise money for a growing company is known as a *business plan*. The most popular types are written for entrepreneurial companies seeking a private placement of funds from venture capital sources. Internal venture management teams of larger companies also write business plans. Although these venture plans seldom circulate to external private placement sources, they do progress upward within the organization for approval by corporate management.

Modest differences exist between the entrepreneurial plan and internal venture group plan. The major difference rests in the enterprise's risk and reward structure and not in the reading or writing of the document. The objectives of both types of plan are the same—launching a new business or expanding a promising small business. The ultimate responsibility for success or failure in one case rests with an entrepreneur/venture capitalist and in the other with a manager/vice president. But no matter what its origin, the document that consummates the financing is called the business plan. In both cases, the document must be thorough and well done to be successful in securing new capital.

The vast majority of business plans are prepared by entrepreneurs seeking venture capital. New venture groups within large companies are expanding their activities, but they do not approach the number of existing small companies seeking the same goal. As a comparison, there are about 14 million small businesses in the U.S.A. while only several thousand larger companies exist in the country. In addition, start-up companies, which still appear despite current depressed economic conditions, require a special breed of entrepreneurial business plan. This third category of brand new companies is the least common source of business plans.

The term *business plan* is the more formal name for the document; however, many within the financial and legal communities prefer the nickname *deal*. Although the latter is crude and a bit harsh, it does have shock value, which makes it a realistic and descriptive phrase. Some financiers carry this nicknaming one step further and compare the fund raising process to the television program "Let's Make a Deal." In any case, the word *deal*, which embodies the excitement of the chase, becomes *business plan* when the chase is successfully completed.

THE BUSINESS PLAN*

Why should you go to the trouble of creating a written business plan? There are three major reasons.

1. The process of putting a business plan together, including the thought put in before beginning to write it, forces you to take an *objective, critical, unemotional* look at your business project in its entirety.
2. The finished product—your business plan—is an operating tool which, properly used, will help you manage your business and work toward its success.
3. The completed business plan is the means for communicating your ideas to others and provides the basis for your financing proposal.

The importance of planning cannot be overemphasized. By taking an objective look at your business, you can identify areas of weakness and strength, pinpoint needs you might otherwise overlook, spot problems before they arise, and begin planning how you can best achieve your business goals. As an operating tool, your business plan helps you to establish reasonable objectives and figure out how to best accomplish them. It also helps you to red-flag problems as they arise and aids you in identifying their source, thus suggesting ways to solve them. It may even help you avoid some problems altogether.

In order for it to work it is important that *you* do as much of the work as possible. A professionally prepared business plan won't do you any good if you don't understand it thoroughly. This understanding comes from being involved with its development from the very start.

No business plan, no matter how carefully constructed and no matter how thoroughly understood, will be of any use at all unless you use it. Going into business is rough—over half of all new businesses fail within the first two years of operation; over 90 percent fail within the first 10 years. A major reason for failure is lack of planning. The best

*Copyright permission granted by Andy Bangs of Upstart Publishing, Portsmith, NH 03801. Excerpted from the book *The Business Planning Guide*, Osgood and Bangs. Reprinted with permission.

way to enhance your chances of success is to plan and follow through on your planning.

Use your plan. Don't put it in the bottom drawer of your desk and forget it.

Your business plan can help you avoid going into a business venture that is doomed to failure. If your proposed venture is marginal at best, the business plan will show you why and may help you avoid paying the high tuition of business failure. It is far cheaper not to begin an ill-fated business than to learn by experience what your business plan could have taught you at a cost of several hours of concentrated work.

Finally, your business plan provides the information needed by others to evaluate your venture, especially if you will need to seek outside financing. A thorough business plan automatically becomes a complete financing proposal that will meet the requirements of most lenders.

PREPARING A BUSINESS PLAN FOR LENDERS OR INVESTORS*

This is a true story. In the late 1960s a sightless entrepreneur raised two million dollars at luncheon with the partners of one of New York's most prestigious investment banking firms. The purpose was to launch a new company whose objective was to merge computer technology and education to solve social problems. I don't mean the partners of the investment banking firm set off after lunch to raise $2 million. I mean that following the dessert, the entrepreneur left the luncheon with a certified check for two million in his hands. Nothing in the annals of venture capital has happened before or since, so don't hold your breath until it happens again!

The late 1960s were fascinating times on Wall Street. Venture capital could be raised for any purpose via a public offering. The stock price of any new company from 1967 to mid-1969 went up. One prospectus from that era described the background of a man and his wife, each about 23 years of age, who intended to use the proceeds of the public offering to identify and promote a new business. The prospectus, or business plan, provided no more information than that. The public poured millions of dollars into small underwritings to launch companies whose names they did not know. Little or no due diligence was performed by the brokerage firms that were underwriting these new issues. Today, when most of the new companies of the late 1960s and

*Reprinted with permission from A. David Silver, *Preparing a Business Plan for Lenders or Investors,* published by the Competere Group, New York, New York, 1979.

their underwriters are out of business and the public is reluctant to return to a stock market that cost so dearly, the process of launching a new company is considerably different.

As the 1960s passed into the early 1970s, private venture capital firms became the primary source of start-up and expansion capital. The new issue public market was laid to rest. For example, in 1974, the only new issue I can remember was that of a small firm whose business was liquidating brokerage firms. Between 1975 and 1976 there were a handful of new issues and in 1977 and 1978 perhaps twenty. The few private venture capitalists, beaten about their wallets by the stock market's decline, began to demand substantially more information from entrepreneurs about their objectives, the costs of achieving those objectives and myriad other details. In addition, someone had to take the blame for the huge portfolio losses. Rather than blaming themselves for their Koros, Ubris, and Ate', as would the good Spartans carrying their dead on their shields, the venture capitalists of the early 1970s pinned the blame on the entrepreneurs. They told them, in effect: "I'll finance your company, but I have to own most of the stock and I must have voting control of the board." This did not encourage new company formation, although a few interesting enterprises were launched between 1973–1975, which will be discussed later. The primary effect of this attitude was to reduce the number of new companies launched in the early 1970s, shrink the number of venture capitalists, and usher in competitive government programs to assist in new company formation. For specifics, see *Everything You Need to Know about Raising Money for a New Business,* by A. David Silver and published by The Competere Group, New York, New York, 1979.

The venture capital industry is new, immature, and seemingly in perpetual transition. This industry is constantly trying to grasp and absorb the various changes that affect it. Entrepreneurs are not aware of this. All too frequently entrepreneurs think that a venture capitalist is J.P. Morgan or Jacob Schiff reincarnate: very wealthy, ultra-conservative and poised to press a buzzer under the desk that will call in a runner with the bags of cash to pour on the table for the entrepreneur to scoop up. Not true! Venture capitalists are intelligent young men and women seeking to simultaneously recommend to their investment committees the next Syntex, Polaroid, or Xerox and prevent erosion of capital in their fund through portfolio demise. Therefore, when an entrepreneur and a venture capitalist meet, the entrepreneur should bear in mind the following ideas.

    a. The venture capitalist wishes that the information he or she is given by the entrepreneur is true.

    b. The venture capitalist, if sold, must resell the idea to his or her investment committee and must be given the facts with which to do so.

  c. The venture capitalist has twenty other situations on his or her desk each competing for time and attention.

  d. Venture capitalists make judgments about a new company's projections based on their recollection of past projections, both realized and unrealized.

The latter is a process similar to the description in Plato's *Republic* of the artisans in the cave chained in place all day staring at shadows. They are not permitted to turn around and see the shadowcaster; they can only stare straight ahead at the shadow. But they must form judgments about the shadowcasters based on the shadows.

Similarly, venture capitalists literally stare at projections all day, unable to see the actual future operating statement numbers. If the projections remind the venture capitalist of the sales and earnings trend to Intel, City Investing, or Teledyne, he or she will be inclined to dig into the deal. If they evoke memories of Stirling Homex or Viatron, the venture capitalist will not be so inclined.

The uncertainty surrounding the entrepreneur is the ability to realize the projections. He or she may be merely a good projection maker and a lousy accomplisher. The venture capitalist does not know which. Herein lies a duel: The venture capitalist tries to attack the business assumptions on which the projections are based to determine their credibility, *i.e.,* the ability of the entrepreneur to make the projections come true. The entrepreneur jabs with upside potential. The venture capitalist counters with downside risk. The projections are dissected to their most minute ratio to try to see if the business plan has credibility. The battle lasts on into the night for day after day, until finally the seller and buyer become joined in their enthusiasm for the new business and have but to agree on a price in order to complete the funding.

This all sounds a bit romanticized, and yet there is no denying that raising money is a battle in the war called Wealth. It is but an early battle in a three to five year war and the entrepreneur has far less experience in fighting it than the venture capitalist. Knowing how to prepare a credible business plan helps put the two on an equal footing.

CHAPTER TWO

The Five Minute Reader

Business plans are comprehensive documents that often require several months to compile. Although they vary in length and complexity, the process of writing them requires the coordination of external legal, financial, and accounting assistance. In addition, the internal analysis of manufacturing, finance, and marketing must coincide with the external activities; this coordination adds to the time required for a preparation. Spending $2,000 to $20,000 for outside services to prepare a business plan is typical. The preparer intuitively believes that the plan's thoroughness and sophistication reflect on the enterprise's likelihood of success. Consequently, there is a tendency to do the plan well and sometimes to do it and redo it.

Despite all this care during the preparation, most business plans are not read in detail from cover to cover. Although five weeks may have been required to compile it, potential investors will initially invest only *five minutes* in reading it. A venture capitalist who receives a dozen plans a day—hundreds annually—simply does not have enough time to read through each one. In fact, a leading venture capitalist at a large Boston bank claims he never reads any plan. "They all say the same thing and it's never true," he comments, "so I never read them."

In spite of this, you should not conclude that a business plan is unnecessary; it is essential to raising new money for internal or external entrepreneurs. The business person without a plan will be immediately conspicuous and will be turned away by a venture capitalist. The fact of financial life is unlikely to change, even though the plan may not be read initially, the entrepreneur must write one, if for no other reason than to prove that he eventually can do it. It will be read from cover to cover if you are successful in writing it.

Multiple exposures are often given to a single business plan, one of the reasons hundreds of deals arrive at a single venture capitalist's office. An entrepreneur in dire need of funds will often mail the plan to a long list of venture capitalists. Such lists are available from several sources. This multiple exposure, frequently described as "shopping the deal," often seriously weakens rather than improves the chances of raising the needed capital. On the other hand, not showing the plan to anyone assures failure. A thin line exists between exposure to too few or too many potential investors. Incidentally, the Security Exchange Commission (SEC) frowns on exposing a deal to more than thirty-five potential investors. This issue is in constant flux; first you must comply with the federal government's regulations for an offering, and secondly you must comply with each state's so-called blue sky offering laws. Just as you'd guess, these two regulatory bodies (state and federal government) don't always have common laws. For instance, in Massachusetts, a deal can only be shown to 25 potential investors while the federal limit is 100 potential investors. Hence, both rules must be observed. Also, these rules vary depending upon the amount of money you seek. Lately, it's been significantly more attractive to raise less than $100,000 within any consecutive twelve-month period to avoid costly registration problems. Check with your lawyer on this issue as the guidelines are constantly changing.

GOING PUBLIC

If you're thinking of taking your company public while the window is still wide open, you'll have to comply with both federal and state securities laws, as well as investing considerable time and money to make it happen. The chart below highlights some of your options.

An excellent booklet, *A Businessman's Guide to Capital-Raising Under the Securities Laws*, by Michael M. Coleman and Irving P. Seldin, offers a valuable appendix dealing with the new and popular Regulation D and Form S-18. This booklet is available from Packard Press, 1528 Walnut St., Suite 2020, Philadelphia, PA 19102; (215) 236-2000.

EQUITY CAPITAL RAISED BY COMPANIES WITH A NET WORTH OF UNDER $5M

Year	Number of Offerings	Millions of Current $
1968	358	745.3
1969	698	1,366.9
1970	198	375.0
1971	248	550.9
1972	409	896.0
1973	69	159.7
1974	9	16.1
1975	4	16.2
1976	29	144.8
1977	13	42.6
1978	21	89.3
1979	81	506.5
1980	237	1,401.0
1981	306	1,760.0
1982	112	617.0

THE TWO MOST COMMON EXEMPTIONS FROM REGISTRATION OF SECURITIES ACT OF 1933

Requirements in General	Less than $1,000 in any rolling 12 month period Rule 240 (§3(b))			Sophisticated investors Rule 146 (§4(2))	
	Rule 504	Rule 505	Rule 506	Section 4(2)*
Limitation on Amount Sold	$500,000	$5,000,000	None	None
Limitation of No. of Offerees	No Limit	No Limit	No Limit	No specific numerical limit, but cannot rise to level of public offering
Limitation on No. of Purchasers	No Limit	35 non-accredited purchasers. Unlimited number of accredited purchasers	35 non-accredited purchasers. Unlimited number of accredited purchasers	No specific numerical limit, but cannot rise to level of public offering
Qualifications for Purchasers or Offerees	None	None	All non-accredited purchasers must be sophisticated	All offerees and purchasers must be sophisticated and/or must be able to bear the economic risk

*There is considerable uncertainty concerning the precise factors requisite to the availability of the Section 4(2) exemption, and there are numerous, sometimes conflicting, court decisions interpreting that exemption. Accordingly, the factors specified in this column of the table should be viewed with some caution.

THE TWO MOST COMMON EXEMPTIONS FROM REGISTRATION OF SECURITIES ACT OF 1933 (cont.)

Requirements in General	Less than $1,000 in any rolling 12 month period Rule 240 (§3(b))		Sophisticated investors Rule 146 (§4(2))	
Prohibition on Advertising and General Solicitation	Yes, except for certain state-registered offerings	Yes	Yes	Yes
Mandatory Disclosure	None specified	None specified if all investors accredited. If non-accredited investors, disclosure requirements vary.	None specified if all investors accredited. If non-accredited investors, disclosure requirements vary.	None specified, but must furnish or make available same kind of information as registration would provide
Financial Statement Requirements	None specified	Yes, but requirements vary	Yes, but requirements vary	None specified, but see box immediately above
Limitations on Issuer	Not available to 1934 Act reporting companies or investment companies	Not available to investment companies or issuers disqualified under certain provisions of Reg. A.	None	None
1934 Act Reporting Obligations Triggered	Not unless 500 or more shareholders and $3,000,000 or more in total assets	Not unless 500 or more shareholders and $3,000,000 or more in total assets	Not unless 500 or more shareholders and $3,000,000 or more in total assets	Not unless 500 or more shareholders and $3,000,000 or more in total assets
SEC Filings	Yes, Notices	Yes, Notices	Yes, Notices	No
Resale Restrictions	Yes, except for certain state-registered offerings	Yes	Yes	Yes

THE TWO MOST COMMON EXEMPTIONS FROM REGISTRATION OF SECURITIES ACT OF 1933

Requirements in General	Less than $1,000 in any rolling 12 month period Rule 240 (§3(b))	Sophisticated investors Rule 146 (§4(2))

TABLE OF CERTAIN FEDERAL SECURITIES OFFERING ALTERNATIVES

	Section 4(6)	Rule 147	Reg. A	Form S-18
	$5,000,000	None	$1,500,000	$5,000,000
	No Limit	No Limit	No Limit	No Limit
	No Limit	No Limit	No Limit	No Limit
	All purchasers must be accredited investors	All offerees and purchasers must be residents of single state	None	None
	Yes	No	No	No

THE TWO MOST COMMON EXEMPTIONS FROM REGISTRATION OF SECURITIES ACT OF 1933 (cont.)

Requirements in General		Less than $1,000 in any rolling 12 month period Rule 240 (§3(b))	Sophisticated investors Rule 146 (§4(2))
None Specified	None Specified	Yes	Yes
None	Must be organized and doing business in state where securities offered and sold	Unaudited financial statements for two fiscal years	Audited financial statements for two fiscal years
		Unavailable for sale of oil or gas or mineral rights and to investment companies	Unavailable to investment companies, insurance companies and 1934 Act reporting companies
Not unless 500 or more shareholders and $3,000,000 or more in total assets	Not unless 500 or more shareholders and $3,000,000 or more in total assets	Not unless 500 or more shareholders and $3,000,000 or more in total assets	Yes, but reporting obligations reduced for first year
Yes, Notices	No	Yes, Offering Statement	Yes, Registration Statement
Yes	Yes, Out-of-state re-sales prohibited for nine months.	No	No

WRITING FOR A FIVE MINUTE READER

The primary problem in writing a business plan is making it comprehensive and shaping it for the reader for whom it is intended—the prospective investor with five minutes to read it. The entrepreneur should accept the inevitable: A potential investor will initially invest only five minutes to read a plan; therefore, the plan should be adapted to this time span.

Many authors concerned with the writing of business plans focus on checklists, blank sample forms, and tables of contents. As guides, they help catch items that might be overlooked because they force a full and balanced consideration of the many intertwined issues. In the appendices of this book are a number of actual table of contents of business plans as well as an actual business plan that secured bank debt for a solar industries business in New Hampshire. Excerpts of a business plan or a table of contents from a typical plan or a checklist can be useful guides and are strongly encouraged.

A central message of how-to-write-a-plan advice is that you should tailor the document to meet the needs and desires of the potential investors. This sound advice does not mean that you should exaggerate, lie, or inflate the sales projections. It does mean that you should emphasize items of special interest for a specific potential investor. In some cases, a business plan is written in modular form, the appropriate modules being combined to appeal to the characteristics of the investor. A single plan rarely suffices for all possible uses. However, every plan eventually has its moment and is given a once-over lightly.

Insight into what happens to a plan when it finally reaches the top of the pile is scarce. What happens during the five minutes the venture capitalist examines the plan? How is it read? How is it analyzed? An understanding of the reading and interpretation process may help to direct the writing style and the focus of the plan. On the basis of field research involving several dozen venture capitalists and several hundred entrepreneurs, I have concluded that all knowledgeable investors use the precious five minutes of reading time in about the same way.

CHAPTER THREE

HOW A BUSINESS PLAN IS READ

In order to determine how a business plan is analyzed, I conducted in-depth interviews over the past three years with two dozen venture capitalists and twice as many others (including bankers, lawyers, accountants, and consultants) in the financial community. The reading process is naturally a private affair between the company and the money source. Each source prides itself in the sophistication it has developed for analyzing investment opportunities. I spent several days actually observing several venture sources; and, as an investor in several entrepreneurial companies, I have read hundreds of business plans.

Almost everyone, the study revealed, analyzed the plans in the same way; the initial five minute reading is a good average if all the plans that are never read are excluded. The following steps are typical of the reading process (less than a minute is invested in each step):

Step 1. Determine the characteristics of company and industry.
Step 2. Determine the terms of the deal.
Step 3. Read the latest balance sheet.
Step 4. Determine the caliber of the people in the deal.
Step 5. Determine what is different about this deal.
Step 6. Give the plan a once-over lightly.

Determine the Characteristics of Company and Industry

Each venture capitalist has preferred areas for investment. Some like high technology and others like low technology; some others computers; others like consumer goods; and still others prefer publishing. A single venture capitalist is seldom at ease in every industry, just as a single entrepreneur cannot manage with equal skill in diverse industries. The venture capitalist's area of expertise is developed over the years and is based upon past successes; success in a particular industry will cause him to be receptive to deals in the same industry. Consequently, many of the potential investors may never read a business plan beyond Step 1, regardless of the terms of the deal, if they have little interest in the industry.

Consequently, it is well worth your time to be careful in selecting the venture capitalist who will read and analyze your plan. Several good venture capital guidebooks exist that not only identify venture capital sources but highlight their industry preferences. These are listed in the appendix.

Every potential investor also factors the current glamour of the specific industry into the analysis. Are there any larger publicly traded companies in the same industry? If so, how high is the stock price earning multiple (P/E ratio) of these firms? Or, better yet, is there a larger company that is extremely successful in this industry? How well has it done? Companies find it easier to raise funds when another company has pioneered successfully. For example, in the computer industry the Data General Corporation could point to Digital Equipment Corporation; in the consumer goods industry, many smaller companies have pointed to Avon Products or Alberto-Culver. A specialty chemical company that eventually failed, Lanewood Laboratories, Inc., raised $500,000 based a business plan that pointed to Lestoil. The B.L.T. Company in the appendix, the carwash gas station, successfully raised over $1,000,000 just after Robo-Wash went public with an initial offering. However, B.L.T. went bellyflop in less than 2 years.

Industry glamour rises and falls much like the length of women's skirts. Ten years ago, the glamour field was electronics, followed by franchising, and then by computers. Currently, the glamour field is energy, and tomorrow it will be genetic engineering. Despite the obvious problems with financial fads, everyone accepts them as a reality. They exist and they do make a difference; if one's industry is momentarily glamourous, one's chances of securing funds suddenly increase.

The reason for the glamour is important. Investors must hope to get out of their investments eventually. They must become liquid again to be able to invest in the next business, as that is their business. So, determining the salability (glamour) of an industry before investing is crucial. Otherwise, no other financial source will buy out their investments and they will be locked into a business.

After the potential investor examines and evaluates the industry, he or she will quickly categorize the company within the industry. The potential investor will determine the following six facts about the company.

1. annual sales for the past twelve months
2. profit or loss for last year
3. number of employees
4. share of market
5. degree of technology
6. geographic location of facilities

The fundamental value of carefully highlighting these items in a front page summary of the business plan is that it saves time.

Depending upon his or her interpretation of these facts, the investor will soon be able to determine whether the company matches the venture capitalist's profile of an ideal investment. Is it too large or small? Is it too far away? There are numerous acceptable reasons for not making the investment. Seldom, if ever, is a venture capitalist faulted for the investments not made. More often and more intense is the criticism of the investments he or she actually selected. The sequence in Step 1 is first to check the industry and then to check the company.

Determine the Terms of the Deal

How much of a company is being "sold for what price" are the terms of the deal. The peripheral issue is the form (debt or equity) of the deal being offered. Many venture firms strongly prefer convertible debt (or debt with warrants) to a straight equity deal. Their profit-seeking structure may require the venture firm to generate annual income to pay current overhead, in addition to the capital gains expected from the capital portfolio. Naturally, these firms would prefer interest-bearing debt to help cover this overhead, and a few of them will discourage deals that do not satisfy this basic requirement. In these cases, form is not a peripheral issue; but in the majority of cases the more substantive issue of "how much for how much" is of more concern.

Accordingly, a well-done business plan informs the reader of the following financial items on the first page. Other items should also be included in this summary, such as number of employees, geographic location, types of products, annual sales, and profits.

A. Percentage of company being sold (after dilution)
B. The total price for this percentage of the company (per share figures also included)
C. The minimum investment (number of investors sought)
D. The total valuation (after the placement) being placed on the company

E. The terms of the investment
   1. Common stock
   2. Preferred stock
   3. Debt with warrants
   4. Convertible debentures
   5. Subordinated convertible debt
   6. Straight debt

Following is a more complete explanation of these last six terms.

1. *Common stock:* Common stock is the term used to describe the documents that represent the value on the books of the business. When the funds are initially put into a company, common stock is known as capital stock. These certificates of common stock describe the ownership of the company.

2. *Preferred stock:* This is a special category of stock which, in some ways, is preferred or treated better than simple common stock. Most of the time, preferred stock has certain advantages, such as guaranteed dividends or prior rights in a liquidation, and it is a separate category above common stock.

3. *Debt with warrants:* The debt of a company is simply an obligation to repay a certain amount of money over a certain period of time at an agreed-upon rate. In the simplest terms, it's a loan. Some loans are risky, and a high interest rate is not enough to make the loan financially attractive. Hence, stock warrants are attached to the debt to sweeten the attractiveness of the investment. Warrants are the right or privilege to buy shares of common stock at a fixed price within a specified time period. If the price of the common stock rose above the predetermined stock warrant price within the time period, the holder of the warrant could opt to exercise the warrant. If, for instance, the warrant was at $3.00 per share and the stock was trading at $5.00 per share, a holder of 1,000 warrants could buy stock from the company for $3,000 and supposedly resell the same stock for $5,000, less appropriate commissions. Hence, a warrant is like a stock option and it has some value. The value is only realized after the warrants are exercised and the stock is sold.

A classical example of a debt with warrants type of investment occurred in the mid-1960s. Fred Fideli of the Worcester-based firm, State Mutual Life Assurance Company, traveled to Chicago in order to evaluate a growing chain of hamburger stands. Although only 100 units were operating at this time, after personally visiting about 75 of the chains, Fideli offered a loan of $750,000 with an interest rate of $7\frac{1}{2}\%$ to this business now headed up by the famous entrepreneur, Ray Kroc. In addition, to sweeten the financial attractiveness of this loan, Fideli obtained warrants to purchase 10% of the common stock of the chain.

About ten years later, State Mutual had received full payment for its loan, exercised the warrants on the company, and sold the stock in the public market. Rumor has it that this conservative life insurance company realized about $12,000,000 in turn for making this loan. The McDonald's Corporation was the most successful of all of State Mutual's investments.

4. *Convertible debentures:* A debenture is a loan and it is a type of debt. The convertible feature allows the debt holder to choose whether or not to convert the remaining outstanding debt into stock. For instance, a five year note for $500,000 at 10% simple annual interest, payable monthly, is a form of debt. The convertible feature would add the possibility that the note holder could convert any remaining debt into common stock at a specific price. Consequently, when and if it becomes attractive, a note holder could trade in the remainder of the debt for common stock at a predetermined price. The difference between this technique and debt with warrants is simple. Under convertible debts, the note holder might not retrieve all the loan before purchasing the stock. In the case of debt with warrants, all of the debts must be repaid and, in addition, the note holder is given warrants which he may or may not exercise. Consequently, most venture capitalists prefer a debt with warrants rather than convertible debt.

5. *Subordinated convertible debt:* This is a special class of debt. The adjective *subordinated* refers to the ranking in event of liquidation of this debt as compared to other forms of debt. Subordinated debt is usually senior to any equity but subordinated to any other debt, especially bank borrowing. In case of bankruptcy or liquidation, subordinated debt is paid after all other debts, usually including trade payables, are satisfied. The stockholders are traditionally the only group of investors with lower priority than holders of subordinated debts. The convertible feature remains the same as described in 4 above. The difference between 4, convertible debenture, and 5, subordinated convertible debentures, is only that 5, subordinated convertible debentures, is also subordinated to other debt.

Following is a common possible ranking of rights in a bankruptcy.

1. certain IRS liens
2. secured creditors
3. unsecured creditors (trade payables)
4. subordinated debt
5. stockholders

6. *Straight debt:* This is simply a loan or debenture. An obligation to

pay back an amount of borrowed funds at an agreed-upon rate over an agreed-upon time period. There are two basic forms of straight debt: secured and unsecured. Secured debt is further backed up by an asset that is pledged to guarantee the payment of the debt. In the event of default, the secured lender would seize the pledged asset to recover the outstanding debt. A house mortgage is a good example of secured debt. Any debt without an asset pledged as collateral is considered unsecured debt.

This information is most helpful if it is presented both clearly and quickly to the potential investor. There is a considerable amount of detail and intracacies in every business plan and the terms mentioned only cover a few points of interest.

Unfortunately, many deals do not spell out these financial details plainly. The short time invested by a venture capitalist in looking over the plan is spent in digging out these pieces of needed information. If they were clearly stated at the beginning, potential investors could spend more time analyzing the plan's more positive selling features (such as the product literature). A summary sheet saves everyone's time and increases an interested reader's enthusiasm.

Finally, after the terms are known, the follow-up analysis focuses on these related issues; depending upon the specifics, the following may also be included in the summary.

How does the price per share of this placement compare with the founder's price per share?

Are the founders reinvesting in this placement?

What was the value of the company at the last placement and why has it changed?

How will the new funds be used, and, more specifically, will they be used to repay old debts or to undertake new activities that, in turn, will increase profitably?

Read the Latest Balance Sheet

A current balance sheet is usually located at the end of the written business plan, just before the appendix and future estimates of (*pro forma*) cash flow and income statements. The most current balance sheet is often the first page of the financial exhibits; and often it is also the ONLY financial page glanced at during an initial reading of a business plan. This historical document exposes the company's history, whereas most other financial documents in the appendix describe the company's future hopes.

Much preferred to any pro forma analysis is a one-minute process for interpreting the balance sheet and income statement. (Merrill, Lynch, Pierce, Fenner & Smith publishes a free twenty-four page brochure, *How to Read a Financial Report,* which contains greater detail on the same subject. Call any of their local offices to receive this free brochure.) The following four-step process, which is used to read a balance sheet from the top down, offers most of the financial information needed to make a quick evaluation of the deal.

A—Determine liquidity
B—Determine debt/equity structure
C—Examine net worth
D—Examine assets and liabilities

A—DETERMINE LIQUIDITY

Check working capital or current ratio, each of which measures about the same thing. Working capital is equal to current assets minus current liabilities, while the current ratio is current assets divided by current liabilities. Below is a typical balance sheet illustrating these relationships.

Cash	$ 50,000
Accounts Receivable	200,000
Inventories	+ 250,000
Total Current Assets	$500,000
Accounts payable	$250,000
Notes payable (within one year)	75,000
Accrued expenses payable	100,000
Federal income tax payable	+ 25,000
Total Current Liabilities	$450,000

Working Capital=$50,000 ($500,000−$450,000)
Current ratio = 1.1 ($500,000/$450,000)

A firm's working capital should be positive while the current ratio should be greater than 1 (those two statements say the same thing in different words). A current ratio closer to 2 indicates a more financially stable company. A company with less than a positive $100,000 of working capital will be tight on cash. A quick check will determine the firm's payroll; and then relating payroll to cash (or working capital) will place the firm's needs for cash in a better perspective. For instance, if the firm above needs $100,000 per month for payroll, its cash is only two weeks of payroll and its working capital is only half a month of payroll. This analysis indicates the firm's need for cash, and is a fair indication of how well they are doing.

B—DETERMINE LONG TERM DEBT/EQUITY STRUCTURE

It is important to remember that the debt/equity ratio is equal to total debt divided by total equity. The ratio reveals how much credit a debt source (such as a bank) has already extended to the company. In addition, it offers insight into the remaining borrowing power of the company. A 400 percent debt/equity ratio, where a lender advances three dollars for every equity dollar, is a ballpark upper limit for this ratio. Seldom will debt sources advance three long term debt dollars for every equity dollar in a small company. Consequently a debt/equity ratio of 3:1 is rare, while a ratio of 1:1 usually indicates the company has some borrowing power remaining.

The numerator usually consists of long term debt, such as bonds or mortgages, and never includes current liabilities (due within one year), such as accounts payable. The denominator is tangible net worth or owner s equity at the time of the placement. This is not to be confused with the initial investment of the owners, which may have been made some time ago. Many times, small companies have unusually high (larger than one) debt equity ratios. This often indicates that outside assets other than those on the company's balance sheet are securing the debt. A wealthy owner may have countersigned the bank note or pledged an asset in order to obtain more debt. The debt/equity ratio often uncovers this discrepancy. In the following example, the debt/equity ratio is ⅔.

C—EXAMINE NET WORTH

The potential investor extracts from the balance sheet the amount of money initially invested in the firm, which is the initial capitalization provided by the founders. The cumulative profits (or loses) that are contained within retained earnings offer another benchmark of the company's success to date. These two items added together algebraically determine a company's current net worth. Below is a typical balance sheet:

Long term debt (current portion that is due this year is shown under current liabilities)	$100,000	Line 1
Capital stock (initial capitalization)	+ 250,000	Line 2
Retained earnings (profit or loss to date)	(100,000)	Line 3
*Owner's equity (combines capitalization and retained earnings)	150,000	Line 4

*Owners equity is what is initially put in to start the company plus or minus the earnings to date which is equal to Line 2 + Line 3.

$$\frac{\text{Line 1}}{\text{Line 2} \pm \text{Line 3}} = \frac{\text{Debt}}{\text{Equity}} = \frac{\$100}{\$150} = .667 = \text{⅔}$$

A prospective investor interprets this information by noting that the founders began the company with $250,000 and that they have lost $100,000 since its inception. The company has a long term interest-bearing note that was probably awarded when the company was founded and was based upon the initial capital of $250,000. A further check to determine what, if anything, is offered as security for the long term debt would follow by examining the footnotes to the balance sheet. However, due to the losses to date, the company probably has little remaining borrowing power. The investor will make a quick check to determine which assets (accounts receivable, inventory, and fixed assets) are pledged to secure any of the debt. Free and unencumbered assets would indicate more borrowing power.

Remember the debt to worth ratio is only one factor to consider in determining a business's borrowing power. There are three other issues of concern to any lending source. First and foremost, is the ability to repay the loan. This vital element is a function of the two other variables mentioned: (a) the strength of any personal endorsements and (b) the profitability of a business enterprise.

As a rule of thumb, a debt source will allow the following amounts of debt shown in column 2 to be secured against the assets shown in column 1.

COLUMN 1 Asset As It Appears on Balance Sheet	COLUMN 2 Percentage of Balance Sheet Value Which Can Be Borrowed Against
Cash or marketable securities	100%
Accounts receivable	75–85% of those under 90 days
Inventory....................	20–30% (Percentage will depend upon market value, not on book value)
Fixed assets	75% (Percent will depend on market value, not on book value)

D—EXAMINE ASSETS AND LIABILITIES

A potential investor will quickly check to be sure all assets are real (tangible); and then he or she will check liabilities to verify that debt is owed to outsiders, not to insiders (such as notes to stockholders). This determination also hinges on the reputation of the accounting firm that prepared the financial statement. An unaudited, company-generated financial statement is seldom even interpreted, since the investor needs some independent assurances that the financial reporting is accurate. Without this assurance, investors will undoubtedly pass over the deal, at least at the initial reading.

By examining the asset categories, investors check to be sure soft assets (such as good will, patents, or trade secrets, formulas or capitalized research and development) are not large or unreasonable. For some unexplained reasons, small companies often choose to capitalize research and development (R & D) or organizational expenses rather than write off these expenses during the period in which they occur. This practice is frowned upon by all potential investors because it distorts the balance sheet, impairs future earnings, and is a sure sign of danger. If this "asset" is large, it can dampen an investor's interest. Furthermore, entrepreneurs and friends and relatives of entrepreneurs often choose to make their initial investment in small companies as debt rather than equity. This makes these founders feel more secure because it offers some protection in the event of·bankruptcy. By making a quick check, a potential investor uncovers the identity of the company's creditors and the amount of debt.

This four-step process (A through D) usually takes less than one minute of reading time from beginning to end. In the initial reading of the business plan, potential investors are not probing the balance sheet in depth but are searching for red flags. Before an investment is consummated, the balance sheet, income statement, and pro formas will be analyzed in considerable detail. However, during the first glance, the balance sheet analysis and a quick look to determine the magnitude of last year's sales from the profit-and-loss statement are the extent of the financial investigation. The balance sheet, along with a magnitude of sales, provides sufficient data to judge whether or not a more detailed financial investigation is warranted.

Determining the Caliber of the People in the Deal

This step, most venture capitalists claim, is the single most important aspect of the business plan. A potential investor begins by examining the founders, board of directors, current investors, outside professionals (accountants, lawyers, bankers, consultants, directors) in hopes of uncovering a familiar name. The reputation and "quality" of the team are the issues in this measure. Unfortunately, this is a subjective area, and, as such, is open to a wide range of individual interpretations; what is good to some is not so good to others. Because it is subjective, opinions and assessments fluctuate dramatically.

Potential investors usually know someone associated with the company (at least they will know someone who knows someone), and this person will set the tone for the whole deal, regardless of his affiliations with the company. Even if he is only a small investor, the company loses its identity and the business plan becomes known as "John Smith's deal" around the office. These known insiders become the links for further information sought by the potential investors.

Consequently, the reputation of *all* the individuals surrounding the business is of serious concern in securing additional funds. For start-up deals or for situations where the company is unknown to the potential investors, a number of questions are asked in order to determine management's abilities. This format is about the same for both internal and external businesses. However, internal venture teams are greatly assisted when the project directors are highly regarded by corporate management. Many times this *golden boy syndrome* becomes the crucial variable in approving new corporate funds. Here are the issues.

What is the track record of founders and managers, including where they worked and how well they performed in the past? Without a doubt, this is the single most significant ingredient when assessing management's abilities.

How much balance and experience does the inner management team possess? How long have the members worked together, and what is the degree of balance among marketing, finance, and manufacturing represented by the operating managers?

Who, is the financial man (or bank or accountant), and what are his credentials? Potential investors much prefer a deal with one strong full-time financial type. He speaks their language and is more at home with money than products. Potential investors like to envision this financial type as a caretaker for any newly arrived funds.

Determine What is Different About This Deal

This difference is the eventual pivotal issue on whether or not a specific venture capital firm chooses to invest. The same holds true for obtaining headquarters approval for internal venture management teams in larger companies.

Is there an unusual feature in the product? Does the company have a patent, an unusual technology, or a significant lead over competition? Is this a company whose critical skill rests in marketing, manufacturing, or finance? Does the company's strength match the skills needed to succeed in this industry? Or is there an imbalance? What is different about this company, and how much better is its product? The answers to these questions are the investor's chief concerns.

Does the company have the potential to open up a whole new industry, such as Polaroid, Xerox, IBM, Digital Equipment Corporation, McDonald's, or Hewlett-Packard did? Or is this a modest idea with limited future growth? A venture capitalist needs a return of greater than ten times his or her investment just to stay even (one in ten succeed). He or she is seldom intrigued with companies that hold a marginal advantage over competing firms or products. In essence, this is what Rooser Reeves has called the Unique Selling Proposition (U.S.P.)! Good ideas or products that are better than others attract capital. Marginal improvements do not possess enough potential to offset the risks inherent in a new business venture.

Give the Plan a Once-Over Lightly

After this analysis, the final minute is usually spent thumbing through the business plan. A casual look at product literature, graphs, unusual exhibits, samples, letters of recommendation, and letters of intent is the purpose of this last check. Seldom, if ever, are new opinions formed during the final minute. However, the fact that everyone engages in this leafing through process supports the argument for unusual enclosures. A product pasted on a page, a letter with a meaningful letterhead, or an unusual chart or two can be helpful in maintaining interest. Although enclosures will not make the big difference in the final analysis, an eye-catching enclosure can extend the readership of a business plan.

After this final step, the analysis is over and the investors decide whether to obtain more information or to return the plan. Ninety-nine times out of a hundred, the deal is turned down. A few investors make phone calls at this stage, and then reject the deal after a detail or two is confirmed. But it is important to remember that deals are actually turned down during the first reading even though the act of formal rejections is postponed a few additional days.

CHAPTER FOUR

THE PLAN PACKAGE

Most entrepreneurs assume that a positive relationship exists between time invested in reading the plan and the likelihood of obtaining capital. "If they would only read my plan," mumbles the unsuccessful entrepreneur, "they would be chasing me instead of vice versa." With this goal in mind, and assuming that the product is only as good as the package, business plans are often dressed in their Sunday best, in leatherbound jackets sometimes costing over ten dollars each.

In research with several dozen venture capitalists, I conducted some small tests to determine the method used to select a single business plan from a group of five to ten. Several deals were randomly placed on a table and the investors were asked to examine only the covers of the business plans before selecting which of the half dozen plans they would read first. The plans that received the most initial attention were not the ones with pretty covers; instead the company name was more crucial. Next in importance was the geographical location of the company. The third element was the thickness of the plan; the shorter plans received more attention.

In these tests, nothing else was revealed about any of the business plans other than what appeared on the cover. The position of the deals on the tables was random, and I observed each venture capitalist as he or she glanced over the deals. To conclude, I have ranked the variables in descending order of importance.

1. company name,
2. its geographic location,
3. length of business plan, and
4. quality of cover.

The next question I explored was, "How can an entrepreneur increase the likelihood that a capitalist will read a business plan once past the cover?" Should the entrepreneur send it along in installments with the final chapter first, or should he or she send along a summary? In my research, I concluded that summaries and "miniplans" are not effective documents. A teaser summary that is not an integral part of the plan only delays the eventual reading of the entire plan, and the teaser is often vague or incomplete. It is much better to have the entire document available to each and every potential investor and highlight the plan with a succinct and informative summary page as the first page of the business plan.

Two additional variables were uncovered that help to determine a plan's eventual reading, and, to a lesser extent, the likelihood that a venture capitalist will make an investment. The first is the method of dispatching the plan. The second is the *preselling*, which precedes the plan. Months may be spent preparing the plan, but only a few minutes are spent deciding how to deliver it. The naive entrepreneur follows the suicidal path of a blind mass mailing. Armed with a directory and helped by a secretary, the plan is mailed with a form letter to a sampling from the directory. This wastes everyone's time and the entrepreneur's money, because this procedure never works.

Another bad approach for the entrepreneur is to make a personal visit with the business plan tucked under his arm. This humble, straightforward approach is like going to a doctor as an unreferred patient. Everyone asks, "Who sent you?" The key man is often away from his office or unable to see the visitor, who then begins to feel like an intruder.

The best method of delivering a business plan is through a third party. Unless the entrepreneur is already established and successful, a third-party referral adds credence to the plan, and, as a result, increases the likelihood that it will be read. Anyone from the following groups is acceptable as long as the reputation and liaison with the venture capitalist are positive (it need not be the same person for each potential investor): consultants, bankers, lawyers, accountants, or other entrepreneurs.

The second level of improvement—a good job on *preselling*—is invaluable. If the potential investors are told about the exciting company six months before the plan arrives and then about current developments each month for the intervening six months, they will be more receptive to reading the plan when it finally arrives. *After all, the best time to raise money is when it isn't needed.* The same holds for arousing potential investor interest. A well-managed company planning to expand will invest time in such preselling often and early. The preselling is as important as any aspect of the process.

The same person should both presell and eventually deliver the plan. With the company name and address and location clearly spelled out on the cover page, it should be hand-carried by a mutual friend to a select group of venture capitalists.

If the process is depressing, always remember that the two most successful venture capitals deals in the Northeast were turned down a number of times before receiving a "yes." In 1958, Digital Equipment Corporation (DEC) finally convinced American Research & Development to invest about $70,000. Rumor has it that the investment today is worth over $500 million.

A spin-off from DEC occurred in 1968 when three engineers in their twenties approached Fred Adler, a New York attorney, who agreed to a modest investment in a struggling new company known as Data General Corporation. It is rumored that the four principals each made in excess of $10 million within four years of launching this venture. The rewards are high for those who play and win. Unfortunately, those who play lose most of the time, and plans of this type significantly outnumber the winners.

Explaining the format for reading a business plan suggests that the document's preparations should be based on the process that will inevitably be used to read and interpret the plan. Whether the writer is an internal or external entrepreneur, it is his responsibility to put the company's best foot forward once the business is underway. Thus, a well done business plan will be tailored to the reader.

The definition of a "good" business plan is one that raises money; a "bad" plan does not attract investors. It is that simple; but the entrepreneur must remember that the terms "good plan" and "good business" are not synonymous. A good plan may raise money, but the business may still fail. However, a bad plan almost always means business failure. In order to succeed in reaching the more crucial objectives of a profitable business, a good plan plus a good business is required.

The five-minute process is so cold in concept that it may seriously alienate many business people. The business becomes part of life and the plan becomes the essence of the business. Hence, to add a degree of warmth and a bit more understanding to the central aspect of small business, actual business plans should be interpreted against the above process.

While dealing in this abstract area remember a quotation that links entrepreneurs and venture capitalists.

The men who manage men, manage the men who manage things, *but,* the men who manage money manage the men who manage men.

Pecking order	Ease of handling	
	Venture capitalist	Entrepreneur
1. Money	High	Low
2. Men	Medium	Medium
3. Things	Low	High

CHAPTER FIVE

WRITING A
BUSINESS PLAN

The business plan is such a personal document that actual hard advice on its proper preparation is like giving any extremely personal counsel. Usually this type of guidance is not specific enough to be of applied value. Yet there are some common, helpful ideas that can and should be embodied in a business plan.

The most important first stage of development for a business plan is the development of the table of contents. This should be done before any serious writing occurs. The process of then subdividing the actual writing of each module that appears in the table of contents is an extremely common practice. Although sub-dividing is an efficient and reasonable practice, any plan that is developed by the modular approach runs the risk of appearing pieced together. Naturally, this nonintegrated business plan risks the substantial danger of lacking an overall thrust.

The purpose of writing a business plan is to raise capital by the direct sale of securities to one or more private investors. The transaction is exempt from registration with the Securities and Exchange Commission (SEC) provided that it conforms to certain SEC established laws. Very often a business plan does not seek to sell equity but rather to arrange for long term debt financing.

In many cases, particularly in the past few years, the condition of the public stock market prohibits companies from securing new financing through an initial sale of common stock. In the late 1960s, it was not uncommon to have several thousand small companies *go public*; but the early and middle 1970s were years when this figure fell from several thousand to fourteen or sixteen per year. In those lean years, the only viable alternative was the long term debt market. These facts give some indication of why the development of the business plan should be integrated with the needs of the financial markets.

To offer guidance in writing a business plan, a typical table of contents follows.

A.1   History of the Company
A.2   Business Summary
A.3   Manufacturing Plan
A.4   Production and Personnel Plan
A.5   Products and Services
A.6   Marketing and Sales
A.7   Competition
A.8   Research and Development
A.9   Management
A.10 Financial Reports Supplied by the Company and Accompanying Explanations, Footnotes
A.11 Capitalization or Equity Structure
A.12 Capitalization or Debt Structure

HISTORY OF THE COMPANY

A. Date and place, including state of incorporation as well as pre-incorporation organizational structure.
B. Founding shareholders and directors.
C. Important changes in the structure of the company, its management, or its ownership. Set forth predecessor companies, subsidiaries, and divisions in an easy to understand manner.
D. Company's major successes or achievements in the field to date.

BUSINESS SUMMARY

A. Principal products or services.
B. Describe the unique features of the business and the products. Compare these objectively with the competition. Give specific goals on annual sales growth and profits and relate to actual past performance.
C. Detailed breakdown of sales or services for the current year and for the past five years. Indicate the cost of goods sold and the pretax profit by product line for all products or services that contribute more than 10% in pretax profits.
D. Breakdown of sales by industries, including the U.S. (military versus nonmilitary) and export.
E. Product brandnames, price ranges, and quality.
F. Capital goods versus consumer goods. How cyclical or seasonal?
G. Describe patents, trademarks, and other trade advantages such as geographic or labor advantages. List expiration dates, if any, and impact on sales, profits, and marketing strategy.
H. Give the statistical record of the industry or subindustry in which company operates, with an evaluation of its prospects.
I.   Maturity of the product line. Discuss the problems of techno-

logical obsolescence and product line, and the problems of competition.

J. Describe any technological trends or potentialities within the business environment that might be favorable or unfavorable to the company.

MANUFACTURING PLAN

A. Fill in data below.

1. Plant location.
2. Square feet.
3. Number of floors.
4. Type of construction.
5. Acres of land.
6. Owned or leased.
7. Lease value.
8. Annual rent expires.

B. Describe levels of current operations. Estimate the capacity and the current percentage utilization of plant and equipment.
C. List auto equipment, including delivery trucks, number of vehicles, and whether rented or owned. What are the lease arrangements?
D. Describe the company's depreciation policies. How are they accounting for wear on their assets? Over what time period and at what rate are these assets being depreciated?
E. What manufacturing and/or office equipment is leased?
F. Condition and description of plant equipment (enclose evaluation if possible):

1. List major equipment.
2. Condition.
3. Location.
4. Owned or leased.
5. Value estimate.

G. Is the plant layout efficient? Describe.
H. What is the general housekeeping condition?
I. Is the operation job-shop or mass-production oriented? Do they build custom products per individual jobs or is it a mass-produced product that can be manufactured under large cost-efficient methods, and inventoried?
J. Incremental increase in space and equipment required for $1,000,000 increase in sales. For each major increment of expansion in revenue, is an equal, more, or less increment necessary in facilities, people, and equipment?

K. Logic for plant location(s).
L. What future capital expenditures for plant and machinery are planned? How will they be financed?
M. What major capital improvements have been made in the past few years? What was their cost and how were they financed?
N. Any sale of assets planned—on what basis, cash or deferred payments?
O. Number of shifts being worked daily. Percentage of overtime. Breakdown by departments. Economics of a two or three shift schedule.

PRODUCTION AND PERSONNEL PLAN

A. Brief description of manufacturing operation.
B. Number of personnel (breakdown by functions).
C. Union affiliation. State address and representative.
D. Strike history.
E. Turnover and morale.
F. Labor market (description of important skills) and competition for labor.
G. Percentage of labor content in cost of goods sold by product.
H. Fringe benefits provided and their cost percentage to wages.
I. Does the company rate itself as a low-cost, high-cost, or average-cost employer? What is the unemployment rate based upon the business's past hiring and firing practice charged to the company by the state government?
J. Steps being taken to improve production methods.
K. Are competent people assigned to production planning?
L. Describe quality control procedures.
M. Unit costs versus production levels, detailing fixed and variable costs.

PRODUCTS OR SERVICES

A. Principal suppliers; location; product; volume; officers dealt with
B. A brief description of significant materials and supplies, including availability. Are the storage and material handling facilities adequate?
C. Are purchase economies available? Are purchase discounts available?
D. Are make-or-buy decisions made?
E. What is the average inventory turnover within the company's industry? Explain any deviations for your firm.
F. Does the finished inventory have a shelf-life?
G. Methods of inventory valuation.
H. Current inventory status of distributors and ultimate users.

MARKETING AND SALES

A. Describe the market. History, size, trend, and your product's position in the market. Identify sources of estimates and assumptions.
B. Is the market at the take-off stage? Project the market back five years and forward five years.
C. Where are the products sold, and who is the essential end user?
D. Are the products sold by salaries or commissioned sales force, by distributors, by brokers, or ?
E. Are accounts receivables sold, discounted, or pledged? If so, to whom, at what discount, with or without recourse, and so forth? If receivables are pledged to a loaning source, either the lender or the borrower actually receives the cash. If they are discounted, the lender gives a percentage of the receivables at the moment they are pledged as collateral. Resource means that the lender can recover any bad debt on an uncollectable receivable from the borrower, thus lowering the lender's risk.
F. Number of customers or active accounts, and the amount of accounts receivable due over 90 days.
G. How many customers make up 80% of the sales? Please list.

   1. Principal customers
   2. Location
   3. Product
   4. Volume
   5. Percent of Company's Sales
   6. Officer Dealt With

H. Describe any special relationships with customers.
I. Describe pricing policies with respect to all product lines. How sensitive are prices to costs?
J. Current backlog and current shippable backlog. The shippable backlog can be shipped and billed immediately upon completing the manufacturing of the product.
K. How many purchase orders are on hand at present (dollar amount)?
L. Warranties on present products (enclose copies).
M. Advertising: annual budget and media used (enclose recent copy).
N. Is business seasonal? If so, explain peaks in production, sales, and so forth.
O. Selling costs as a percentage of revenues. How will these vary with more or less sales volume?
P. Customer primary motivation to purchase your product: price, delivery time, performance, and so forth.
Q. Are any proposed government regulations expected to affect your market?

COMPETITION

A. List major competition, location, sales earnings, percent of market and strengths and weaknesses.
B. Nature of competition: cut-throat or permissive; poorly or well financed.
C. Competitive advantages; disadvantages. Be specific.
D. Is new competition entering the field?
E. Compare your company's prices with those of the competition.
F. Share of the business you receive by market area.
G. Describe service arrangements and service experience.
H. Describe advertising and promotional efforts. Discuss the importance of brand names and trademarks.
I. Independent firms, publications, or outside agencies which have evaluated your firm against competitors.
J. Effects of regulatory agencies, including government.

RESEARCH AND DEVELOPMENT

A. Amount of percentage of sales spent per annum in the past five years and projected. Compare with competitors. Detail any capitalized R & D costs.
B. Number of employees in this area. Advanced college degrees.
C. Detail product developments and R & D that is not related to specific products or services, which is basically research and not development.
D. Percent of current sales generated by past R & D.
E. State any new field your firm contemplates entering: Is it complementary to the present product or service line?
F. List any outside consulting R & D relationships such as firms, universities, individuals, and so forth; and state the percentage of total R & D budget let to outside sources.
G. Funding and its consistency from government sources.

MANAGEMENT

A. Is an organization chart included?
B. Are résumés included?
C. Are references included?
D. Have credit and personal investigation checks been performed?
E. Analysis or reputation, capabilities, and attitude. Analysis of team: one man show, executive turnover, morale.
F. Profit consciousness: Is there an on-going profit improvement plan? An executive incentive program?
G. Innovative ability. Be specific. How is creativity fostered?

H. Schedule of past, current, and proposed salaries and other compensation for each member of management and/or owners, including bonuses, fee arrangements, profit sharing, and so forth. Please list.

    1. Key personnel.
    2. Annual salary.
    3. Bonuses, fees, and so forth.

I. If a stock option or other management incentive plan is in effect, provide an outline.
J. How are salary increases for management controlled?
K. Directors—other than officers and employees: Please list.

    1. Name and identity.
    2. Compensation.
    3. Shares of stock owned.
    4. Common or preferred.

L. Life insurance on officers (amount and company).
M. Enclose any contract or proposed contract between the firm and any member of management, any stockholder, or any outside consultant.

FINANCIAL REPORTS SUPPLIED BY THE COMPANY AND EXPLANATIONS

A. Reports

    1. Audited annual reports for the past five years, including balance sheets, profit and loss statements, and statements of sources and applications of funds.
    2. Current financial reports, with officer's statements as to material changes in condition.
    3. Pro forma balance sheets giving the effect of the proposed financing on a quarterly basis for two years.
    4. Month by month projections of profit and loss, cash receipts, and disbursements for the two year period.
    5. Yearly projections of revenues and earnings for five years.
    6. Analysis of sales by markets, products, and profits.
    7. Record of the industry or subindustry in which the company operates to contrast with the performance of the specific business.

B. Describe accounting principles regarding depreciation, R & D, taxes, inventories, and so forth.
C. Are the tax returns of the company and its subsidiaries for the past five years included?

D. If the business is seasonal, explain its cycle and relate it to the company's financial needs.
E. Discuss the aging of accounts receivable and accounts payable.
F. List the losses from bad debts over the past five years.
G. Describe the trend and give percentages for the following:

1. Sales, increases or decreases.
2. Cost of goods sold.
3. Overhead, fixed and variable.
4. Selling expenses.
5. Research and development.
6. Taxes.
7. Pretax and after-tax profit margins.
8. Return on total capital, including long term debt.
9. Return on total equity.
10. Industry trends in each of the above areas.

H. Does the balance sheet contain hidden or undervalued assets or liabilities?
I. Discuss any nonrecurring items of income or expense in recent financial statements.
J. Describe the company's profit improvement plan.
K. What years' tax returns have been audited?
L. Are all taxes paid?
M. Are there any disputes between the company and any taxing authority?

CAPITALIZATION: EQUITY

A. Total shares authorized: Common _____ Preferred _____
B. Total shares outstanding: Common _____ Preferred _____
C. Describe principal terms, including voting rights, dividend payments, conversion features, and so forth for each class of stock.
D. If a private company, list all shareholders. If a public company, list all shareholders who directly or indirectly control more than 5% of the outstanding voting stock.

1. Name and identity.
2. Consideration for shares.
3. Number and class of shares.
4. Percentage owned of outstanding stock.

E. If any of the shareholders listed in D are not members of the company's management, describe their motivation for becoming shareholders.

F. If individuals or entities who might be considered founders, promoters, or insiders under any law are no longer shareholders, describe the reason for their withdrawal from the business.

G. Provide a chronological list of sales of stock, stating prices, terms, number of buyers, and their names.

H. Describe any other transactions involving the principal shareholders and the company—such as those involving real estate, equipment leases or sales, loans to or from shareholders, and voting trusts.

CAPITALIZATION: DEBT

A. Principal bank. Name of officer handling account.

B. List the following for each long term debt obligation.
   1. Lender and contact
   2. Total amount
   3. Initial date
   4. Length of term
   5. Sinking fund
   6. Date of maturity
   7. Security or collateral

C. Are seasonal loans required? What was the largest amount borrowed in each of the past two years? Minimum?

D. Amounts of current lines of credit, and with whom.

E. Describe all contingent liabilities.

F. Debt to equity ratio: for company; for industry.

G. What guarantees are currently required by lenders?

SOURCES OF INFORMATION ON PREPARING A BUSINESS PLAN

1. Small Business Reporter, P.O. Box 37000, Bank of America, San Francisco, CA, 94120 (Tel: 415-622-2491). $2.00 per copy. The "Business Operations" series is helpful for general information on running a business. Titles include: *Operating Your Own Business, Small Business Success, How to Buy or Sell a Business, Financing Small Business, Personnel for the Small Business, Steps to Starting a Business.* Other series are "Business Profiles," which cover specific small businesses and "Professional Management" for doctors, dentists, veterinarians.

2. One of the finest pieces of information for understanding financial statements is offered free of charge by the world's largest securities firm,

Merrill Lynch Pierce Fenner & Smith. This 24 page red book, entitled "Understanding Financial Statements" is so good it is often used as a free handout in graduate level college finance courses. It offers an understanding of the three basic financial tools.

1. Balance Sheet
2. Cash Flow Statement
3. Profit & Loss Statement

May I suggest you call your local Merrill Lynch office, which can be found in your local telephone directory.

3. Several excellent articles on developing a business plan are contained within the books offered by the most professional source of venture capital information, Capital Publishing Company. These books provide some of the articles on the business plan that are truly excellent and tips are practical and worthwhile.

Write:

The Center for Entrepreneurial Management, Inc.
83 Spring St.
New York, NY 10012
212-925-7304

4. I have edited an excellent book of readings for entrepreneurs which is known as the *Entrepreneurs Handbook.* This two-volume handbook is described as excellent because the books contain all the good articles on business plans (plus other entrepreneurial subjects) ever written. There are six articles on how to prepare a business plan in these two volumes. Write:

Artech House
610 Washington Street
Dedham, MA 02026

or

The Center for Entrepreneurial Management, Inc.
83 Spring St.
New York, NY 10012
212-925-7304

5. The Small Business Administration offers several excellent pamphlets on writing a business plan. These are very inexpensive and surprisingly good. They even offer further information on where to obtain further information on writing a business plan. I'd suggest your local SBA field office for current information.

a. Small Marketeer Aid # 153
   Business Plan for the Small Service Firm
   24 pages

b. Small Marketeer Aid #150
   Business Plan for Retailer
   24 pages

c. Management Aid for Small Manufacturers #218
   Business Plan for Small Manufacturers
   22 pages

A new center was established in February 1978 to speed up the delivery process of SBA pamphlets. All requests to this high speed center should be on SBA Form 115A, which is a list of available SBA publications. Form 115A can be requested from the center. Write:

> The Small Business Administration (SBA)
> Box 15434
> Fort Worth, Texas 76119

Nationwide toll free number is 800-433-7272. In Texas call 800-792-8901. The telephone recording service is available 24 hours per day, seven days per week.

6. Another source of information on a business plan's development is a two part document. Part I is a five-page approach to developing a business plan and Part II describes how to prepare a business plan. $30.00.

> Institute for New Enterprise Development (INED)
> 385 Concord Avenue
> Belmont, MA 02178
> 617-489-3950

CHAPTER SIX

THE ENTREPRENEUR'S LIFE CYCLE

Having a business of your own is not too different from having a child. You experience many of the same emotions and problems. And, as with a child, starting one is half the fun. However, only being a business starter is less than one half of the job. The hard part is to make a business successful. As I pointed out earlier, a successful business plan alone is not sufficient to ensure a profitable business. A successful plan plus a sound entrepreneurial team are the basic cornerstones for a successful business enterprise.

All successful small businesses start with an idea and proceed through the classic entrepreneur's life cycle. Following is a life cycle for entrepreneurs.

Stage I   The entrepreneur's early development
Stage II   The idea stage
Stage III   The start-up problem
Stave IV   The venture financing
Stage V   The growth crisis
Stage VI   The maturity crisis
Stage VII   The impossible transition

One of the interesting aspects of small business is the team built around the entrepreneur. A talented entrepreneur recognizes that the central fact of management is *accomplishing tasks through other people*. An ineffective entrepreneur tries to do everything himself. This raises the classic issue of delegating, which is often contrary to the entrepreneur's natural tendencies.

The vast majority of successful small companies were built around an entrepreneur team and not a single entrepreneur. In fact, partnerships are an increasingly effective method of balancing each entrepreneur's strengths and weaknesses to produce a well-balanced top management team.

Some of the most successful companies were launched by two equal partners who complement one another. Rolls and Royce, the founders of the prestigious British motor car company bearing their names, were totally opposite in philosophies and lifestyles. One was Mr. Inside and the other Mr. Outside, but together they were an effective entrepreneurial team. The same holds for the largest consumer goods company, Proctor & Gamble. David Packard and William Hewlett of Hewlett-Packard electronics fame in California is another example. In discount retailing it was Two Guys from Harrison who started the revolution; not one individual.

The team allows balance and strength to exist in the enterprise. The stronger the team, the more powerful the company. It's the synergistic concept of two plus two being equal to five.

Franklin Delano Roosevelt summed up the process this way. "I'm not the smartest fellow in the world, but I can sure pick smart colleagues." He claimed: "Because I'm not so smart, I have to surround myself with real talent." The entrepreneur who can adopt this same philosophy will select the following members of the team.

1. Partners
2. Lawyers
3. Advertising Agencies
4. Accountants
5. Bankers
6. Board of Directors—Angels
7. Consultants
8. Manufacturer's Representatives
9. The Controller

Following is a commentary on the roles of these team members. Along with a sound business plan, a team of professionals adds the final ingredient to mixing up a profitable business enterprise.

BUILDING AN ENTREPRENEURIAL TEAM

Partners

A partner can be a blessing or a curse. Whether you take one, or more, into your business venture depends on your needs for additional depth in management, marketing, technology, or financing.

Selecting your business partners is not much different from choosing your spouse, and it should be done with the same care. More, perhaps, because the wrong partner can put the entire venture in jeopardy. Marriages are relatively easy to start. A marriage license and a blood test only cost a few dollars. If one fails, you can try again. In business it's not so easy.

I advise finding a partner whose talents complement your own, but whose business philosophy, personality, and background differ. The most successful companies are formed with two partners whose combined abilities give depth to the enterprise, and whose different backgrounds serve as a buffer against excesses of any kind. You both may disagree and you both may have conflicts, but usually they are over business issues rather than personalities. A good marketing/financial man is an ideal partner for a strong production/engineering type, but two optimists or two pessimists can kill a business before it has a chance to get off the ground. The outside and inside philosophy has also been applied to David Packard, former Secretary of Defense (Mr. Outside) and to his equally talented, but less outgoing partner, William Hewlett (Mr. Inside).

Once you have selected your partner, you should immediately agree to disagree. From my experience in mediating between partners I never become concerned about disagreements. They are akin to fights between alley cats: After all the scrapping, the only result seems to be more cats. The success of a partnership depends on arriving at sensible business decisions through cooperation and equal participation.

Every partnership should have a *godfather*. Not the kind made famous in Mario Puzo's recent novel about the underworld, but one who is trusted and respected by both partners and who can serve as a mediator to help resolve conflicts. This helps unstick the sticky problems in the 50-50 partnerships.

This godfather should be unbiased; he should have little or no vested interest in the company. He can be a business acquaintance, a friend, a college professor, or someone respected in the technology of your business. Bring him into the picture right at the beginning and keep him abreast of what goes on so he can understand the causes of any problems.

If you're lucky and if the situation is very unusual, you may never require him to do more than settle minor disputes or serve as a sounding board for new ideas. If worst comes to worst, however, and you must dissolve the partnership, the godfather may be the only one who can keep the pieces together long enough for the company to gain its equilibrium and survive. Remember, nothing lasts forever. But the business, if it survives at all, will most likely outlive the partnership.

Lawyers

How to Form Your Corporation Without a Lawyer for Under $50 (and imitations by dozens of other writers), a book written by Ted Nicholas and published by Enterprise Publishing Co., Wilmington, Delaware, 1971, seems to imply that incorporating a small business can be a homemade process. I don't disagree. It can be done cheaper on your own, but I suggest that the first step in the starting a business game is to see a lawyer. Not just so he or she can incorporate the business to avoid the legal disadvantages in a proprietorship, but to begin a long relationship. Selecting a proprietorship as the form of your new business can leave you and your assets exposed to law suits by unsatisfied creditors. Using a corporate format will strongly discourage unsecured creditors from suing any individual management member to collect unsecured unpaid corporate bills. However, the corporate form of organization will seldom protect an individual from repaying secured bank debt, as almost all banks require a small business person to sign two ways—first, as the president of the corporation and second, as an individual. Hence, secured creditors such as banks, receive payment from either the corporation or the individual responsible for the management of the business. Unsecured creditors, traditionally known as the accounts payable, are legally discouraged from pursuing any management individual to collect unsecured debts. This level of legal protection for a corporation is not available to a sole proprietor, and often the small business person is responsible for all debts, secured and unsecured. It's not the money you save that counts but the headaches you avoid by having competent legal advice from the beginning. I say step one in the start-a-business-process is to see a good lawyer. You can still buy Ted Nicholas's book, but I would not recommend any homemade legal advice.

The lawyer is one of the critical elements in any business. He or she is a full-fledged team member and many times captains the team. Hence, he or she must be well qualified. I'd suggest going into the city to select your lawyer and choosing a young one who specializes in Securities and Exchange Commission (SEC), which regulates security markets, or a corporate specialist at one of the prestigious law firms. Your lawyer will know how to take companies public, how to set up tax shield stock plans, and how to keep all the liabilities to a minimum. One good lawyer is worth a dozen bad ones; a good lawyer is a critical player on your management team.

Advertising Agencies

Most entrepreneurs tend to avoid advertising agencies or they put off hiring one until they hit an impasse in their marketing plans. Then it may be too late. I believe in finding a good, small (no more than ten people) agency early.

With advertising agencies, unlike law firms or public accounting firms, the largest is not always the best for the small businessperson.

With a small agency, you'll get the attention—and probably plenty of it—of the top person.

The agency is often a junior member of the team but they should be selected early. An integrated corporate communications concept for letterheads, business cards, envelopes, and logos will establish a corporate identity that blends well together. It makes a big difference when all communications are well coordinated from the beginning. It avoids the embarrassment of not looking professional or of not being taken seriously.

Once you've found the right advertising agency, give them their head. Don't tell them what colors *you* like. Be candid and honest, and give them all the information you can about your product and your markets—but don't impose your artistic talents. The more you give them, the more they'll be able to give you.

When it comes to agency compensation, please don't rely on the old fifteen percent of the media costs method. This old method of compensating for agency efforts was very simple but it is now antiquated. Most approved media will allow an accredited agency to deduct a 15% discount very much like the airlines allow a travel agency a 7% discount. Hence, an advertising agency that annually placed $100,000 of media billing for a client would be indirectly compensated by paying the various media $85,000 while billing the client the published rates of $100,000. First of all, it's impossible for an agency to work profitably on a straight commission basis unless your media expenditures are considerable. Remember, they're in business to make a profit, too. Furthermore, it tends to create a conflict of interest for the agency, since it is to their advantage if your advertising dollars go into a commissionable media. The best course for your company may be direct mail or some other noncommissionable medium. Do you want the agency working for your company or for the commissionable advertising media? There is a possible conflict between what is good for the media and what is good for the client. An agency that is singularly reimbursed for commission media, print or electronic, may be unreceptive to designing brochures or trade literature because the printing commissions may be less than the earned discount from the commissionable media. An estimate of the annual advertising budget should be the foundation for determining an agency's compensation. This allows a fuller, fairer choice of the optimal allocations between commissionable and noncommissionable activities.

The most practical and fairest method of agency compensation is a monthly retainer fee that amounts to about ten percent more than the commissions they would receive on annual forecasted commissionable media expenditures. This method eliminates the conflict of interest and lets the agency worry about what's best for you, not about what's best for them.

Accountants

Another person you'll want to get on board at the earliest moment is a top-flight certified public accountant (CPA). Numbers are the language of business management, and intelligent decisions require an understanding of the quantitative factors involved.

If you have hopes for expansion or for going public, line up one of the big accounting firms. A merely adequate accountant is suicide. A big, well-known firm immediately lends credibility to your numbers; and, when the time comes for that public offering, three years of audited statements from one of the big names adds plenty of status. Don't worry about a big firm being too expensive. Most of them have separate divisions for small businesses. They'll install a one-write check system (which can save hours of work and improve your accuracy) and an accounts-payable voucher register (so you'll know who you owe money to), proof your receivables (so you'll know who owes you money), and set up all the necessary systems to help you avoid unnecessary false starts.

Next, introduce your lawyer and your accountant to your banker. There will be plenty of decisions where their functions overlap, so they should know one another from the outset.

Bankers

Pick a banker, not a bank. If he is with a large bank, or a bank with a captive small business investment company (SBIC), so much the better. Many bankers are really venture capitalists in disguise and they can be sources of valuable financial assistance.

Here again, forget the big titles and pick a young loan officer or assistant vice president: Then gain his confidence. Supply him or her with detailed pro forma cash flow projections to show what your cash needs will be. Simply stated, this is a cash plan that estimates the future incoming cash and subtracts the estimated future cash needs of the business. The difference will be the estimated future cash needs (or excess cash) generated by the business. Then meet or exceed your projections. Getting financial aid will be easy from then on.

In working with your friendly banker you'll soon learn that he or she expects you to countersign your company's bank debt personally. Don't let it throw you. It's the only way he or she has to certify your numbers and your confidence in what you're doing. But don't take this responsibility lightly, either. It's easy for you to be overly optimistic and that can get you into a lot of trouble. Before you sign that note, take a good, hard look at those figures again. That signature on the back of the note isn't an autograph—unless you become very, very famous. The countersignature on a bank note means that you, as an individual, are personally responsible for the debts. In the event that the business goes into bankruptcy and is unable to meet the financial obligation that bears your countersignature, the lender can seek the difference between what is collected and what is owed from you as the countersigner of the debt.

If you have inventory and/or receivables, you may be able to avoid the countersignature; or you may at least be able to limit your personal vulnerability by assigning them to the bank. I like the concept of limited personal guarantee and banks are more receptive to a limited guarantee than to no guarantee at all. It usually is reasonable grounds upon which a compromise can be established.

If the worst happens and the bank has to go after your security, it is better that the bank secures the company's inventory, not your wife's diamond ring. Some states protect your home from creditors or bankers trying to collect against a bankrupt company under the Homestead Act. The Homestead Act originated years ago to protect farmers who often lost their farms when they were unable to meet the payments for large farm equipment. The states individually passed legislation in the 1800s that protected a person's primary residence from creditors other than the principal mortgage holder. But, to gain this level of additional legal protection, a short two-page document must be filed prior to any seizure attempts by creditors. It's all very complicated, very legal and it varies from state to state. But all of these issues point out the reason you selected a good lawyer first. Ask your lawyer how to do it, that's why lawyers are paid so well.

Board of Directors

There is no doubt that the most crucial single personification of an entrepreneur's management team is the board of directors. A board of directors is charged with establishing policy level decisions. A well-balanced board of directors adds depth to a small, understaffed enterprise. When the board is composed of respected business advisors who meet periodically and debate policy and develop corporate strategies, then the company is operating on a solid foundation.

Unfortunately, too many small businesses do not have actual boards of directors. The entrepreneur who is concerned with day to day activities often ignores the potential advantages of establishing a balanced board of directors. The board of directors is often comprised of a wife and father who never influence business issues. They are rubber stamps in the true sense of the word.

Whether to choose accountants, lawyers, bankers, or others to serve on the board of directors is a puzzle with no single answer. Rather, the answer depends on the other talents of the individuals and on the needs of the company. The only group who consistently offers a universal appeal as board members is a group affectionately labeled "angels." These seasoned investors/businessmen are often the nucleus of a good working board of directors.

Angels are hard to find, but they do exist. They're those marvelous people who descend from the heavens just to invest in small companies. No, they're not supernaturals. Usually they are just successful, wealthy businessmen, who, instead of putting their money in the stock market, investing in a mutual fund, or buying savings bonds, invest a portion of their wealth in young businesses.

This is the best sort of investor/director. Such an individual usually joins the team at the founding level and stays with the company until it makes a public offering. Often he makes useful contacts for the company. When more money is needed, he is usually the first to step forward. Most angels have invested between $100,000 and $200,000 in several small businesses, keeping their stake in each venture below $50,000. They are likely to be the only nonemployee investors in the companies. To top it off, they're usually the salt of the earth: nice people—but smart. As venture capitalists, they are better to do business with than with any other alternative. They don't value their advice as highly as a professional venture capitalist, even though it's usually better; they don't value their money as highly as a professional venture capitalist, because they don't have large fixed costs for offices and the like. Compared to doctor and lawyer money, angels are seldom nervous or irrational over business problems as they grew up in business, not in law or medicine. If you can find one (in a city the size of Boston there are probably only 100 angels), you can't go wrong by bringing him into the financing arrangements. Then go the extra step to involve him in a balanced board of directors who meet monthly and debate business policies vigorously.

Management Consultants

Entrepreneurs, more than most businesspeople, rely on other people—such as professional management consultants, college professors, other company presidents, or anyone else who can intelligently offer advice and objectivity.

These people serve as sounding boards for the entrepreneur's ideas and help him or her weigh alternatives before making the final decision. In other fields—such as government, the military, and even sports—these sounding boards exist internally in the form of staff assistants.

Since small businesses can't afford droves of staff assistants, they have to rely on external sources; and this leads to the emergence of professional management consultants for small businesses. The management consultant (M.C.) is usually a person with a broad range of knowledge in the management of businesses, and he or she applies that experience to your problems in order to guide you in the right direction. Ultimately, the decision is always yours; but the M.C. plays a vital role in helping you see flaws and correct them before you implement the plan. The M.C. is often the source for new creative concepts, too.

In order to demonstrate the emergence of the management consultant, I counted the number of consulting firms listed in the Yellow Pages in various cities and noted their increase over the years. The results are shown in the table below. Apparently there is no other means to prove this point, as neither the government nor any association compiles statistics on the number of management consulting firms by city. I believe the data demonstrates the growth, and thereby the value, of the service.

NUMBER OF MANAGEMENT CONSULTANT FIRMS IN YELLOW PAGES BY YEAR

City	1951	1960	1963	1964	1965	1969	1970	1974	1975	1976
Boston	17		60			178				365
Chicago					268		449			
Los Angeles		112			225		337	340		
Philadephia					108		158		182	
Washington, D.C.				111						401

Strangely enough, many small businesses use the services of management consultants successfully. They can often provide the frosting on the cake, but should never be over-extended to provide the cake. That's the job of the entrepreneur. This is often confusing or misunderstood by a struggling businessperson who is unsure of the economic return from a small business consultant. If the business succeeds, it's because of the entrepreneur, not the adviser. The same if it fails. The consultant only provides help, guidance and assistance, and he or she is never the pivotal difference between success and failure in a small growing enterprise. That's the job of the entrepreneur.

Manufacturer's Representatives

Manufacturer's representatives or reps are the mainstay of the sales force of most small businesses. They are independent businesspeople, entrepreneurs in their own right, peddling the merchandise of several manufacturers rather than just one.

Reps don't add to a company's fixed costs. They're paid on a commission basis according to what they sell. Because of this, a small company can afford to maintain a respectable sales force without incurring large, fixed overhead costs.

The rep is also a valuable source of industry intelligence. He or she is a kind of mercenary soldier, stomping through the industrial mud as a commissioned member of several armies. If anyone knows what's going on, the rep does. He or she's the sage of his or her industry.

When you latch onto a good rep (there are some poor ones), hold onto him or her—even when it's time to hire an inside person. Many companies make special arrangements with best reps to keep them on. It's good for the company; and it's good for the rep, who lives in fear of selling him- or herself out of a good line. If a rep performs too well in a territory, many small companies get confused and suddenly believe that the best alternative would be to fire the rep and hire a direct salaried person. A manufacturer may eventually decide that a certain territory is lucrative enough to support a full-time company employee. This cost efficient decision will occur at different levels for different companies and products. A cost efficient decision is elusive in practice but easily explained in theory. It's elusive because the opening assumption usually proves to be misleading. The question is, given the same sales in both cases, when is an independent, commissioned agent less expensive than a salaried full-time company salesman? The pivotal assumption (remember *assume* derives from the Greek meaning ass of u and me) is underlined. The answer is, when less commissions are paid to the agents than salary that would have been paid to the salesperson, for a given level of sales. Whenever the crossing point occurs for a sales territory, it is commonly thought to be more cost efficient to replace the commissioned agent with a salaried employee. But watch out for the *assumptions.*

It is useful to clarify this issue in the early stages of business growth, for many small companies begin with manufacturer's representatives and eventually shift to full-time company paid salespeople. The issue is, "What are the trade-offs in making these decisions?" There are both qualitative and quantitative reasons to prefer one type of sales force to another.

The qualitative advantages of each are listed below.

MANUFACTURER'S REPRESENTATIVES

1. A commissioned agent who receives compensation only when he or she sells something.
2. Usually the representative firm has a number of persons covering a single territory instead of just one person.
3. A manufacturer's representative also sells products for other

manufacturers and this can help him or her in merchandising complementary products.

4. The nature of their specialization makes them knowledgeable about their territory and their customers.
5. The marketing effort by a team of experienced reps is usually more efficient than a headquarters-directed effort at identifying and merchandising key accounts.

COMPANY SALESPERSON

1. Loyalty undoubtedly rests with the single employer and is not scattered among many manufacturers.
2. Willing to invest effort to develop new products or to maintain service to customers, both of which may be less income productive than pursuing other activities.
3. More efficient above a certain sales volume.
4. Able to develop better inside managers by having them initially perform at field sales.
5. Able to control sales activities better.

The Controller

Show me a successful small company with great growth potential and I'll show you a company with a talented financial person keeping his or her thumb on the cash flow—the company controller. This is the person who passes on all company expenditures. This person's also the one who manages to get the quarterly audit done, in spite of last quarter's foolish mistakes.

When given the chance, he or she will vote "no" 80 percent of the time. He or she frustrates everyone with pessimism, and is accused of throwing cold water on every good idea. Production doesn't like the controller because he or she refuses to sign purchase orders. Sales doesn't like him or her because he or she gives them a hard time about expense reports.

The controller is never popular but he or she is the one person in the company who can provide the balance it needs. With him or her, there's temperance. Without him or her there could be a drunken spending spree that might cripple a small, young company or one growing old. This financial genius, along with the first mate, are the two most crucial picks in your draft of management talent. Let's call them the first two rounds of the draft, or the number one and two draft pick.

Entrepreneurs often make fatal mistakes in selecting the financial specialist. This is especially true of the Boston Route 128 technical types. Typically, they are unfamiliar with finance, as compared to their extensive engineering and technical knowledge. Hence, in selecting the financial genius, they often rely on those with college degrees rather than on those with proven experience on the job.

Consequently, technical entrepreneurs hire business school MBAs (Masters in Business Administration) the way some large firms hire minority groups. It's the thing to do—especially if those hired are finance majors. Entrepreneurs tend to be infatuated with the MBA—the brash kid in his late twenties who knows all the answers and all the words, like *game plan* and *M.B.O.*—Management by Objectives, a managing technique made famous by Mr. Peter Drucker.

The trouble with most of today's business school graduates is that they have more answers than there are questions, just as there are more horses' asses than there are horses. It may sound strange, but too many solutions can create a problem. Furthermore, it's claimed they get too much money and change jobs too often.

In my experience with MBAs in small business, I have found that they spend most of their time analyzing their employer and the company. The ones who excel in small business management are running their own companies. They won't work for entrepreneurs; they *are* entrepreneurs. Think twice before you offer an unusually high salary for a would-be soothsayer.

If you must hire one of the new MBAs, try to find one who is in his or her second or third job. A little experience under the belt could do you a lot of good. A person with an MBA in finance or marketing, who is looking for his or her third job and who has some small company experience, could be the right medicine for your company. This is especially true for retail businesses because of the unique nature of retailing. In retailing, it's often best to wait until the MBA is past the age of 40, regardless of the number of previous jobs. A certain maturity plus an MBA is extremely powerful medicine, even for a certain sick business.

CHAPTER SEVEN

CAPITAL: WHERE IT IS AND HOW TO GET IT

"The men who manage men manage the men who
manage things but the men who manage money manage
the men who manage men?"

The pecking order in this universal saying is as it is in the entrepreneurial world.

1. Money
2. Men
3. Things

VENTURE CAPITAL TIPS

One of the leading investment bankers of New York, David Silver, who
is also a columnist for *Venture Magazine,* claims all financial forecasts look
like a hockey stick. That is, they start out flat and suddenly take a sharp
steep upward slope one or two years in the future. Silver further claims
there are only three crucial ingredients in a business plan. Silver's
perspective is from the eyes of a venture capital investor, and he claims
all successful plans contain these three ingredients in the following
order.

A. Big market
B. Good product
C. Good management team

He likes to tell the story of one of the most successful venture
capital investments ever, to illustrate his message. This investment
wasn't in some high technology esoteric product but, rather, in a service

business. The rule of thumb has always been that a service business is not candidate for a venture capital investment. But, in this exciting story, a 28-year-old up-shot known as Freddie Smith proved everybody wrong as he raised $94,000,000 to launch Federal Express. Better yet, according to Silver, Smith was able to maintain 4% of the business while providing less than 1% of the capital. (He invested just about $1,000,000).

One of the venture capital sources who invested in Federal Express tells an affectionate Freddie Smith story. It goes like this.

Four people were stranded on an island in the Pacific when a group of leaflets decended from the sky announcing that the island was to be annihilated in five minutes by a nuclear blast. Looking dejected, one of the inhabitants, an older man, walked into the bushes to enjoy his last bottle of wine. Two of the other inhabitants, a young couple, also went into the bushes to spend their last five minutes alone. Freddie Smith was the 4th person on the island and he immediately dove into the vast pacific ocean. The other 3 people eventually emerged from the bushes as they watched Freddie diving and swimming in the ocean. Finally one of them shouted "What are you doing?" Freddie ignored them but shouted over his shoulder "I've got 5 minutes to learn to swim underwater, please don't bother me now."

They say that the original founders of Federal Express so believed in the venture and Freddie Smith that they all hocked their watches just to make payrolls!

In 1980 there were private (nonSBIC) venture capital firms with an average portfolio of $30 million each. Just 10 years ago there were only 3 venture funds that were private. So, the success of past venture investments, such as Federal Express, has spawned a renewed interest in venture capital investing.

What does a venture capitalist look for? According to Silver they have several goals. First, they seek a minimum of five times on their money. In practice, they are often able to turn their money four times in three years, which is a 45% annual return on investment (R.O.I.). To make an investment, they want to know the five answers to these five questions.

1. How much can I make?
2. How much can I lose?
3. How do I get out of the deal?
4. Who is in the deal?
5. Who says the product and the people are any good?

The 400 or so nonprivate small investment companies (SBICs) firms and the 150 Minority Enterprise Small Business Investment Companies (MESBICs) have an average of about $10 thousand of capital to invest. In 1981, more venture capital was available in more funds than ever in the history of the venture capital industry. A record of $900 million of new capital was committed to the venture industry in 1980. Private venture firms received $657 million of this, a figure four times greater than 1979 and greater than any previous single year. Of the $657 million, $42 million in private capital was raised by Small Business Investment Corporations in 1979 and $17 million was raised by Minority Enterprise Small Business Investment Corporations. Since 44 SBICs and 31 MESBICs were licensed in 1980, these totals are not surprising. This total of 75 new firms is the highest number of new licensees since 1964. (Incidentally, these new SBICs combined brought a total of $61,372,723 into the venture capital industry.)

The industry now boasts a total of approximately 4.5 billion in venture capital broken out in the following way.

Independent venture firms	$1.8 billion
SBIC's, MESBIC's	1.4 billion
Corporations	1.3 billion
Total	4.5 billion

Watch the growth of the venture capital industry as another 30 groups, many headed by experienced venture capitalists, attempt to raise another $600 million in 1982, which would bring the total capital available to over 5 billion dollars in 1982.

While the philosophy of venture capital is similar throughout the United States, there are several regional differences which might be useful to know before making your final selection. Here is the regional focus of venture capitalists around the United States.

South: (Texas) The emphasis is on "who are your people?"
East: (New York) The emphasis is on "who do you know?"
Midwest: (Chicago) The emphasis is on "who do you work for?"
West (California) The emphasis is on "What's your package?"

The only axiom which seems to hold no matter what part of the country you are from is a very simple but very true expression. "Speak Yiddish but dress British, when raising money."

For the very reasonable cost of one dollar, you can obtain all the information you ever wanted to know about SBICs (including the names and addresses of those closest to you) by sending for the directory of SBIC.

National Association of Small Business
Investment Companies (NASBIC)
618 Washington Bldg.
Washington, DC 20005
(202-638-3411)

BREAKEVEN

A breakeven analysis is a critical calculation for every small business. Rather than calculating how much your firm would make if it obtained an estimated sales volume, a more meaningful analysis determines at which sales volume your firm will break even. The other statistic is really pie-in-the-sky because the estimated sales volume is very questionable. Don't assume a sales volume and determine your profits; do it in reverse; determine the sales volume necessary for your firm to break even. Above the breakeven, the firm makes money, below it loses money. A breakeven point, then, is a level of sales volume over some period of time. An example would be: "My firm broke even on $10,000 a week in sales."

$$T.C. = V.C. + F.C.$$
Total costs = variable costs plus fixed costs

T.C. = Total costs = All costs to operate the business over a specified time period.

V.C. = Variable costs = Those costs which vary directly with the number of products manufactured. Sometimes called direct costs, they typically include material and labor costs plus a percentage of the overhead costs.

F.C. = Fixed costs = Costs which do not vary with the number of products produced. Also known as indirect costs, these costs typically include executive salaries, rent, insurance, and are considered fixed over a relevant range of production.

B.E. = Breakeven point = Where total costs are equal to total revenues.

Here is an example for a plant which produces only one product.

A. The fixed costs are $100,000 per year. These costs include
   –lights and power and phones (utilities),
   –rent,
   –insurance,
   –administrative salaries.
   These costs are fixed over 20,000 units to 40,000 units manufactured annually.

B. The variable costs over the 20,000 − 40,000 unit range are:
   $2.00 material
   $3.00 labor
   $1.00 overhead (50% of material)
   $6.00 per unit

Note: A word of caution. In a small business, there is no such item as a truly fixed cost. No costs are fixed forever. Insurance can be cancelled, executives can be fired and rent can be renegotiated. Hence, a fixed cost should be thought of as a fixed cost only over a period of time or over a finite range of production.

C. Sale price per unit is $10.00

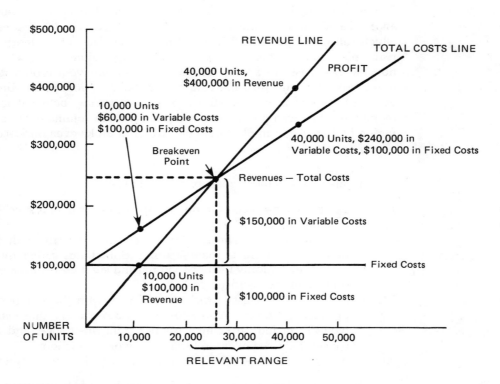

A BREAKEVEN CHART REVENUE = $10/UNIT FIXED COSTS = $100,000
VARIABLE COSTS = $6/UNIT

Creation of the Breakeven Chart

A breakeven chart (also known in more optimistic circles as a *profit* graph) translates the three known facts into linear terms: The fixed costs of $100,000, the variable costs of $6 per unit, and the sales price of $10 per unit.

The fixed costs line is horizontal because the fixed costs are $100,000 regardless of production volumes. To determine the revenue line, calculate that at 10,000 units the revenue is $100,000 (10,000 × $10) and that at 40,000 units it will be $400,000, and draw a line through those two points. From the revenue line, you can determine the revenue if you know the number of units or the number of units if you know the revenue.

The total costs line is determined by calculating what the variable costs would be at any two volumes, adding the $100,000 in fixed costs to each of these numbers, and drawing a line through the two points. The total costs at 10,000 units are $160,000 (10,000 $\times$ $6 = $60,000 + $100,000), and at 40,000 units the total costs are $340,000. The total costs line through these two points shows the total costs at different volumes.

When you have drawn the fixed costs, revenue, and total costs lines, you see the breakeven point is 25,000, which is the intersection of the revenue and total costs lines. At volumes greater than 25,000, there will be profit since revenues will be greater than total costs.

The Breakeven Formula

Although the breakeven chart is probably the most useful means of visualizing breakeven analysis, the following formula provides the same information.

$$\text{Breakeven} = \frac{\text{Fixed Costs}}{(\text{Revenue/Unit} - \text{Variable Costs/Units})}$$

Using the figures from the example, there is a breakdown equal to $100,000 $\div$ ($10 $-$ $6) $=$ 25,000 units. Being able to determine the specific breakdown point is handy, but the main value of breakeven analysis comes in applying the concept to evaluate a variety of business problems.

Pricing Decisions

A common business problem is estimating the effects of raising or lowering a product's price. How many more would need to be sold to maintain the profit level if you lowered the price a dollar? How many fewer would need to be sold to maintain that profit level if you raised the price a dollar? A rough estimate can be quickly made by drawing new revenue lines on the breakeven chart. If you do draw new revenue lines on the chart in the figure, you will confirm the finding that if the price is raised a dollar, the breakeven point drops from 25,000 to 20,000 units. If you lower the price a dollar, the breakeven jumps to 33,333 units. As you change the revenue line, you will also see how much the profits rise and fall with other price changes.

Breakeven is a valuable tool, but only one of many useful tools for analyzing your business. Breakeven oversimplifies decision. While the advantage is that it makes it easier to comprehend difficult small business issues, it also has some disadvantages. The assumptions are its disadvantages and some of them are listed here.

1. All fixed costs are not really fixed, even over the relevant unit range. They can and do vary.
2. A changing product mix can change the breakeven. The assumption that one plant produces one product can be misleading.
3. Costs do not vary directly with production. Material or labor costs often vary even over very narrow ranges.
4. Selling price is seldom fixed.
5. Inventory costs are seldom calculated within a breakeven and these costs can be large.

As a final tool in *understanding* pricing decisions, the following formula can also be helpful for determining prices.

S.P. = T.C. + P.
S.P. = Selling Price = Per unit selling price
T.C. = Total Costs = Variable costs plus fixed costs per unit.
  P. = Profit = Profit per unit.

100%   Selling Price

P
V.C.
F.C.

0%

A further understanding of this breakeven calculation can be gained by comprehending a concept known as contribution analysis. Contribution is a difficult concept in practice but easy in theory. Any revenue above the variable costs for a product can *contribute* to fixed costs plus profit.

As the example above, with

$$S.P. = \$10.00 \text{ per unit}$$
$$V.C. = \$6.00 \text{ per unit}$$

$$F.C. \div 40{,}000 \text{ units} = \frac{\$100{,}000 \text{ F.C.}}{40{,}000 \text{ units}} = \$2.50 \text{ per unit.}$$

$$\text{Profit} = S.P. - T.C.$$
$$= \$10.00 - (\$6.00 + \$2.50)$$
$$\text{Profit} = \$1.50/\text{unit}$$

Hence at 40,000 units, the firm will show a per unit profit of $1.50 per unit.

The crucial question in a contribution analysis usually occurs when the customers suddenly announce he or she will pay $9.00 for your 40,001st unit of production. Take it or leave it.

The classical school that discounts the contribution type analysis suggests you refuse the order. The contribution school claims, if this is your only choice, take the order for the 40,001st unit at $9.00 as you will still be making 50 cents of profit [$1.50 – ($9.00 – $8.50)].

In fact, the contribution school further argues, on this rare example, that any revenue above the level of variable costs would be better to accept than to reject. For instance, a price of $6.01 per unit would be the lowest price where the order for the 40,001st unit should be accepted. At this level, the sale produces one cent to be contributed to profit and fixed costs. The decision, in the final analysis, will depend on other variables as well. But the purpose of this exercise is to outline the rationale of contribution analysis for use in your final decision making.

WHEN IS THE BEST TIME TO RAISE CAPITAL?

The best time to sell is immediately after you've sold. Hence, the best time to raise capital is immediately after you have raised capital or in short, when you don't need it. I call this Mancuso's Law of Small Business. The theory for this phenomenon, which is generally well accepted by practicing salespeople, is founded in some psychological research conducted by Dr. Leon Festinger of Columbia University in the late 1950s. The research comes under the broad category of cognitive dissonance. Cognitive dissonance is one of the most popular areas of academic inquiry, as evidenced by the number of marketing doctoral dissertations. What is cognitive dissonance? *Cognitive* means being aware and *dissonance* means being stressed.

Therefore, together, it means being aware of internal stress. Every individual who makes a difficult decision, including purchasing or investment decisions, suffers from cognitive dissonance. When the cognitive dissonance reaches an intolerable level, the individual will take action to reduce the dissonance and return his or her own state to equilibrium and harmony. There is no more difficult and stressful decision than to invest money in a small business.

What action does an individual take to reduce dissonance? Consider the example of an automobile buyer.

Assume you are an individual torn between purchasing one of two or three medium-sized cars. On a Saturday, you rush first to the Ford dealership and then across the street to the Chevy dealership and eventually down the street to the Plymouth dealership. Because you are a value-conscious buyer, you compare the features and prices of each car but after the comparison you are still undecided on the best value. Finally, as the Saturday wears on, and your need for a car increases, you finally make a commitment with one of the three car dealers. (The one you trust). For you it was a difficult decision.

This process occurs every day and because 10,000,000 new cars are sold annually under this back and forth dissonance producing method, many of us have experienced it. Yet everyone claims to have secured a "good deal" in buying a car. I don't know one person who has ever admitted to a "bad deal" during the process. Do you? Can it be so?

This decision is known as a *stressed-decision* and the purchaser's dissonance is very high. When you bring the car home, you take the following steps to reduce that dissonance and justify the purchase.

1. You may inadvertently choose to leave the new car in your driveway rather than the garage. Or to drive it and park it where it will be conspicuous to your peers.

2. The night you bring home the car, you will undoubtedly read the

owner's manual and begin searching for new pieces of information about what a wonderful car you have chosen. You probably will never read the owner's manual again and you will either proceed to lose it or bury it in the glove compartment.

3. You may become extremely receptive to TV, newspaper, and magazine advertisements about the car you just purchased. You will ignore other automobile ads. That car will become the single most exciting thing for you for a period of time. You will reject the chance to read other automobile advertisements, preferring only to read advertisements that reinforce new features about the wonderful car you just purchased. Because motor car companies are aware that you suffer dissonance, the President of General Motors will send you a personal letter congratulating you on such a wise automobile choice. They may even send you a questionnaire seeking feedback information about the purchasing process that occurred during your selection of a car. Beside the value of the information you feed back to them (they can learn these facts through less costly sampling techniques) the questionnare allows you a chance to vent any residual dissonance.

So the message is simple. The best time to sell is immediately after you've sold. The best time to make a sales call is immediately after you make the sale. The best time to send a sales message is immediately after you made a sale. Hence, the best time to raise money is when you don't need it and just after you received money. That finding is built on Leon Festinger's concept of cognitive dissonance and it works.

THE ENTREPRENEURIAL RAISING CAPITAL MODEL

The raising capital process often follows a specific sequence of actions. The one I like is the six-step process. Understanding the process often helps improve the results.

Step 1. Locating sources
Step 2. The approach
Step 3. Qualifying the source
Step 4. Presenting the business plan
Step 5. Handling objections
Step 6. Gaining commitment

Step 1—Locating sources: Without a doubt, prospecting is the hardest part of the raising capital process. Once you find the right person, the business plan can help by taking over. Some of the Center for Entrepreneurial Management's directories are the best first step in the locating process.

Step 2—The approach: During the approach, two major actions should occur. First, you should seek to reduce relationship tension. In other words, you and the capital source should feel at ease. Raising capital is not you doing something to the venture source, but a shared experience, where you are going to make money together. Secondly, the entrepreneur should simultaneously build a degree of task tension. While reducing relationship tension there should be a reciprocal concern about the task at hand such as, "I understand you have a $100 million portfolio to invest." The task that needs to be accomplished creates task tension. Your visit is not a totally social exchange. You can't just kid yourself and say that you are there just for the fun of it. You're there to raise money.

Step 3—Qualifying the source: This is "the hot button" and it focuses on the reason the capital source will eventually do the deal. Within every situation there are certain salient features and attributes. Among the product's features, certain benefits are more important to certain capital sources. Not everyone invests in the same product or business plan for the same reason. Most of the time, the same plan is bought by different people for different reasons. The issue is to determine what turns this specific source on. What button do you push to get the order? What is it that this source needs? This can only be gained through a very careful questioning of the source's needs.

Step 4—Presenting the plan: Within this model, most entrepreneurs do this step best. They are so familiar with their product, having presented it numerous times, they are almost always able to make a convincing presentation about its benefits. The only issue here is to stress the benefits: What is the perceived value the customer receives from the product versus what your product does? What are its features?

Step 5—Handling objections: There will be some objections, or attempts to postpone the investment and some discussion on the weaknesses of your product. How do you handle objection? I offer you a very simple conceptual method, which I call the "feel, felt, found method" and it works like this: When you are given an objection don't disagree with it, don't be negative. Whatever you do, respond to the objection in a sincere way. Before you do, remember you should do three things.

1. Empathize with it

2. Legitimize it
3. Introduce some new information to show why the objection is without foundation.

In other words, when you're given the objection, you respond by saying, "I understand how you feel about that, it's very understandable to think that an individual would feel that way about that issue." Second you say, "I felt that way too," and you legitimize it, "and several other sources, who I just visited, felt the same way about that issue so it is a very legitimate feeling." But you must remember that you are here to raise capital. Therefore, you have to introduce new information to more completely inform the source of the relevant issues. The first two steps reach out and agree with the objection, but the third and final step must change the source's opinion. The mood is set and the guard is down and the objection is about to vanish.

The new information should be introduced something like this, "you are really only partially informed; I want to show you some new test information that we just completed in the field, and that will really put your mind to rest about our product's whatever." The venture source is never wrong! Occasionally, they are partially informed and that's how you turn your objection inside-out. You say, "we found . . ."

Step 6—Gaining Commitment: This has traditionally been classified as the most important step in raising capital. It just is not so. Actually, the most vital step is qualifying the source. (Step 3) If steps 2 and 3 are completed properly, then gaining commitment is a very small step and actually the least stressing step in the entire process. To gain commitment, you may want to create an opportunity to close on an objection. Many times you are given an objection that can be handled by exercising the feel, felt, found technique, and you really want to close to get on with running the business. How do you do it? I call it a "trial close." Frequently an entrepreneur enjoys the raising capital process so much, that he or she goes past the close, and keeps presenting the plan rather than trying to make the deal. Don't be afraid to close early. Try closing the deal several times as the venture source will only invest in your enthusiasm. You can't be too enthusiastic so keep trying to make the deal.

Raising capital is the art of reaching agreement. It is an art and a process of building trust and confidence. Unfortunately, the reason entrepreneurs are often held in low esteem is that many of them are ineffective capital raising artists. This damages the image of the good ones. The professional is an artist with a set of listening skills and an inner desire to perform. Entrepreneuring is fun when you are good at it.

DIFFERENCE BETWEEN A MARKETING
AND SELLING ORIENTATION
WHILE RAISING MONEY

The difference between a marketing versus a sales orientation can be determined by how the entrepreneur handles the subtle difference between a product's features and the corresponding customer benefits. A *customer benefit* is a product feature turned inside-out. A marketing oriented business emphasizes the perceived customer benefits of a product.

An example of this is often highlighted by the quarter-inch drills story. Last year 3,250,000 quarter-inch drills were sold in this country and the drills have come to represent the product feature. On the other hand, last year customers bought 3,250,000 quarter inch holes. It just happened that the drill was necessary to produce the hole. If anyone is ever able to package a hole (put it in a small plastic container) customers would begin buying the holes to solve their problems. Mr. Charles Revson, the entrepreneur founder of Revlon, the famous cosmetic company, once said the same thing in another way. He said, "In my factory we make cosmetics, but in my stores we sell hope." Customers buy benefits while you make features.

A marketing orientation requires a customer looking for a product; while a sales orientation requires a product looking for a customer. It's really only a matter of perception and direction, as visualized in the following chart.

CUSTOMER		*PRODUCT*
Marketing		*Sales*
Product	*Feature*	*Benefit*
Cosmetics	Special fragrance	Hope
Drill bits	Characteristics of drill	Hope
Encyclopedia	Volumes of information	Knowledge

—Venture capitalists buy stock and sell money
—Entrepreneurs sell stock and buy money
—It's all a matter of orientation

S.B.I.R.

The Small Business Innovation Research Act directs that small firms receive at least a fixed, minimum percentage of research and development awards made by Federal agencies with sizeable R & D budgets.

The act was signed into law by President Reagan on July 22, 1982. The Small Business Administration (SBA) estimates that $47 million will be awarded in Fiscal Year 1983. *That amount is expected to increase tenfold by Fiscal Year 1987.* Each participating agency will make awards to small firms on a competitive basis. Selection criteria will be included in each solicitation.

Background

In 1977, the National Science Foundation (NSF) pioneered seed-money grants to entrepreneurial companies. Since then, NSF has provided roughly $20 million in funding through the SBIR program, with follow-up funding expected to exceed $47 million. Firms completing the second phase of funding have received $41 million to date. *Nearly 40% of all awards have been to firms with ten or fewer employees.* The same ratio holds true for the Department of Defense, which became involved in seed-money funding two years ago. Of the 1,103 proposals received by DOD thus far, just over 100 awards have been made.

There have been five NSF solicitations since 1977, and one DOD solicitation. Each year there has been a consistent ratio of about one winner for every eight proposals submitted. Last year, NSF received 764 proposals and 154 of these were recommended for Phase I awards; however, only 108 were actually funded.

The real attraction of the SBIR programs is not so much the initial seed money ($30,000 to $50,000), but the fact that approximately 40% of all first round winners go on to receive second round funding ($200,000 to $500,000) within 12 months. *And as the odds for receiving funding go up, so do the odds of finding outside financial investors, particularly venture capital firms.* Endorsement from the SBIR is not taken lightly by the private sector in Phase III.

Present and Future

If none of the foregoing information provides you with the incentive to go after this seed money, the future of the Small Business Innovation Act should. This legislation, which is being phased in over a five year period, will eventually provide as much as $450 million in grant money. Therefore, those of you making the initial effort to win these grants will be in on the ground floor. It is estimated that as many as 2,000 Phase I proposals and 1,000 Phase II proposals will be funded in the final 12 months of this program.

Specifically, the SBIR program requires Federal agencies with R & D budgets of over $100 million to eventually devote 1.25% of their research funds to establish Small Business Innovation Research programs within the respective agencies. As we said, the program will be phased in gradually, beginning this year, and continuing through 1987. This total expenditure will go from about $50 million in 1983 to about $470 in 1987-88.

SBIR

SBIR PROPOSALS, AS OF AUGUST 1, 1983

Agency	No. of Proposals Received	Estim. No. of Awards
Dept. of Energy	c. 1700	100
Environmental Protection Agency	214	10
Dept. Health & Human Services	727	100
Dept. of Transportation	372	8-10
Dept. of Defense	c. 2900	c. 200
Dept. of Interior	105	6
Nuclear Regulatory Commission	172	7-8
NASA	978	c. 100
Dept. of Agriculture	268	8-10
Totals	7,436	544

The word from the respective government agencies is, that the quality of the SBIR proposals being received is in general high, with more good proposals than can be funded, so that careful and difficult choices must be made. This is, of course, good for the SBIR program. If the situation were reversed it would justify the sniping the established big research centers have been directing at the program since its inception (let alone trying to keep the SBIR act from passing in the first place). The latest and quite subtle attempt to undermine the program has come from Representative John Dingle of Michigan, who buried three seemingly innocuous amendments in the appropriations bill of the Department of Health and Human Services, which, if passed, would make it possible to reject SBIR proposals on the basis of quality and return the unused monies to the Department's general research fund. Mr. Dingle was acting on behalf of the powerful medical research community. This attempt at subversion was spotted, and it is expected that the amendments will be removed before the bill's passage. However there will probably be further attempts of this kind, at least until the SBIR funded projects start to prove themselves. It is therefore doubly important that the quality of the proposals remain high.

Agency SBIR Program

REPRESENTATIVES

Department of Agriculture

Ms. A. Holiday Schauer
Office of Grants
and Program Systems
Department of Agriculture
1300 Rosslyn Commonwealth
Building Suite 103
Arlington, VA 22209
(703) 235-2628´

Department of Defense

Mr. Horace Crouch
Director, Small Business
and Economic Utilization
Office of Secretary of Defense
Room 2A340 Pentagon
Washington, DC 20301
(202) 697-9383

Department of Education

Dr. Edward Esty
SBIR Program Coordinator
Office of Educational
Research and Improvement
Department of Education
Mail Stop 40
Washington, DC 20208

Department of Energy

Mr. Mark Kurzius
c/o SBIR Program Manager
U.S. Department of Energy
Washington, DC 20545

Department of Health and Human Services

Mr. Richard Clinkscales
Director, Office of Small
and Disadvantaged Business
Utilization
Department of Health and
Human Services
200 Independence Ave., S.W.
Room 513D
Washington, DC 20201

Department of Interior

Dr. Thomas Henrie
Chief Scientist
Bureau of Mines
U.S. Department of the Interior
2401 E. St., N.W.
Washington, DC 20241
(202) 634-1305

Department of Transportation

Dr. James Costantino
Director, Transportation
System Center
Department of Transportation
Kendall Square
Cambridge, MA 02142
(617) 494-2222

Environmental Protection Agency

Mr. Walter Preston
Office of Research Grants
and Centers—(RD 675)
Office of Research and Development
Environmental Protection Agency
401 M. Street, S.W.
Washington, DC 20460
(202) 382-5744

National Aeronautics and Space Administration

Mr. Carl Schwenk
National Aeronautics and
Space Administration
SBIR Office—Code R
600 Independence Ave., S.W.
Washington, DC 20546
(202) 755-2450

National Science Foundation

Ritchie Coryell
Roland Tibbetts
SBIR Program Managers
National Science Foundation
1800 G. Street, N.W.
Washington, DC 20550

Nuclear Regulatory Commission

Mr. Francis Gillespie
Director, Administration
and Resource Staff
Office of Nuclear
Regulatory Research
Nuclear Regulation
Commission
Washington, DC 20460

PROJECTED SBIR FUNDING BY AGENCY

AGENCY	PROJECTED FUNDING									
	%	1983	%	1984	%	1985	%	1986	%	1987
Department of Defense	.1	$16,340	.3	$ 49,020	.6	$ 98,040	1.0	$163,400	1.25	$204,250
NASA	.2	5,500	.6	16,500	1.0	27,500	1.25	34,375	1.25	34,375
Department of Energy	.2	4,161	.6	12,483	1.0	20,805	1.25	26,006	1.25	26,006
Health & Human Services	.2	6,476	.6	19,428	1.0	32,380	1.25	40,475	1.25	40,475
National Science Foundation	.2	5,500	.6	6,000	1.0	9,700	1.25	12,125	1.25	12,125
Department of Agriculture	.2	579	.6	1,737	1.0	2,895	1.25	3,619	1.25	3,619
Department of Transportation	.2	491	.6	1,473	1.0	2,450	1.25	3,062	1.25	3,062
Nuclear Regulatory Commission	.2	391	.6	1,173	1.0	1,955	1.25	2,444	1.25	2,444
Environmental Protection Agency	.2	288	.6	864	1.0	1,440	1.25	1,800	1.25	1,800
Department of Interior	.2	231	.6	693	1.0	1,155	1.25	1,444	1.25	1,444
		$39,957		$109,371		$198,320		$288,750		$329,600

This chart is a projection of the funding for the SBIR program through 1987, based on current budget levels. In illustrating the effect of annual percentage increase against agency budgets, the chart assumes zero inflation and zero expansion. All dollar figures are in thousands.

UNUSUAL SOURCES OF CAPITAL

Lending institutions prefer to loan money against collateral because they retain the option of liquidating the collateral to repay the loan. Following is the rule of thumb for what can be loaned against different forms of collateral from the balance sheet of an entrepreneurial venture.

In practice, the actual ratios are even more pronounced. In other words, banks prefer not to lend against inventory as contrasted to lending against receivables. In turn, easily liquidated fixed assets are the most attractive type of collateral (automobiles) and they usually command both a high percentage of their lendable market value as well as a subsequently lower interest rate.

A lender is basically unsure of an inventory's value until it is converted to cash by being sold. That's the underlying reason that lenders shy away from accepting inventory or certain types of fixed assets as collateral for a loan. Thus, the role of T.H.E. Insurance Company is to write an insurance policy to protect a lender against bankruptcy. Insurance companies essentially appraise the collateral asset and insure to repossess it from a lender at the assessed rates.

Rather than the insurance policy paying off at death, the policy is paid upon default in the loan. Here's how it works.

1. T.H.E. appraises the assets to be pledged, including both inventory and fixed assets.
2. T.H.E. then issues an insurance policy for the amount of their appraisal.
3. The company hands this policy over to the lender and then borrows 100 percent of the value of the policy in a loan.
4. If the company defaults, T.H.E. takes title to the collateral and sells it. The lender is paid in full using T.H.E.'s credit and capital to be reimbursed.

What Does All This
Insurance Protection Cost?

1. Appraisal fee: minimum amount $1 thousand. This is for the appraisal and it is 1 percent of the appraised value of the collateral plus out-of-pocket (travel) expenses.

2. A 2 percent add-on interest rate on the outstanding loan balance, not on the full appraisal of the collateral. The premium interest rate of 2 percent is charged only on what's borrowed or what is at risk.

The value of T.H.E. policy allows more capital to be secured from existing lenders. On the one hand, a lender typically allows only 10 percent of inventory value to be used as loan collateral. With a policy the inventory allowed as collateral might be above 50 percent of its value, depending upon T.H.E.'s assessment. This arrangement often allows a two or three times greater amount to be loaned against an asset.

Often an asset or inventory can be borrowed against when it was given zero valuation by a bank because of the T.H.E. formula. On a theoretical basis, the lending interest rate can be reduced if you can convince the lender of the merits and security of the guarantee. In effect, given the policy, the lender should advance funds on T.H.E.'s credit, not the credit of your entrepreneurial venture.

	Percentage to be Loaned Against
Accounts Receivable	75%–80% under 90 days
Inventory	10%–20%
Fixed Assets	70%–80% market value

In practice, you are seldom ever able to negotiate lower bank interest rate by securing a T.H.E. guarantee and, in total, you are paying 5–6 percent above prime rate for this type of lending. If your entrepreneurial venture can service debt, write to Mr. Ed Shifman, Vice President, T.H.E. Insurance Company, 80 Bent Street, Cambridge, MA 02141, (617) 494-5300.

ENTREPRENEURIAL BANK BORROWING

There is a small but developing trend that may be of interest to entrepreneurs currently searching for a new banking relationship. Recently two major changes have occurred in the overall United States banking structure that have created some measurable differences between banks. The first of these changes is foreign banks doing business in the United States. In 1972, when the Federal Reserve started keeping statistics on such issues, there were 52 foreign banks with 100 offices in the United States. By mid-1978, the number of foreign banks had more than doubled to 123 and they operated 268 offices. The assets of these foreign-owned United States-based banks have grown more than four times during the five-year period and today their assets are over $100 billion. The second change is the two-tier prime rate structure now being charged to small business. But more about that in a minute.

Why are these foreign banks expanding in the United States? There are two basic answers: the relative devaluation of the United States dollar and the ability of these banks to avoid United States banking regulations. Because of these factors, these banks have generally been taking a more aggressive posture toward loans to entrepreneurial ventures. This is not true for every banker at every bank, but it is true as a generality. So, if you're considering a banking relationship why not consider Britain's Barclay Bank, or the Bank of Montreal, or any of the host of Japanese, Swiss or French banks.

These foreign-owned banks are allowed to open branches outside their countries (U.S. banks are not) and they often have offices in the major cities of the country. They are seldom located in small towns, much preferring the New York or Los Angeles type of city. This ability to operate across counties can also be a feature for your company if they operate in the same cities where branches of your business are located. Beside this benefit, these banks are not required to tie-up a portion of their assets with the Federal Reserve System because they most often choose to operate under state banking regulations. These two fundamental reasons allow these banks the slight tendency to be more aggressive in securing new business. Hence, it may prove to be to your advantage to do business with them.

Further, with this expansion continuing, I would predict a major overhaul in United States banking restrictions to allow United States banks to compete on more favorable terms with these foreign banks. Hence, if this happens, this opportunity for more aggressive banking will prove to be available only for a moment in time.

There are the obvious advantages of doing business with a foreign-based bank, if your entrepreneurial venture business happens to sell or buy from the host country. For the bank nearest you, consult the Yellow Pages of the largest city near you.

The second major change was triggered by the heros of small business at The Mellon National Bank in Pittsburg, Pennsylvania. They began offering small businesses a borrowing rate below the prime rate. They did this during money shortages (now) to help entrepreneurs, and they deserve pioneering recognition! For an up-to-date list of banks who offer a revised two-tier lending rate, write to Chief Counsel for Advocacy, SBA, 1441 L St. N.W., Washington, DC 20416.

WHERE ARE THE HIDDEN SOURCES OF CAPITAL?

Turn Around Technique

One of the most interesting problems in small business is turning around unsuccessful companies. A condensed story of how Mr. Bill Frustajer (the founder of several highly successful businesses) and his

consulting team turned around the H.S. Scott Hi-Fi Company in May-
nard, Massachusetts serves a point. H.S. Scott is one of the leading
quality manufacturers of stereo equipment in the United States. Some
years ago they ran into terrible price competition from foreign suppliers, mainly Japanese, and the company was tettering on the verge of
bankruptcy. Payroll had been paid intermittently, bills were overdue,
and the large Boston-based State Street Bank had closed in. Bill
Frustajer's first chore was to discover any sources of short term cash.
Cash would stay-off the creditors and pay past due payroll to keep the
employees working. The technique he used was to uncover a heretofore undiscovered asset. Three years previously, the earnings of the
company had been sufficient to warrant the company paying income
taxes of $1,200,000 on that year's profits. The losses the last two years
had been staggering, but profits were respectable the preceding year.
Bill Frustajer rewrote his financial statements and filed IRS form 1139 in
order to go back and get a tax refund against those assets. A tax loss can
be either carried forward for five years or back for three years. Below is
a simplified statement of the company's performance.

	SIMPLIFIED PROFIT AND LOSS			
	1971	1972	1973	1974
Sales	$12,000,000	$13,000,000	$14,000,000	$12,000,000
Profit before taxes	2,400,000	(250,000)	(2,700,000)	
Taxes	1,200,000	—	—	
Profit after taxes	1,200,000	(250,000)	(2,700,000)	

While this statement is simplified to demonstrate the example,
income taxes are not due until April 15th of the following year for a
company with a calendar year end. Consequently, by filing an amended
set of financial statements and tax returns plus IRS form 1139, he was
able to obtain a tax refund for the taxes paid in 1971. In the H.S. Scott
case mentioned, although these are not the actual numbers, the tax
refund saved the day and in turn, the company.

Actually, the turn-around-time on receiving an IRS rebate is too
long (months) to ordinarily save a faltering business. So, Bill pledged
this refund to the bank along with the documents filed to secure the IRS
refund and was able to borrow against this asset, thereby shrinking the
processing time to receive the needed cash infusion. He received the
funds in less than a month.

Hidden assets don't always appear on financial statements in
plain view. Examples of other hidden assets are foreign rights to
products, licensing arrangements, patents, and goodwill.

Farmers Home Loan

The SBA is supposedly the government agency charged with helping the entrepreneur, but, in practice, other federal agencies also provide a great deal of help. The FmHa is the loan program of the Farmers Home Administration, which offers guaranteed loans to growing businesses. Unlike the SBA's program with a $500 thousand ceiling, the FmHa loan program has no ceiling. In fact, loans have ranged from $7 thousand to $33 million with an average of about $900 thousand.

The FmHa loan gives preference to distressed areas, and rural communities of less than 25,000 inhabitants. It will loan money for any worthwhile business purpose. The minimum equity requirement is 10 percent and, if your venture can be shown to be job creating, your loan has a greater chance of approval. Unlike the SBA, you do not have to prove to be an unbankable company to secure a FmHa loan. The loans are for fairly long terms, thirty years for construction, fifteen years for equipment and seven years for working capital. The interest rate is about the same as can be negotiated with a bank, but the FmHa has a one-time fee that is calculated by multiplying one percent of the principal loan amount by the percentage of the guarantee. Even given the one-time fee, the good standing of the United States Government stands behind the guaranteed portions of the loan and the interest rate eventually negotiated often effects these favorable considerations. Why not write the FmHa in care of the (USDA) United States Dept. of Agriculture, Washington, DC 20250, or look in your nearest largest city yellow pages for one of the 1800 county offices. Look under United States Government—Agriculture.

Help in Applying for SBA Loan

A Complete Guide to Getting Your Own SBA Loan, published by Business Aids and Investment Associates, Houston, Texas, 1980. It is "dedicated to all small business people."

Anyone who has a realistic proposal for a small, entrepreneurial venture but who lacks the financial backing to launch it will most likely consider an SBA guaranteed loan. But where does the budding entrepreneur begin? What are the filing procedures? *A Complete Guide to Getting Your Own SBA Loan* can answer all of your questions and dispel many misconceptions about a Small Business Administration loan. This guide leads you from start to finish through the SBA process and saves you money, too. A correctly completed application can eliminate needless waste of time and energy and get you an SBA loan in 4–6 weeks instead of 6 months, as is commonly believed. Perhaps you don't qualify. Maybe you think you don't qualify and in fact you do. One sure way to find out is to read this guide, which is written in easily understood terms. For a comprehensive outline to SBA guarantee loans, send for *A Complete Guide to Getting Your Own SBA Loan* from Business Aids and Associates, Inc., P.O. Box 37065, Houston, TX 77036. The price is $29.95 with $1.50 handling and postage, add $3.00 for first class mail.

SOURCES—OTHER SBA NONBANK LENDERS

Money Store Investment Corporation, Springfield, NJ (201) 467-9000. Offers SBA Guaranteed Loans in branch locations in 12 states.

Merrill Lynch Small Business Lending Company, New York, NY, (212) 637-7455. Loan program functions nationwide.

Allied Lending Corporation, Washington, DC, (202) 331-1112. SBA guaranteed loans for the Washington area.

NIS Capital Funding Corporation, White Plains, NY, (914) 428-8600. Provides SBA guaranteed loans locally.

Independence Mortgage Company, Inc., Odessa, TX, (915) 333-5814. SBA guaranteed loans for the Odessa area.

The First Commercial Credit Corporation, Los Angeles, CA, (213) 937-0860. Provides SBA loans in Los Angeles.

ITT Small Business Finance Corporation, Minneapolis, MN, (612) 540-8509. Offers SBA loans on a national basis. (This is a subsidiary of International Telephone & Telegraph Finance Corporation.)

SBA's BUSINESS LOAN PROGRAMS

Under a congressional mandate, the United States Small Business Administration (SBA) assists the nation's small businesses through a number of programs and efforts. SBA helps new or growing businesses meet their financial needs, counsels small firms with problems, offers special assistance to minority and women-owned businesses, helps small businesses to secure government contracts, and acts as a special advocate for small business with other federal agencies, with states and within the private sector.

Basic Types of SBA Loans

SBA loan proceeds can be used for working capital, purchase of inventory, equipment, and supplies, or for building construction and expansion. The SBA offers two basic types of business loans.

1. Loans made by private lenders, usually banks, and guaranteed by SBA. SBA *bank guaranteed loans* are tied to funds appropriated by Congress. The amount of loans that SBA can guarantee is much larger than funds appropriated for direct loans. Thus, the majority of SBA loans is of the guaranteed type. By law, SBA can guarantee up to 90 percent of a loan made by a bank or other private lender.
2. Loans made directly by the agency. Monies for *direct loans* also come from funds appropriated specifically by Congress for this purpose. Those direct loan monies are limited, however, and demand invariably exceeds supply. In addition, in recent years the SBA has approved an increasingly larger share of its direct loans for small firms that have unusual difficulty raising funds in the private market—*i.e.,* firms headed by women, handicapped persons, and representatives of socially and economically disadvantaged groups.

In general, direct SBA loans carry interest rates lower than those in the private financial markets. They are available only to applicants unable to secure private financing or an SBA-guaranteed or participation loan.

SBA also offers special *economic opportunity* loans for socially and economically disadvantaged persons (mostly representing minorities). These loans help small firms adversely affected by government regulations. Loans are also made to small firms engaged in manufacturing, selling, installing, servicing, or developing specific energy measures. Local development companies obtain loans for projects aiding small business in urban or rural communities.

The SBA licenses, regulates, and financially helps private firms called *Small Business Investment Companies* (SBICs), which supply equity capital and regular loans to small firms with unusual growth potential. Details concerning special loan programs can be obtained from any SBA office.

Even with its varied programs, the SBA cannot assist all the small businesses, or all the persons interested in starting a small firm. Agency funds and personnel are limited. Therefore, in recent years, the SBA—as small business' advocate—has increased its liaison and cooperation with the private sector. The primary aim is to widen assistance and make more funds available to the millions of small entrepreneurs in the country. The nation's banks have been made more aware of the advantages of participating in SBA guaranteed loans, and have been urged to respond through their own loan programs to small business' needs and wants. The SBA has instituted a special arrangement with a number of certified banks to cut down on red tape and paperwork in SBA guaranteed loans. Other companies have been organized as SBA nonbank lenders, and can make small business loans guaranteed by the Agency.

This approach, involving greater cooperation with the private financial markets and putting the Agency more and more into a role of a *wholesaler,* will be emphasized in the months and years ahead. The private lender will be more and more the *retailer* of small business lending, while SBA takes on the role of *wholesaler.*

Who Is Eligible for an SBA Loan?

By law, the Agency may not make or guarantee a loan if a business can obtain funds on reasonable terms from a bank or other private source. A borrower therefore must first seek private financing before applying to the SBA. This means that a person first must apply to a bank or other lending institution for a loan. In a city of over 200,000 population, a person must be turned down by two banks before applying for an SBA loan.

A company must be independently owned and operated, not dominant in its field and must meet certain standards of size in terms of employees or annual receipts. Loans cannot be made to speculative businesses, newspapers, or businesses engaged in gambling.

Applicants for loans also must agree to comply with SBA regulations stating that there will be no discrimination in employment or services to the public based on race, color, religion, national origin, sex, or marital status.

What Is a Small Business?

At present, eligibility for loans varies by industry and SBA program. For business loans, the general size standard eligibility requirements are as follows.

Manufacturing—Number of employees may range up to 1,500 depending on the industry in which the applicant is primarily engaged.

Wholesaling—Yearly sales must not be over $9.5 to $22 million, depending on the industry.

Services—Annual receipts not exceeding $2 million to $8 million, depending on the industry in which the applicant is primarily engaged.

Retailing—Annual sales or receipts not exceeding $2 to $7.5 million, depending on the industry.

Construction—General construction: average annual receipts not exceeding $9.5 million for the three most recently completed fiscal years.

Special Trade Construction—Average annual receipts not exceeding $1 to $2 million for the three most recently completed fiscal years, depending on the industry.

Agriculture—Annual receipts not exceeding $1 million.

What Are the Credit Requirements?

A loan applicant must:

1. Be of good character.
2. Show ability to operate a business successfully.
3. Have enough capital in an existing firm so that with an SBA loan the business can operate on a sound financial basis.
4. Show that the proposed loan is of such sound value or so secured as reasonably to assure payment.
5. Show that the past earnings record and future prospects of the firm indicate ability to repay the loan and other fixed debt, if any, out of profits.
6. Be able to provide, from personal resources, sufficient funds to have a reasonable amount at stake to withstand possible losses, particularly during the early stages of a new venture.

How Much Can a Person Borrow?

Loans made directly by SBA have a maximum of $150 thousand. The bank guaranteed loan program permits the Agency to guarantee up to 90 percent of a loan, or a maximum of $500 thousand, whichever is less. (Legislation is pending in Congress to increase this figure to $750 thousand).

Economic opportunity loans are limited to $100 thousand under each type of lending program. Handicapped assistance loans have a limit of $350 thousand under the guaranteed program. A handicapped assistance loan made directly by SBA is limited to $100 thousand. Energy loans carry a ceiling of $500 thousand for the guaranteed type and $350 thousand for direct or immediate participation types.

Note: A new standard definition of a small business has been proposed based on a single measurement of size—total number of employees per firm. SBA field offices can advise firms which standard applies to them, if this proposal is formally adopted.

Note: When neither private financing nor a loan guarantee is available, SBA may provide loan funds on an *immediate participation* basis with a bank. The bank disburses part of the loan, at market interest rates, and the balance of the loan is disbursed directly by the SBA, at a lower interest rate. The SBA's share of an immediate participation loan may not exceed $150 thousand.

Loans to businesses affected by federal legislation, regulation, or actions have no statutory maximum. The amount of economic injury is the governing factor. Small companies are eligible if they are displaced as a result of government action, or adversely affected by occupational safety and health legislation, strategic arms limitation actions, air and water pollution control legislation, military base closings, or emergency energy shortage situations.

Local Development Company loans carry a maximum of $500 thousand.

Terms of SBA Loans

Regular business loans generally have a maximum maturity of 10 years. Working capital loans are limited to seven years. Loans that include construction or acquisition of real estate have a 20-year maximum.

The SBA regularly sets a maximum allowable interest rate that banks can charge on guaranteed loans. Interest rates on direct loans and the SBA's share of an immediate participation loan are tied to the cost of money to the federal government and adjusted periodically.

Economic opportunity loans carry a maturity of 15 years. Handicapped assistance loans carry a 15-year maturity. The interest rate is 3 percent for SBA's share of a handicapped assistance loan.

Displaced business loans and other loans to alleviate economic injury resulting from federal legislation or other action have maturities of 30 years and carry the same interest rates as direct loans. Emergency energy shortage economic injury loans are subject to these same terms.

Collateral

One or more of the following may be acceptable security for a loan.

1. A mortgage on land, a building and/or equipment
2. Assignment of warehouse receipts for marketable merchandise
3. A mortgage on chattels
4. Guarantees or personal endorsements, and in some instances, assignment of current receivables

How to Apply for a SBA Loan

Those already in business should:

1. Prepare a current financial statement (balance sheet) listing all assets and all liabilities of the business.
2. Have an earnings (profit and loss) statement for the current period to the date of the balance sheet.

3. Prepare a current personal financial statement of the owner, or each partner or stockholder owning 20 percent or more of the corporate stock in the business.
4. List collateral to be offered as security for the loan, with an estimate of the present market value of each item.
5. State the amount of the loan requested and exact purposes for which it can be used.
6. Take the foregoing material to your banker. Ask for a direct bank loan and if you are declined, ask the bank to make the loan under the SBA's Loan Guarantee Plan or Immediate Participation Plan. If the bank is interested in an SBA guaranteed or participation loan, ask the banker to contact the SBA for discussion of your application. In most cases of guaranteed or participation loans, the SBA will deal directly with the bank.
7. If a guaranteed or a participation loan is not available, write or visit the nearest SBA office. The SBA has 110 field offices that often send loan officers to visit many smaller cities as the need is indicated. To speed matters, make your financial information available when you first write or visit the SBA.

Those wanting to start a business should:

1. Describe the type of business you plan to establish.
2. Describe your experience and management capabilities.
3. Prepare an estimate of how much you or others have to invest in the business and how much you will need to borrow.
4. Prepare a current financial statement (balance sheet) listing all personal assets and all liabilities.
5. Prepare a detailed projection of earnings for the first year the business will operate.
6. List collateral to be offered as security for the loan, indicating your estimate of the present market value of each item.
7. Follow steps 6 and 7 for those already in business.

CHAPTER EIGHT

FACTS ABOUT SMALL BUSINESS AND THE U.S. SMALL BUSINESS ADMINISTRATION*

FACTS ABOUT SMALL BUSINESS

Small Business In General

There are an estimated 14.4 million businesses in the U.S. Of this total, 3.4 million are farms and 11 million are nonfarm businesses. Of the nonfarm businesses, 10.8 million (8.2 percent) are considered "small" by the SBA's loan application size standards. Approximately 99 percent of the 3.4 million farms are considered small businesses by the Agency's size standards.

The number of small businesses in the U.S. has increased annually in most of the last 30 years. New business incorporations increased by 10 percent in 1979, to 524,565 from 478,019 in 1978. Incorporations increased by 16 percent in 1977 and decreased by 3 percent in 1974 (Dun & Bradstreet statistics).

Business failures (bankruptcies and discontinuances for other reasons) increased by 14 percent in 1979, to 7,564 from 6,619 in 1978. Nearly 55 percent of failures (bankruptcies or closures with losses for creditors) among small businesses occur within their first 5 years of operation. 92 percent of all business failures are a direct result of poor management.

Estimates for 1976 (the latest year available) indicate small business produces 39 percent of the Gross National Product (GNP). (For these statistics, a small business is defined in Internal Revenue Service data as one with 0 to 499 employees.)

Approximately 62 percent of nonfarm businesses have annual sales or receipts of less than $25,000. 82 percent have sales or receipts of less than

*Reprinted from the U.S. Small Business Administration, Public Communications Division, February 1981.

$100,000 and 98 percent have sales or receipts of less than $1,000,000 (IRS data, 1975).

Small businesses account for nearly $8 of every $10 earned by construction firms (excludes farms).

Small businesses account for nearly $7 of every $10 in sales made by retailers and wholesalers (excludes farms).

Small nonfarm businesses account for nearly $6 of every $10 of receipts in the service industries.

Small nonfarm business provides 58 percent of U.S. business employment.

Small business directly or indirectly provides the livelihood of over 100 million Americans.

⅓ of all small nonfarm businesses are in the service industries.

Nearly ¼ of all nonfarm small businesses are in retail trade.

75% of all U.S. businesses are sole proprietorships, and virtually all of these are small businesses.

Nearly 80% of all U.S. nonfarm businesses employ less than 10 people.

The small business sector of the economy creates more jobs than any other: Between 1969 and 1976, 16 million new jobs were created. One million of these jobs were created by the 1,000 largest corporations. Three million of the new jobs were in state and local governments. The remaining 12 million were created by small business.

> 66 percent of the total jobs generated between 1969 and 1976 were in firms with 20 or fewer employees.
> 77 percent were in firms with 50 or fewer employees.
> 82 percent were in firms with 100 or fewer employees.
> 87 percent were in firms with 500 or fewer employees.
> 13 percent were in firms with over 500 employees.
> —(David Birch, *The Job Generation Process*)

Minority-Owned Small Businesses

(Except where noted, the Census Bureau figures are for 1972, the latest year available).

561,000 businesses are owned by members of minority groups (Black Americans, Hispanic Americans, American Indians, Asian Americans, Eskimos, and Aleuts), according to 1977 data. Members of minority groups own 4.4 percent of all businesses.

In 1977, Black Americans owned 231,000 businesses, compared with 194,986 in 1972.

Hispanic Americans owned 220,000 businesses in 1977.

Asian Americans, American Indians, and members of all other minority groups owned 111,000 businesses in 1977.

Nearly all minority-owned businesses are small businesses.

Gross receipts for minority businesses were $26.4 billion in 1977.

63 percent of minority-owned non-farm firms are in the retail and service industries.

80 percent of minority-owned firms have no employees.

Women-Owned Small Businesses (Data for 1977)

Women own 702,000 businesses. A Department of Commerce survey in 1977 used the following definition of a woman-owned business: "A women-owned business is one in which the sole owner is a woman or *one half or more* of the partners is a woman, or 50 percent or more of the stock in a corporation is owned by a woman or women." SBA defines a woman-owned business as: "A woman-owned business is one that is at least 51 percent owned, controlled, and operated by a woman or women. 'Controlled' is defined as 'exercising the authority to make policy decisions', and 'operated' is defined as 'actively involved in the day-to-day management of the business'." This definition was changed from 50 percent in March, 1979.

Gross annual receipts for women-owned businesses were $41.5 billion. This represented 6.6 percent of all U.S. business receipts, excluding those of large corporations.

Nearly all women-owned businesses are small businesses.

75.8 percent of women-owned businesses are sole proprietorships. They accounted for 22.8 percent, or $9.5 billion, of the gross annual receipts generated by women-owned businesses.

23.9 percent of women-owned businesses have employees.
70.4 percent of the women-owned businesses that do have employees have fewer than 5 employees.

Average gross annual receipts for women-owned businesses without employees were $11,800. Average gross annual receipts for women-owned businesses with employees were $209,000.

8.4 percent of women-owned businesses were corporations that accounted for 46 percent, or $19 billion, of all gross annual receipts generated by women-owned businesses.

15.9 percent of women-owned businesses were partnerships that accounted for 31.2 percent, or $13 billion, of all gross annual receipts generated by women-owned businesses.

75 percent of all women-owned businesses were in the services and retail trade industries. These firms accounted for 74 percent of the gross annual receipts generated by women-owned businesses.

FACTS ABOUT SMALL BUSINESS AND THE U.S. SMALL BUSINESS ADMINSITRATION

SBA in General

The U.S. Small Business Administration is an Executive Branch agency of the Federal Government. The head of the Agency—the Administrator—reports directly to the President. SBA was created on July 30, 1953 to provide broad assistance to small businesses.

The Agency's government antecedents were:

> The Reconstruction Finance Corporation (1932–1957)
> The Smaller War Plants Corporation (1942–1947)
> The Small Defense Plants Administration (1951–1953)

SBA has 110 offices in 100 cities throughout the U.S. This includes 10 Regional Offices, 63 District Offices, 18 Branch Offices, and 19 Post-of-Duty Stations.

On September 30, 1979, SBA had 4,372 permanent employees. A year earlier, the Agency had 4,402 permanent employees. In 1969, SBA had 4,099 permanent employees.

SBA's operating expenses for FY 1979 were $192.2 million ($171.5 million for the Agency's regular assistance programs and $20.7 million for the disaster loan program). The Agency's FY 1978 operating expenses were $176.0 million ($146.3 million for the regular programs and $29.7 million for the disaster program).

Small Business Size Standards

On March 11, 1980, SBA proposed a new set of small business size standards. These standards would be based on a firm's average number of employees for the preceding twelve months and would vary by industry. The merits of these standards are still being discussed. Until a new set of size standards is adopted officially by the Agency, the following small business size measurements apply to firms seeking SBA assistance.

SIZE STANDARDS (Maximums)

A. **For Loans**	**Annual Receipts Maximum**
Services	*$2–$8 Million
Retail	*$2–$7.5 Million
Wholesale	*9.5–$22 Million
General Construction	*$9.5 Million
Farming and Related Activities	*$1 Million
	Average Employment Maximum
Manufacturing	*250 to 1,500
B. **For Procurement**	**Annual Receipts Maximum**
Services	*$2–$9 Million
General Construction	*$12 Million
	Average Employment Maximum
Manufacturing	*500 to 1,500
C. **For SBIC Assistance**	
All Industries	**Net Worth Maximum**
	$6 Million
	Average Net Income
	(after taxes) maximum $2 Million for the preceding two years
D. **For Surety Bonds**	**Annual Receipts Maximum**
All Industries	$3.5 Million

*Varies by industry

Note: A. and C. standards increase 25% if a firm operates in an area of high unemployment, as defined by the Labor Department.

Finance

INTEREST RATES

SBA sets maximum allowable interest rates for guaranteed and immediate participation loans and for lines of credit. Rates are based on a continuous survey of the market for fixed income securities, both federal and private, and on the prevailing rate for loans as determined by SBA field personnel.

Interest rates on SBA direct loans are based on a formula that considers the cost of money to the federal government.

The interest rates are reviewed quarterly and adjusted at that time and at other periods if adjustment is warranted.

A variable interest rate is also permitted if it is agreed to by both the borrower and the lender at the time a loan is made.

BUSINESS LOANS

Total SBA financial assistance to businesses (loans, surety bonds, and Small Business Investment Company funds) has averaged $4.7 billion in recent years (excludes disaster loans to businesses).

The total number of all business and disaster loans was 107,112 for $4.9 billion in FY 1980.

Since it began and through September 30, 1980, SBA approved 1,251,096 loans of all kinds for $39.7 billion, and 413,982 business loans for $26.2 billion. At the end of FY 1979, the Agency's loan portfolio contained 402,229 accounts outstanding valued at $13.4 billion. The cumulative loss rate on all disbursed business loans since SBA was started is 4.18 percent.

Thirty-nine percent of the Agency's business loans and 53 percent of the business dollar volume since the Agency's beginning occurred in the last five fiscal years.

FISCAL YEARS		
1979	30,176 Loans	$ 3.41 Billion
1978	31,727	3.31
1977	31,793	3.05
1976 Budget Transition Quarter	6,795	0.58
1976	26,078	2.07
1975	22,348	1.59
	148,917	$14.01 Billion

In SBA's first year of operation (FY 1954), 473 business loans were approved for $28 million.

In terms of business loans approved, FY 1973 was the record high year with 33,948 loans approved for $2.2 billion.

June of 1975 was the highest single business loan month in the Agency's history with 3,475 business loans approved for $248 million.

Private sector participation in FY 1979 business loans was $2.9 billion, decreasing from $3.0 billion in FY 1978. In FY 1977, this figure was $2.7 billion.

FY 1979 business loans made directly by SBA totalled 6,066 for $356 million. In FY 1978 the figures were 5,988 direct loans for $311 million and in FY 1977, 6,467 direct loans for $300 million.

Twenty-four percent of the FY 1979 business loans were used to create 7,328 businesses. In FY 1978, 30 percent of the business loans were used to create 9,657 new businesses.

Of SBA's 10 organizational regions throughout the country, Region 6 (Texas, New Mexico, Oklahoma, Arkansas, and Louisiana) approved the highest number of business loans in FY 1979; 4,342 loans for $470 million. Region 5 (Illinois, Ohio, Michigan, Indiana, Wisconsin, and Minnesota) approved the highest number of loan dollars: 4,090 loans for $556 million. In FY 1978, Region 6 approved the highest number of business loans for the highest dollar amount: 4,893 loans for $470 million.

Ninety-five percent of all SBA business loans are for one year or more.

The average maturity of SBA business loans is 8¾ years.

The current average size of a guaranty business loan is $85,000.

10,000 of the 15,000 banks in the U.S. (66 percent) participate in SBA loans.

DISASTER LOANS

69,943 natural disaster loans for $1.2 billion were approved in fiscal 1980, compared with 69,413 loans for $1.4 billion in FY 1979.

Eighty-one percent of the natural disaster loan dollars went to businesses in FY 1979. In FY 1978, this figure was 86 percent.

The largest single natural disaster to which SBA has responded was Tropical Storm Agnes, which occurred in 1972 and was the most destructive storm in recorded U.S. history. SBA assistance for business owners, homeowners, renters, and nonprofit institutions victimized by Tropical Storm Agnes totalled 144,738 loans for $1.3 billion, a record high for any single disaster.

Since the beginning of the disaster program in 1953, SBA has made 837,114 disaster loans for $9.4 billion.

DETAILED CHART OF BUSINESS LOAN PROGRAM FOR FY 1980 AND FY 1979

LOAN PROGRAM	FY 1980		FY 1979	
	Number	Dollar Amount In Millions	Number	Dollar Amount In Millions
Regular Business	28,168	3,604	26,776	3,200
Disaster	69,943	1,202	69,413	1,400
Economic Opportunity	2,434	90.9	2,841	100.7
Economic Injury Disaster	1,138	78.5	980	49.3
State Development Co. Loans & Local Development Co.	476	79.2	479	79.7
Seasonal Line of Credit	Not Available		254	35.0

LOAN PROGRAM	FY 1980		FY 1979	
	Number	Dollar Amount In Millions	Number	Dollar Amount in Millions
Handicapped Assistance	258	20.6	288	22.4
Contract Loan Program	Not Available		224	22.0
Displaced Business	155	35.8	80	15.1
Small Business Energy	183	27.2	108	14.4
Water Pollution Control	18	3.0	18	4.6
Economic Dislocation Disaster	1,422	56.6	88	4.5
Occupational Safety & Health Disaster	19	8.0	14	4.3
Air Pollution Control	26	6.5	11	3.6
Consumer Protection Disaster	7	1.7	6	1.7
Emergency Energy Shortage Economic Injury	24	2.1	5	1.0
Base Closing Economic Injury Disaster	14	1.3	5	0.5

SURETY BONDS

In FY 1979, there were 31,972 Surety Bond guarantees resulting in 18,071 contracts valued at $1.4 billion, a record high dollar figure. In FY 1978, there were 32,125 guarantees on 19,044 contracts for $1.4 billion and in FY 1977 29,932 guarantees on 15,435 contracts for $1 billion. The Surety Bond Program has grown more than 1,387% since 1972, its first year of operation.

Investment (Data for FY 1979)

SMALL BUSINESS INVESTMENT COMPANIES

There were 327 operating SBIC's licensed by SBA in 40 states, the District of Columbia, and Puerto Rico as of September 30, 1979. In FY 1978, there were 294 SBIC's operating in 38 states and Puerto Rico. SBIC's had $1.2 billion in assets. This compared to $1 billion in FY 1978.

SBIC's made 2,221 small business financings for $267.1 million, an increase from 2,097 financings for $232.2 million in FY 1978. Figures for

FY 1977 and FY 1976 were: 1977–2,071 financings for $206 million; 1976—1,720 financings for $129 million.

Equity-type financings represented 52 percent of the dollars disbursed by the SBIC's. The remainder of the dollars were for debt financing. Outstanding SBIC loans and investments totalled $604.5 million.

38 percent of SBIC financing involved new firms. Since the SBIC program was started in 1958, SBIC's have made more than 59,000 investments for $3.6 billion.

Procurement, Property Sales, and Technology Assistance (Data for FY 1979)

Total federal procurement was $82.4 billion. Prime contracting awards to small business were $19.6 billion, an increase of $435 million over FY 1978.

Small business set aside contracts were $5.8 billion, 29.7 percent of the prime contracts awarded to small business. Subcontracting dollars awarded to small business were $10.7 billion, 43.4 percent of the total.

Total federal contracting dollars were $24.6 billion.

The Certificate of Competency Program resulted in the award of 425 COC's totaling nearly $105 million. This represented a savings of $8.8 million for the government.

8(a) CONTRACTS TO FIRMS OWNED AND CONTROLLED BY SOCIALLY AND ECONOMICALLY DISADVANTAGED PERSONS

Since its first full year of operation (1969), the 8(a) Business Development Program has grown from 28 contracts valued at $8.9 million to over 22,097 contracts valued at nearly $4 billion through FY 1979.

Of the 1,583 companies receiving 8(a) contracts during FY 1979, approximately 36 percent were in the construction industry, 19 percent were in nonprofessional services, 36 percent were in professional services, and 9 percent were in manufacturing. There were 3,919 8(a) contracts for $1 billion issued in FY 1979. This was an increase from 3,409 contracts for $768.0 million in FY 1978. The number of firms assisted by the 8(a) program in FY 1979 was 1,593, an increase from 1,140 firms in FY 1978.

PROPERTY SALES ASSISTANCE

During Fiscal Year 1979, more than 2,800 individual sales of federal timber worth $1.3 billion were awarded to small businesses. These sales resulted in the purchase of 5.7 billion board feet of federal timber by small business. This was an increase from more than 2,700 sales for $951 million in FY 1978.

TECHNOLOGY ASSISTANCE

In FY 1979, SBA's Technology Assistance Program helped approximately 2,500 small businesses utilize technology that had been developed by the federal government or by private industry at the expense of the government.

PROCUREMENT AUTOMATED SOURCE SYSTEM (PASS)

PASS is a SBA-developed computerized data base of small firms interested in bidding on government contracting opportunities. The capabilities of small firms registered in the system are available when requests are made by federal procurement officers or private sector buyers. More than 35,000 small businesses were registered in the PASS system at the end of FY 1980.

At the end of FY 1979, direct terminal access to the data base was available at 30 locations at SBA, the Department of Energy, and other government departments. Additional terminals were added to the system in FY 1981.

Management Assistance (Data for FY 1979)

SBA's Management Assistance program reaches millions of individuals annually. Over 700,000 current or prospective small business owner/managers were counseled or trained. For FY 1978, this figure was 650,000. 229,000 businesses were provided sustained MA counseling.

1979 Detail:
 Counseling—423,000 individuals
 Training—284,000 individuals in 7,635 training units

Six million SBA Management Assistance publications were distributed to the public. In FY 1978, this figure was 5.5 million.

Highlight: 23 Business Basics self-study booklets on small business management subjects were distributed to more than 450,000 readers.

SCORE, the Service Corps of Retired Executives, was developed by SBA in 1964. ACE, the Active Corps of Executives, was developed by SBA in 1969 as an adjunct to SCORE. There are 12,000 SCORE/ACE volunteers in 365 chapters in 49 states, the District of Columbia, and Puerto Rico. SCORE/ACE volunteers counseled nearly 150,000 business men and women. Historically, SCORE/ACE volunteers have counseled over 730,000 small business firms.

The SBI (Small Business Institute) program was started by SBA in 1972 at 36 participating colleges and universities. Nearly 500 colleges and universities participate in the SBI program.

During FY 1979, 10,000 SBI graduate and undergraduate students and 2,000 SBI deans and professors counseled more than 8,000 current and prospective business owners.

There are 18 SBA-chartered Small Business Development Centers at the following universities.

> The University of Georgia at Athens
> The University of Missouri at St. Louis
> The University of Nebraska at Omaha
> The University of West Florida at Pensacola
> Rutgers University
> The University of Maine at Portland
> The California State University at Chico
> The California State Polytechnic University at Pomona
> Howard University
> The University of South Carolina at Columbia
> The University of Wisconsin at Madison
> St. Cloud State University at St. Cloud, Minnesota
> The University of Arkansas at Little Rock
> The University of Utah at Salt Lake City
> Washington State University at Pullman
> The University of Pennsylvania at Philadelphia

The SBDC program was started by business in December, 1976. In FY 1980, SBDC's were established at the University of Alabama at Birmingham and the University of Massachusetts at Amherst.

In FY 1979, 160 firms were awarded "406" Call Contracts for a total of $11 million. In FY 1978, 83 such contracts were awarded for $8 million. Under the Call Contracting Program, SBA gives contracts to qualified firms and individuals so they can provide services (accounting, marketing, engineering, etc.) for other SBA clients.

Assistance to Members of Minority Groups (Data for FY 1979)

5,518 business loans for $428.3 million were approved for members of minority groups. In FY 1978, there were 6,118 loans for $401.6 million and in FY 1977, 6,180 loans for $352.3 million. The average size of an SBA minority business loan is $77,619.

Minority business men and women received 13 percent of the dollar value and 18 percent of the number of all SBA business loans. In FY 1978, they received 12 percent of the SBA loan dollars and 19 percent of the total number of loans.

Six percent of all SBA business loan dollars went to Black Americans, 6 percent to Hispanic Americans, and 1 percent to members of other minority groups. In FY 1978, 5 percent of the loan dollars went to Black Americans, 5 percent went to Hispanic Americans, and 2 percent went to members of other minority groups.

Financings to start new minority-owned businesses totalled 1,838 for $124 million. In FY 1978, there were 1,964 such financings for $112 million.

Minority business owners and homeowners received 4,878 disaster loans for $42 million, a decrease from 7,607 loans for $56 million in FY 1978. In FY 1977, disaster loans to members of minority groups totalled 2,001 for $31.8 million.

There are 110 "301(d)" Small Business Investment Companies licensed to assist members of minority groups in 29 states, the District of Columbia, and Puerto Rico. These companies are capitalized at $79.4 million. At the end of FY 1978, there were 86 such companies in 29 states, the District of Columbia, and Puerto Rico, capitalized at $61.9 million.

"301(d)" SBIC's made 467 financings for $33.7 million, an increase from 454 financings for $29.2 million in FY 1978. In FY 1977, there were 344 such financings for $13.6 million. Forty-three percent of the businesses financed by "301(d)" SBIC's were new firms. In FY 1978, 36 percent of the businesses financed were new businesses.

54,025 minority business men and women received SBA management counseling, compared with 47,957 in FY 1978 and 25,478 in FY 1977. 62,109 minority business men and women received SBA management training, compared with 55,671 in FY 1978 and 45,693 in FY 1977.

Business loans approved for minority women in FY 1979, FY 1978, and FY 1977 compared as follows:

	FY 1979*		FY 1978		FY 1977	
	Number	Dollars	Number	Dollars	Number	Dollars
Black Women	404	$22,794,846	442	$21,861,454	427	$19,439,170
Puerto Rican Women	93	$ 3,363,600	126	$ 3,658,500	102	$ 3,310,212
Other Hispanic Women	242	$15,132,100	277	$13,855,484	229	$10,645,800
American Indian Women	48	$ 3,433,300	48	$ 3,531,000	69	$ 3,605,626
Asian American Women	156	$12,921,683	162	$11,592,200	127	$ 7,512,271
Eskimo and Aleutian American Women	0	$ 0	4	$ 551,600	3	$ 183,000
Totals	943	$57,645,529	959	$55,050,238	857	$44,696,079

*SBA defines a women-owned business as: "A women-owned business is one which is at least 51% owned, controlled, and operated by a woman or women. 'Controlled' is defined as 'exercising the authority to make policy decisions', and 'operated' is defined as 'actively involved in the day-to-day management of the business'." This definition was changed from 50% in March, 1979.

Assistance to Women
(Data for FY 1979)

61,109 women received SBA Management Assistance counseling, an increase over the 55,856 women counseled in FY 1978. In FY 1977, 19,806 women received this counseling.

130,026 women attended SBA-sponsored Management Assistance training conferences, seminars, and workshops, an increase from 122,109 in FY 1978.

4,817 business loans for $381 million were approved for women-owned businesses, a decrease from 5,699 loans for $444 million in FY 1978. In FY 1977, 4,665 loans for $325 million were approved for women-owned businesses.

Women in business received 16 percent of all SBA business loans approved and 11 percent of the business loan dollars. In FY 1978, women received 18 percent of the number of loans and 13 percent of the dollars. The average women's business enterprise loan size is $79,046.

SMALL BUSINESS ADVOCACY ISSUES

THE IMPACT OF TIGHT CREDIT POLICIES ON SMALL BUSINESS

The debt-equity ratio for smaller firms tends to be greater than that for large firms, particularly in manufacturing, construction, and the distributive trades.

The percentage of short-term debt to total assets tends to be higher for smaller firms than for larger firms, and this percentage has been growing in recent years.

The ratio of indebtedness to banks to total indebtedness has been growing more rapidly for smaller manufacturers in recent years than for larger manufacturing firms.

SMALL BUSINESS AND REGULATORY AND REPORTING PAPERWORK

The small business community spends $12.7 billion a year when filling out required government forms and reports.

Small businesses file more than 305 million federal government forms a year totalling over 850 million pages containing over 7.3 billion questions.

About $10 billion of small business' overall $12.7 billion paperwork expense is the result of federal reporting requirements. The balance is spent on state and local paperwork requirements.

One hundred and three federal agencies require small businesses to fill in one or more reports.

Forty-three percent of the federal forms are mandatory, 33 percent are voluntary, and 24 percent are required for small business to derive some benefit from federal programs.

SMALL BUSINESS AND GOVERNMENT COMPETITION

Small firms could gain more than $2 billion worth of business annually if the federal government produced less of its own goods and services and bought more from the marketplace. The federal government directly engages in more than 21,000 commercial and industrial activities at a taxpayer cost of at least $10 billion annually.

Small Business Innovation

Independent small business entrepreneurs have been responsible for more than half of all the product and service innovations developed in the United States since World War II.

A recent review of the leading 500 technological innovations in the United States between 1953 and 1973 showed that small firms (defined as those with up to 1,000 employees) produced four times as many innovations per research and development dollar as medium-sized firms (defined as those with 1,000 to 10,000 employees).

Nearly every major energy-related innovation in the past 100 years has been developed by small business, such as the electric car, the air conditioner, the gasoline engine, the electric light, petroleum cracking, gasoline, and transformers.

Of the seven major innovations in the areas of petroleum refining since 1945, all were developed by small business.

SMALL BUSINESS INVESTMENT CORPORATIONS

SBICs are government-backed, flexible financing devices for furnishing equity capital and long-term loan funds to enable small businesses to operate, grow, and modernize.

These companies are formed to operate under the regulations of the Small Business Investment Act once they have followed the simple steps to obtain an SBIC license. Recent changes in law and regulations offer new incentives to investors, who stand to gain from the government leverage funds and the tax advantages provided.

When SBICs were developed, they were visualized as potential sources of capital and expertise for small firms previously limited to short term financing. Since that time, they have proved to be adaptable to inner city as well as rural economic development. SBIC funnels much-needed investment capital into economically depressed communities, and to socially or economically disadvantaged small business entrepreneurs.

Defining an SBIC

An SBIC is a privately owned and privately operated small business investment company that has been licensed by the Small Business Administration to provide *equity* or *venture* capital and long-term loans to small firms. Often SBICs also provide management assistance to the companies they finance. These are their only functions. They cannot, for instance, sell insurance, trade in property, or become holding companies for groups of operating businesses.

New SBICs derive their initial capital from private investors and normally become eligible to obtain funds from the government or from private financial institutions through government-guaranteed loans.

An SBIC finances small firms in two general ways—by straight loans and by equity-type investments that give the SBIC actual or potential ownership of a portion of a small business' stock. In general, financings must be for at least five years, except that a borrower may elect to prepay indebtedness.

SBICs invest in practically all types of manufacturing and service industries, and in a wide variety of other types of businesses, including construction, retailing, and wholesaling. Many seek out small businesses offering new products or services because they believe these firms have unusual growth potential.

Some SBICs specialize in electronics companies, research and development firms, or other types of businesses that the SBIC's management has special knowledge of. Most companies diversify and will consider a wide variety of investments.

SBICs are intended to be profit-making entities. Their major function is to make *venture* or risk investments by supplying equity capital and extending unsecured loans and loans not fully collateralized to worthy small enterprises. Some SBICs have been organized and utilized as subsidiaries, on a profit-making basis, by national concerns. These SBICs provide equity capital and long term loan funds to enterprises owned and managed by socially or economically disadvantaged persons. Counseling, legal aid, and management training for the benefit of the business community is coordinated on a volunteer basis. This type of SBIC, dedicated solely to assisting disadvantaged small business entrepreneurs, is eligible for SBA purchases of its 3 percent preferred stock and for a subsidized interest rate on its debentures during the first five years. It may also be organized on a nonprofit basis to obtain additional tax benefits for itself and its investors. Some SBICs may be incorporated bodies or limited partnerships, with corporate general partners.

Advantages to Investors

With good management, an SBIC can achieve impressive profit figures. Among the available benefits are certain tax advantages, granted by Congress as an incentive for those providing venture capital to small business through the program. Recent changes liberalizing the legislation and the regulations governing SBICs have made these companies even more attractive.

The leverage available to SBICs through government or government-guaranteed loans can be very important. An SBIC may be eligible for such a loan equal to three times its paid-in capital and paid-in surplus. These loans may be subordinated and have maturity of up to 15 years. SBICs that specialize in venture capital financing and are adequately capitalized may qualify for a fourth layer of leverage. Qualified SBICs may obtain SBA loans or SBA-guaranteed loans aggregating $35 million. There is no limit to the private capital that may be used in the formation of an SBIC.

An SBIC, as a flexible financing vehicle, can serve and has served many corporate and community purposes. It is adaptable to urban and rural economic development needs and to financing of innovative and high-technology small business concerns, and also constitutes an ideal instrument for concentrating much-needed investment capital within economically depressed communities. Especially significant in the fact that, in addition to accumulating capital for economic development, an SBIC is designed and authorized to provide one of the prime requisites for success of new business ventures—adequate management assistance.

The Need for SBICs

Small businesses generally have difficulty obtaining equity capital to finance their growth. Without up-to-date operating records and strong financial statements, small business concerns have difficulty in obtaining long term financing.

To help close this financing gap, Congress passed the Small Business Investment Act of 1958, which authorized the SBA to license, regulate, and help finance privately organized and privately operated

SBICs, which in turn would provide equity-type and long term financing to small concerns.

Present Status of Industry

As an industry, the SBICs have total assets amounting to over $75 million dollars. They have outstanding investments in small businesses of more than $50 million dollars.

The majority of SBICs are owned by relatively small groups of local investors. However, the stock of 21 SBICs is publicly traded, and 73 are partially or wholly owned by commercial banks. A few are subsidiaries of other corporations.

Defining a Small Business

In general, the SBA considers a firm to be *small* and therefore eligible for SBIC financing if its assets do not exceed $9.0 million, if its net worth is not more than $4.0 million, and if its average net income after taxes for the preceding 2 years was not more than $400 thousand.

If a business does not qualify as small under these provisions, it may qualify under certain other criteria established by the SBA for its business loan program, or for assistance to firms that are located in areas of substantial unemployment. In determining the size of a business, the SBA also considers the size of any affiliates, including a parent company that controls the firm, and any other companies controlled by the same parent company.

Income Tax Aspects

The SBIC industry has a number of different kinds of tax advantages. One, for example, is a major tax inducement to investors contemplating commitment of funds to an SBIC. It permits an SBIC shareholder to treat gains on sales of stock as long term capital gains, whereas such a shareholder may take an unlimited ordinary-loss deduction on losses arising from the sale, exchange, or worthlessness of the stock.

A special benefit arises from the fact that SBICs are allowed a deduction of 100 percent of dividends received from a taxable domestic corporation, rather than the 85 percent deduction allowed most corporate taxpayers.

SBICs are granted relief from the tax on excess accumulations of surplus and may qualify for relief from the tax on personal holding companies.

Specific provisions are contained in the Internal Revenue Code to allow SBICs to take full deductions against ordinary income for losses sustained on convertible debentures, or on stock received through conversion of convertible debentures.

Recent legislation provides for licensing SBICs organized as partnerships, with a corporate general partner.

Advantages to Banks

A bank may, through a wholly-owned SBIC subsidiary or partial ownership of an SBIC, add a new dimension to its services to customers. A federally regulated bank may invest up to five percent of its combined capital and surplus in stock of an SBIC. Investment by state chartered member banks is subject to the applicable provisions of state law.

How an SBIC Gets Started

WHAT ARE THE GENERAL REQUIREMENTS?

The initial private investment may vary upward from a minimum of $150 thousand, depending on the area to be served. The amount must be adequate to assure a reasonable prospect of sound and profitable operation. Provisions should also be made for funds to cover organization expenses. The articles of incorporation, bylaws, partnership agreement or certificate, capitalization, and proposed policies of an SBIC are subject to SBA approval, and background information must be furnished for all officers, directors, and persons who will hold 10 percent or more of the SBIC ownership interest. Those proposing to form an SBIC must be prepared to have a reasonably accessible office with qualified management readily available to the public during normal business hours.

MUST PAID-IN PRIVATE CAPITAL OF AN SBIC BE IN CASH OR MAY IT BE IN MORTGAGES OR SECURITIES?

Paid-in capital must consist of cash or eligible government securities.

IS THERE ANY RESTRICTION ON A PROSPECTIVE OWNER OF A PROPOSED SBIC BORROWING FUNDS FOR HIS OR HER INVESTMENT IN THE SBIC?

Yes. He or she may not borrow funds for investment in the SBIC unless he or she can show a net worth equal to at least twice the amount borrowed. The SBA may require that balance sheets be submitted in this connection.

WILL THE OPERATION OF AN SBIC AUTOMATICALLY BE EXEMPT FROM SECURITIES AND EXCHANGE COMMISSION REGULATIONS?

No. The SEC will determine, from the circumstances in each case, whether or not the activities of the SBIC are subject to acts and regulations administered by that agency.

CAN AN SBIC BE PUBLICLY HELD?

Yes. Although most SBICs are owned by relatively small groups of local investors, the stock of 24 is publicly traded.

WHAT GUIDES ARE AVAILABLE ON REGULATORY ASPECTS?

Every holder of a license to operate an SBIC is furnished a copy of the Small Business Administration regulations for SBICs and automatically receives all amendments to the regulations, as well as policy and procedural releases that provide additional information.

What an SBIC Does

MAY AN SBIC FREELY PERFORM ANY AND ALL ACTIONS ASSOCIATED WITH LENDING OR INVESTMENT?

An SBIC may engage in all activities contemplated by the Small Business Investment Act, but not in any other activities.

CAN AN SBIC SPECIALIZE IN A PARTICULAR INDUSTRY?

Yes, except for real estate investments.

CAN AN SBIC BE USED FOR REAL ESTATE FINANCING?

A new company will not be licensed if it proposes to put more than one-third of its assets into real estate investments. However, loans secured by real estate mortgages are not counted as real estate investments if the proceeds of the loans are to be used for purposes other than real estate investments.

ARE THERE PENALTIES FOR FAILURE TO OBSERVE THE REGULATIONS?

Yes. The SBA can conduct investigations and revoke or suspend licenses in the event of false statements or omissions of material facts or for wilful or repeated violations of the Act or regulations. The SBA may issue cease and desist orders, request injunctions, and act as receiver for an SBIC. Also, the SBA can suspend any director or officer of an SBIC for due cause. The Act and regulations require the filing of certain reports with the SBA. Failure to submit these on time may subject a licensee to penalty of up to $100 per day.

CAN AN SBIC CONVERT TO ANOTHER LINE OF BUSINESS?

A licensed SBIC can engage only in the activities authorized by the Small Business Investment Act. However, a license can be surrendered if prior SBA approval is obtained. SBA approval will be conditioned on payment or acceptable settlement of any indebtedness to the SBA and elimination of any existing violations. Dissolution of the entity is not required, but its charter must be changed in accordance with its changed purposes.

CAN THE LICENSE OF AN SBIC BE TRANSFERRED?

An SBIC license cannot be transferred from one corporation or partnership to another except in connection with mergers approved by the Small Business Administration. Sometimes a license might in effect be transferred through transfer of control of the ownership interest of an SBIC. This type of transfer also requires prior approval by the SBA.

How an SBIC Grows

WHAT ACCESS TO LONG TERM FUNDS DOES AN SBIC HAVE?

An SBIC may obtain long term funds from both government and private sources. An SBIC may request the SBA to lend, or to guarantee 100 percent of the loans of private financial institutions, to the SBIC in an amount equivalent to 300 percent of its private capital. The maximum available to an SBIC on this basis is $35 million. The debentures issued by the SBIC for these funds may be subordinated and may have a term of up to 15 years. For SBICs with private capital equal to or in excess of $500,000, funds equivalent to 400 percent of private capital become available if 65 percent of the total funds available for investment are invested or committed in venture capital investments. The maximum available to a qualified SBIC on this basis is $35 million. SBICs dedicated solely to assisting socially or economically disadvantaged small business concerns may borrow from SBA at a subsidized interest rate (usually 3 percent below the going cost of money to the U.S. Treasury) for the first five years of the loan. They may also sell to SBA nonvoting preferred securities on a 1:1 basis in relation to their private capital or (in some cases) portions of their private capital.

MAY AN SBIC BORROW MONEY FOR ITS OPERATIONS FROM SOURCES OTHER THAN SBA AND WITHOUT AN SBA GUARANTEE?

Yes, and it should be noted that SBA funds, or SBA-guaranteed funds, become available only to the extent that funds are not available from private sources on reasonable terms.

CAN AN SBIC MERGE WITH ANOTHER SBIC?

Yes, provided prior approval is obtained from the Small Business Administration.

CAN AN SBIC MERGE WITH A NONSBIC?

Yes, when prior approval has been obtained from the Small Business Administration, and when the resulting company will qualify to hold an SBIC license.

Some Investment Rules

MAY AN SBIC EXTEND LONG TERM LOANS TO, OR PURCHASE STOCK OR CONVERTIBLE DEBENTURE FROM, A SMALL CONCERN? THE CONTROLLING STOCKHOLDERS OF WHICH ARE ALSO STOCKHOLDERS, PARTNERS, OR MEMBERS IN THE SBIC?

Unless an exemption is granted by the SBA, an SBIC may not purchase stock or convertible debentures of, or make a loan to, an officer, director, or owner of 10 percent or more of the private capital of the SBIC. The same restriction applies to any company in which the officer, director, partner or 10 percent owner of the SBIC is an officer or director, or owns 10 percent or more of the stock, or is a partner.

WHAT IS THE MAXIMUM RATE OF INTEREST AN SBIC MAY CHARGE?

In states where state law specifies a maximum interest rate, the SBIC cannot charge a higher rate. If the state law imposes no maximum, SBA regulations specify the maximum interest rate and related charges. In any event, 15 percent is the maximum rate that SBICs are allowed to charge. In the calculation of the actual rate of interest and related charges to a borrower, the SBA requires that all charges, discounts, etc., be taken into account, and that the rate be computed on the basis of the outstanding balance.

DO SBA REGULATIONS GOVERNING SBIC OPERATIONS COVER THE NEGOTIATIONS BETWEEN THE SBIC AND THE BORROWER CONCERNING TYPES OF LOANS, INTEREST RATES, DISCOUNTS, AND CONVERSION FEATURES?

The SBIC and the small business concern negotiate the specific terms and conditions, which must conform to SBA regulations. It is not necessary for the SBIC to secure approval of every transaction; however, the SBIC should ask for approval of any negotiation or transaction which appears doubtful or borderline in relation to the regulations.

IS AN SBIC SUBJECT TO ANY INVESTMENT LOAN LIMITATION?

Yes. Without prior SBA approval, the total funds loaned to or invested in equity securities of a particular small business concern held by a single SBIC may not exceed 20 percent of the paid-in capital and surplus of the SBIC. Two or more SBICs may participate in a single investment thereby providing a larger dollar total of financing in a single firm than any of the participating SBICs could have invested individually. Of course, the company in which the investment is made must qualify as small under SBA standards.

Various Other Rules

IS THE OWNERSHIP OF AN SBIC FREELY TRANSFERABLE?

Yes, with the limitation that transfers of 10 percent or more of the stock, or private capital of an SBIC must be approved by the SBA.

IS THERE ANY RESTRICTION OR LIMITATION ON THE DISTRIBUTION BY AN SBIC WHILE IT REMAINS INDEBTED TO THE SBA?

Yes, where an SBIC is indebted to the SBA, distributions to shareholders or partners can be paid only out of retained earnings.

WILL THE NUMBER OF SBICs IN ANY ONE AREA BE LIMITED? WHAT ARE THE RESTRICTIONS ABOUT THE AREA OF AN SBIC's OPERATIONS?

Yes. A need must be shown. If there is a heavy concentration of SBICs in the area, the license applicant must show that there are types of businesses or industries that can use SBIC financing in a manner advantageous to these businesses and the SBIC.

MAY A GROUP OF RESIDENTS IN ONE STATE ORGANIZE THE SBIC UNDER THE LAWS OF A NEIGHBORING STATE, AND CONDUCT THE SBIC's INVESTMENT BUSINESS IN BOTH STATES?

It depends upon the laws of the particular state. Generally some of the incorporators or partners must be residents of the state in which the SBIC is incorporated or registered.

WHAT ARE SBA REQUIREMENTS CONCERNING THE NAME OF AN SBIC?

Use of "United States," "National," "Federal," "Reserve," "Bank," "Government," or "Development" in the name of the SBIC is not acceptable. Moreover, the name should not be so similar to that of any other organization as to imply that it is associated with the other organization, unless the other organization has given its approval. In addition, the name must be approved by the Corporation Commissioner of the state where incorporated, or other public body with which registered, as well as by the SBA.

MAY AN SBIC ESTABLISH BRANCH OFFICES?

Yes, if the SBA has given its approval to do so. And, in applying for this approval, the SBIC must state the area to be served by each branch.

WHAT RESTRICTIONS ARE THERE CONCERNING THE TYPES OF BUSINESSES TO WHICH LOANS MAY BE MADE BY AN SBIC?

The regulations provide that an SBIC may not provide funds to a small business concern for relending, nor for purposes not contemplated by the Small Business Investment Act, nor for purposes contrary to the public interest, such as gambling activities or fostering a monopoly. It may not provide funds for foreign investment, or for any business not conducted as a regular and continuous activity. Funds invested in real estate enterprises must not exceed one-third of an SBIC's portfolio.

First Steps

WHAT PRELIMINARY STEPS SHOULD BE TAKEN?

Visit the nearest regional office of the Small Business Administration. They are now located in Boston, New York, Philadelphia, Atlanta, Chicago, Kansas City, Dallas, Denver, San Francisco, and Seattle. You also can obtain preliminary information from any of the SBA's field offices located throughout the United States, or the headquarters office of the SBA in Washington, D.C. You are welcome to visit or write the Investment Division at 1441 L Street, N.W., Washington, DC 20416.

HOW DOES YOUR GROUP FIND OUT WHETHER YOU CAN FORM AN SBIC AND PARTICULARLY WHETHER YOU CAN MEET THE LATEST LICENSING STANDARDS?

It is suggested that you furnish SBA Headquarters (Washington, DC) with proposed plans for capitalization, management personnel, operating policies, etc.

IF IT IS THEN INDICATED THAT YOUR GROUP IS IN A POSITION TO FORM AN SBIC, WHAT DO YOU DO NEXT?

Obtain from your nearest SBA office a copy of Form 415, a License Application form. Certain information required by this form may then be submitted to the headquarters of the SBA for informal comment. The formal application for a license may not be filed until the corporation or partnership has been formed and the capital subscribed.

WHAT IS SOME OF THE PRELIMINARY INFORMATION YOU WILL BE REQUIRED TO SUBMIT?

You will need to describe your proposed method of financing, your proposed plan of operation, your proposed articles of incorporation, and bylaws or partnership agreement. You also will need to include personal and business histories of the individuals who propose to form the SBIC. Personal interviews with Washington staff members will follow, if considered desirable by the SBA.

IN ADDITION TO THE RULES AND REGULATIONS OF THE SMALL BUSINESS ADMINISTRATION, ARE THERE ANY IMPORTANT RULES OR LIMITATIONS CONCERNING THE NUMBER AND THE AFFILIATIONS OF THE ORGANIZERS OF AN SBIC?

Various states have rules and regulations of their own. The proponents must, of course, conform to the laws of the state in which they propose to organize with respect to the number and qualifications of incorporators and directors or partners or members and must conform to the laws of the state in other respects.

SBA Liquidation

The Small Business Administration believes it operates at a risk level just above that of a bank. Subsequently, it believes it should experience a higher risk rate (on an average) than a bank. And, in the aggregate, they do. However, many entrepreneurs believe that the SBA should experience an even higher risk rate and take a more aggressive lending position.

Given that the SBA has about 13,000 companies in some form of liquidation, I can't wholeheartedly recommend adopting the policy to increase the SBA's bad debt experiences. But I can advise our readers that many good "deals" exist within the SBA bad loan portfolio. In other words, one person's problem can be another person's opportunity. If you're interested, write to Tim O'Leary, Deputy Administrator, Office of Portfolio Management, SBA, 1441 L Street, NW, Washington, DC 20416.

BDC's—More Opportunity
for Venture Capitalists

Another organizational structure available to venture capitalists is in the form of Business Development Corporations—BDCs. BDCs function as operating companies and are exempt from some aspects of the 1940 Investment Company Act, which has been largely responsible for keeping venture capitalists from going public. The Securities and Exchange Commission's (SEC) regulations have been too severe to allow a private venture capital firm to directly access the public capital markets.

The three major exemptions from the 1940 Investment Company Act offered by BDCs are:

1. The ability to make some affiliate transactions without gaining SEC approval.
2. The asset coverage requirement will be 200 percent rather than 300 percent.
3. Management compensation equal to 20 percent of the BDC's profits will be allowed, a marked improvement over current public venture funds where a venture capitalist draws a salary instead of participating in the fund!

To qualify for these exemptions a BDC must meet 3 requirements:

1. At least 70 percent of its portfolio must be kept in securities that can't be purchased on margin.
2. They must give proven managerial assistance to portfolio companies.
3. The majority of the board of directors must be comprised of outsiders (defined as anyone holding less than 5 percent of the BDC's shares who is not an officer of the company).

The SEC hopes these restrictions will put the burden of regulation onto the board members who could risk lawsuit if they fail to protect shareholders' interests, and that's one of the reasons the SEC is allowing these BDC exemptions. This experiment could be a significant approach toward self-governing the investment community, bringing good news for the entrepreneur.

For instance, E.F. Heizer, Jr. of Chicago, went public with the world's largest venture capital firm, Heizer Capital Corporation. Some say Ned Heizer was the prime mover in having these unnecessary restrictions removed.

Venture capitalists may double or triple the size of the industry by tapping public capital markets. For more information on BDCs contact William S. Coffin, Executive Vice President, National Association of BDCs, P.O. Box 262, Manchester, ME 04351, (207) 724-3507.

State Small Business Programs

A directory. of state small business programs is available. A Small Business Administration survey generated this report that indicates programs each state conducts for small businesses. Included are samples of enabling legislation for small business programs. The booklet is free by writing to Office of Small Business Advocacy (SBA), 1441 L Street N.W., Room 1010, Washington, DC 20416.

Ireland, Land of Manufacturing Opportunity

Interested in a foreign-based plant? Are you interested in an operation overseas? Well, rumor has it that Mr. Ray Stata, the president and founder of Analog Devices, Inc. in Norwood, Massachusetts, that the best source of capital and management assistance he has ever seen comes from Ireland. He has a plant there along with more United States companies than any other single country. The reason for it is the Industrial Development Authority of Ireland, the government's agency in charge of Ireland's industrialization programs. Ireland is now one of the fastest growing and most profitable manufacturing locations in Europe. For a beautiful booklet describing their services and what the state will do for you and why you ought to put a plant there, write to Peter D. Byrne, Director of Small Industry Investments, IDA Irish Development Authority, 200 Park Ave., New York, NY 10017, (212) 972-1000.

EDA Funds

If your company needs funds to expand or strengthen an existing business, you may be eligible for federal funds without knowing it. The federal government has designated two-thirds of all counties in the United States as "economically depressed." If you're located in one of these areas, you may apply for a loan under a special program of the Economic Development Administration.

To qualify for such a loan, a company must show that it has been unable to borrow under similar terms and conditions from other sources. There is no limit on the amount that may be requested. Most of the loans are under $1 million, or $10,000 per job created or saved.

On direct loans for fixed assets, or where there is mortgagable collateral, the interest rate is currently under 10 percent. EDA would provide up to 65 percent of the total funds, but the applicant has to put at least 15 percent of his or her own and get 5 percent from his or her state or a nongovernmental community organization, such as community development corporation. The repayment time is usually the useful life of the fixed assets. The interest rate on a direct loan for working capital or for less mortgagable assets is usually only a ¼ percent higher than fixed assets.

A list of economically depressed areas, the loan application form, and other details of the loan program can be obtained from any of EDA's six regional offices. For the address of the office nearest you, write or call the Office of Business Development, Economic Development Administration, Room 7876, 14th & Constitution Avenue, N.W., Washington, DC 20230, (202) 377-2000.

THE SEC's SIMPLIFIED S-18 STOCK OFFERING PROCEDURE

Form S-18, the Security and Exchange Commission's (SEC) simplified form for the registration of small initial public stock offerings, has had much success since its issue some 18 months ago. The SEC has issued a report that shows that Form S-18 has been used successfully in 111 registrations to issue shares with a total value of $236 million. Form S-18 has almost totally replaced it's more complex predecessor, Form S-1, for such small stock offerings.

If you've been wondering whether raising capital through a public stock offering is right for your company, the SEC report can help you make your decision. The figures provided in the report profile the users of Form S-18 and detail the costs involved in such an offering. Below are some points covered in the SEC report that may help you with your evaluation.

1. About half of the users of Form S-18 are high-technology manufacturers, the remainder are equally distributed into categories of other manufacturers, the services, and wholesale and retail distribution.
2. Fifty percent of the S-18 issues were started by start-up companies that had generated under $500 thousand in revenues in their latest fiscal year at the time of the offering. Half of the companies that were operational when they used the S-18 for their first public stock offering showed annual revenues of $1 to $10 million.
3. Most "start-up" issuer's assets were under $500 thousand before the S-18 registration. Assets for the majority of operating firms were between $500 thousand and $5 million.
4. $1 to $3 million was raised in most of these new stock issues. Sixty-six percent of these companies had $1 to $5 million worth of shares outstanding, prior to the issue.

5. Most of the registrations were filed through SEC regional offices. These regional filings were more efficient and less costly than those filed at the SEC in Washington.
6. Most registrations were handled by regional underwriting firms, or syndicates headed by such firms. Usually, the underwriting fee was one-tenth of the total value of the offering.

CEM Recommendation

Information pertaining to the use of Form S-18 is available from the Securities and Exchange Commission, Washington, DC 20549, (202) 655-4000. Write to the Directorate of Economic and Policy Analysis, at the preceeding address for the report, "Form S-18: A Monitoring Report in the First 18 Months of Its Use".

For further information contact Paul A. Belvin or Douglas S. Perry, Office of Disclosure Policy and Proceedings, Division of Corporation Finance, Securities and Exchange Commission, 500 North Capitol Street, Washington, DC 20549, (202) 755-1750.

The SEC Regional Offices are located in Atlanta, Boston, Chicago, Denver, Fort Worth, Los Angeles, New York, Seattle and Washington, D.C.

RAISING CAPITAL— MADE A LITTLE EASIER

Most small businesses have had difficulty in their raising capital process due to the difficulties of interpreting the national and state laws on securities regulations. One is required to comply with the laws of the Securities and Exchange Commission (SEC) and the laws of one's own state; and because securities laws are significantly different in each state, raising capital is a complex procedure. These dual requirements have prevented many companies from raising money successfully.

In April of this year, the SEC issued Regulation "D," which reduced the red tape for small businesses to raise money within the national securities laws. However, keep in mind that state securities laws were usually more restrictive than even the old SEC law, so that now with the looser SEC regulations, the respective state's Blue Sky Laws are more important than ever in controlling capital offerings.

In simple English, Regulation "D" states that a company seeking up to half a million dollars in a single offering can sell stock through a brokerage firm to an unlimited number of investors, without having to register the offering. The old rule had a limit of one hundred offerees. As a comparison, in Massachusetts, the rule is 35 offerees, so the SEC change does not make a significant difference.

On the other hand, the state Blue Sky Laws are weakly enforced, and are seldom much of an issue; very little prosecution has occurred in that area. But you still should be in compliance with both state and federal securities laws.

If you are looking to raise between a half million and $5 million dollars, it is now easier under SEC's Regulation "D," but you are still limited by the individual states, still 35 offerees in our example of Massachusetts, for instance—unless you can come up with accredited investors.

The legal test cases of what an accredited investor is over the next few years will be quite interesting. Essentially, Regulation "D" says it is someone who has a net worth of a million dollars, or an annual income of $200 thousand for the previous two years and the expectation of at least that amount of income for a third year. Keep in mind that a twelve-month rolling period means that you add the new month and subtract the old month to measure whether or not you have gone over the limit of total offerees in any consecutive rolling period.

In any case, when raising up to five million dollars, a brokerage firm is now allowed to receive commissions. This is important for the smaller offerings.

As usual, these laws are complex and always changing. We seldom recommend trying to raise capital without the advice of a lawyer, because the cry of "Securities Fraud" is one of the easy outs for unhappy individuals who invested in an unsuccessful venture. But be sure to have the lawyer interpret the federal advantages now available under the SEC's Regulation "D."

NEW ISSUES STOCK MARKET

The new issues market is on the rise once again after a roller coaster ride during the 1970s. Many professionals involved in bringing new stocks into the market are suggesting that this revived interest could last for several years. Others caution prospective investors to be extremely selective as many entrepreneurs see the new issues market as an alternative in raising capital for start-up companies.

The volume of new issues this year remains below historic high levels, yet market analysts claim the new issues boom is still in its earliest stages. The new issues market is dependent on the general health of the entire market, and could face disaster if investor speculation falls short.

Nearly all of the new issues in the current market have been in the area of energy or computer related technology, however, the entertainment and food industries are in second place. The SEC claims that during the fiscal year ending Sept. 30, 1980, 450 companies filed to go public through its main office in Washington, DC.

Much of the most speculative new-issues action has taken place in Denver's market for shares in infant oil and gas. No one market has felt the new issues boom as much as Denver, where both the biggest risks and rewards are being found. Many of the new offerings have been in existence less than two years and frequently have limited assets backing their stock. New companies with few assets, little revenue, and no production are represented strongly among the firms that have gone public this year. Although many of the new issues are highly speculative, the current trend has been founded on some genuine success stories.

Two examples of successful new issues stock investments are Apple Computer and Genetech. Apple Computer is a producer of personal computers whose sales are upward to $200 million. Incidentally, in the state of Massachusetts, the sale of Apple Computer shares was curtailed by the Attorney General who believed the cost to be outrageous. He later reversed the ruling and the Attorney General sanctioned the sale of Apple Computer stock in the Massachusetts marketplace.

Genetech is a genetic engineering company, whose genesplicing research went public at $35 a share in October increasing to $89 after the first day on the market. Since then, Genetech shares have dropped to $43.75 per share, but still maintain a margin over the offering price.

Both Apple and Genetech have received several rounds of venture capital, but with the new issues marketplace so receptive now, they have also chosen to go public. These quality, rapidly growing companies could go public in any market, but in a hot market, they really boom.

There are differences between the new issues boom of a decade ago, and the present boom. The high quality and growth records of many of the young companies going public now also encourage market optimists. Underwriters are anxious to handle new issues from which they take 10 percent to 15 percent commission of the money they raise. Of 300 underwriters surveyed, 115 have brought new issues to market in 1980.

The underwriter guarantees an offering by buying all the shares offered by a company and reselling them to the public. Many of the penny stocks underwritten (for example in the Denver market) are brought out as *best efforts* offerings in which the underwriter buys none of the stock itself, therefore assuming no risk. The proceeds are then held in escrow until a given number of shares are sold. If the minimum number of shares are not sold, the entire offering is withdrawn.

Some brokerage firms publish weekly calendars of forthcoming offerings for client information on the subject of new issues. Most brokers also subscribe to the *Investment Dealer's Digest,* a weekly publication that covers the new issues market.

The company sales and earning records, profit margins, accounting methods, competitive position, and other vital information on which an investor would form his or her opinion of the value of an issue appears on a prospectus. Other suggestions to aid the investor are:

1. A reputable underwriter who will not market the stock of any company likely to damage their reputation. Among these are, Blyth Eastman, Paine Webber, Dean Witter, Goldman Sachs, all of New York.
2. If the stock holdings of top officers are being sold, the investor should carefully examine the appeal of the issue.
3. If there is the strong financial support of a venture capital firm, this indicates that the company has been well groomed for the public marketplace, and could be considered a "promising" investment.
4. Check the balance sheet to see if the company's finances are strong enough to keep it going if profits don't meet forecasted figures. Also notice if profit growth is on target, and the risks of plans for continued expansion.

How to Go Public

There are four ways to file a registration statement with the SEC to go public;

1. S-1—Especially suited for companies dealing with oil, gas, and mining ventures. This is the SEC's general filing registration that requires maximum disclosure and reporting in both the offering and quarterly reports. This can be extremely demanding for small firms and start-up companies and should be used only if any other alternative registration statement is not applicable.
2. S-2—Intended for the use of start-up companies with no substantial sales or net income for the past five years. This special filing procedure requires detailed information about what the proceeds will be used for, and the credibility of the individuals who support the business venture.
3. S-18—To help businesses raise relatively large amounts of money (up to $5 million) without filing with SEC headquarters in Washington. These S-18s are processed by regional offices and have to meet the following specific criteria: (1) securities must be sold for cash; (2) the company must be incorporated in and operate in the United States or Canada; and (3) the firm may not be an investment company or offer limited partnerships.

4. Regulation A—This is an exemption from certain filing requirements, such as the 10-K, 10-Q, or interim 8-Q Forms if the
company has fewer than 500 shareholders and less than $1 million
in assets. Regulation A offerings can be filed through SEC regional
offices, but the company cannot raise more than $1.5 million.

If you don't have the stomach to invest directly into one of these
entrepreneurial ventures, why not consider investing in a mutual fund
that does invest in new issues? Here is a list. Some reliable sources of
information to check are:

The 44 West Street Equity Fund, 150 Broadway, New York, NY
10038 (212) 227-0512

Dreyfus Number Nine Fund, P.O. Box 600, Middlesex, NJ 08846
1-800-345-8501; in Pa. 1-800-662-5180

Oppenheimer Special Fund, 2 Broadway, New York, NY 10004
1-800-331-1750; in OK 1-800-722-3600

Fidelity Trend Fund, 82 Devonshire St., Boston, MA 02109
1-800-225-6190; in MA collect (617) 726-0650

Nautilus Fund, Eaton Howard Vance Sanders, 1660 L St., N.W.
Washington, DC 20036 1-800-424-9234

Going Public:
The IPO Reporter

If you are interested in the area of going public, but would like more
information before making the jump into the public offering market, the
IPO Reporter is a monthly publication that can help you to make a well-
informed decision. The *IPO Reporter* is a complete reference guide with
information from investment bankers, brokers, attorneys, accountants,
financial consultants, and venture capitalists. The information is bound
in a three-ring binder, making updated material easily inserted as a
complete reference. A sample entry follows.

ADVEST, INC. 6 Central Row, Hartford, CT 06103 (203) 525-
1421. Randolph Guggenheimer, VP-CF & Synd. 1980 IPOs: None.
1979 IPOs: Bank of New Haven (F$4.0), Greate Bay Casino (S
$25.7). 1978 IPOs: None.

ALLEN & COMPANY INCORPORATED, 711 Fifth Ave., New
York, NY 10022 (212) 832-8000. Harold Wit, EVP-CF; Paul A.
Gould, VP-Synd. 1980 IPOs: None. 1979 IPOs: None. 1978 IPOs:
L. Luria & Son (F $4.6).

ALSTEAD, STRANGIS & DEMPSEY, INC., 609 Second Ave. S., Minneapolis, MN 55402 (612) 339-2800. Jerry A. Alstead, Pres. 1980 IPOs: Flight Transportation (BE$1.8). 1979 IPOs: None. 1978 IPOs: None.

ALTA INVESTMENT COMPANY, 10 Seventeenth St., Denver, CO 80202 (303) 573-7244. Robert W. Sneed, Principal. 1980 IPOs: None. 1979 IPOs: None. 1978 IPOs: Petro Mineral (BE $1.2).

The *IPO Reporter* is prepared and published by Howard and Company, 1529 Walnut Street, Philadelphia, PA 19102, or call (215) 563-8030.

You will also receive, as an added free bonus, complete cumulative data on all 81 companies that went public in 1981 *plus* a two-page profile on *each* company.

Included are *Monthly Reports* for 1982 on all the companies going public during the month, analyzing over 20 different aspects of each offering such as company name, address and phone number, line of business, revenues, date filed and date effective, registration form (S-1, 2, 3 or 18), offering type, security shared, price per share, dollars raised, managing underwriter(s), underwriting syndicate, company counsel, underwriters' counsel, auditor, underwriting fees, cash expenses, aggregate fees and expenses, start-up IPOs, price/earnings ratio, stockholders' equity, price/equity ratio, and aftermarket performance.

1980 IPO Profiles are included and all the profiles updated monthly contain key excerpts from the prospectus and a concise analysis of each offering.

Cumulative reports are updated periodically and offer information on the initial public offering activity in 1980 enabling you to spot trends in the IPO market and make easy comparisons.

Reference Sections are also updated periodically and include:

1. A comprehensive *Guide to IPO Underwriters* listing the name of each investment banking firm that has underwritten an initial public offering since 1978; its address and telephone number; the name of the Corporate Finance Manager and Syndicate Manager; the name of the companies it has underwritten, and the offering type and dollar amount raised for each company.
2. A *Guide to IPO Experts* listing the law firms and accounting firms involved with initial public offerings since 1979.
3. *Articles* on various aspects of going public and an invaluable booklet on the advantages, disadvantages, procedures and consequences of going public.
4. The most current and comprehensive *IPO Bibliography* and reading list available today.

Each month you will receive a new report on the previous month's IPO activities and new profiles on the companies that went public during the month.

Wall Street West

The 17th Street investment marketplace in Denver has been nicknamed "Wall Street West." The Denver market is having a particularly profitable year due to the current boom with new issues and penny stocks. Denver brokers have become very selective in the stocks they underwrite. Many new securities are dealing with energy issues and the use of gas and oil. This energy-concerned market stimulates a great deal of patriotism among brokers, as well as profits for selective investors.

For information on the Denver market, a source to check is *Denver Business World,* a weekly news and financial publication, costing $26 per year. The address is 701 South Logan, Denver, CO 80209, (303) 744-1800.

Also informative is *Penny Stock Preview,* IDWA Marketing Corp., 1901 N. Olden Ave., Trenton, NJ 08618 (609) 882-6880.

New Issue
Sources of Information

New Issues Newsletter, 3471 North Federal Highway, Ft. Lauderdale, FL 33106. Monthly Publication, cost $100.

"Underwriters of Initial Public Offerings," and *Going Public, The IPO Reporter,* Howard and Company, 1529 Walnut Street, Philadelphia, PA 19102, (215) 563-8030.

Growth Stock Outlook, A bi-monthly publication, cost $60 per year. Also, *Jr. Growth Stock Newsletter* at $54 per year. (Prices subject to increase in February). Write or call for sample package. Growth Stock Outlook, P.O. Box 9911, Chevy Chase, MD 20015, (301) 654-5205.

APPENDICES

APPENDICES

APPENDIX A

CHECKLIST FOR STARTING A SUCCESSFUL BUSINESS

INTRODUCTION

Thinking of starting a business? You want to own and manage your own business. It's a good idea—provided you know what it takes and have what it takes.

Starting a business is risky at best. But your chances of making it go will be better if you understand the problems you'll meet and work out as many of them as you can before you start.

Here are some questions to help you think through what you need to know and do. Check each question if the answer is *yes*. Where the answer is *no,* you have some work to do.

These checklists are organized in the following manner:

1. A checklist for going into business that was field tested with a sample of several hundred potential entrepreneurs.
2. A reproduction of the free SBA booklet entitled, "Checklist for going into business. Small marketing aid #71."
3. Information questionnaire for use in the development of a business plan.

The List for Starting
Your Own Small Business

Before entering a new business venture, a checklist can provide the guidance in analyzing all the elements necessary for success. The checklist guide exposes variables that may be forgotten in the rush to start a business. It's also wise to look over a checklist after you begin a new business venture. There are several excellent checklists at the end of this essay. Award yourself points up to a maximum, on varying scales, for each area—then sum up the points. The highest possible number of points on each scale should be awarded when you have an exceptionally strong plus in the area. The lowest number of points (zero) should be awarded when you are weak in an area.

ITEM #1—ARE YOU EQUIPPED FOR A BUSINESS VENTURE?

	Points
1. Have you ever been in business for yourself before?	0–5
2. Have you succeeded in business for yourself before?	0–10
3. Have you ever previously rated your abilities for managing a growing business enterprise?	0–3
4. Have you taken any courses or special training or educational seminars that will help you in your own business?	0–5
5. Have you read any books about starting your own business?	0–3
6. Have you talked to friends who have started their own businesses?	0–3
7. Has anyone in your family—your father, mother, brother, sister, been self-employed? Have you spoken to them about your venture?	<u>0–7</u> Your Sum

Average score on these seven questions, on a sampling of several hundred potential entrepreneurs, was 28 out of a possible 38 points.

ITEM #2—THE IDEA STAGE

	Points
1. Is your idea an original idea? Does it have significant merit or is it a new package for an old idea?	0–7
2. Is it your idea? Will you be able to generate extensions of this idea?	0–3
3. How difficult would it be for someone else to have the same idea?	0–5
4. Have you checked to see if someone else has already had the same idea? Is your idea patentable? Have you checked the patent office?	0–10
5. Have you checked to see if other companies exist who produce the same product?	0–4
6. Have you checked the <u>Thomas Register</u> to see if this product or service is offered?	0–5
7. Have you discussed or disclosed your idea to an expert in the area in which you offer your idea?	0–3
8. Have you talked to inventors about your idea?	0–3
9. Have you analyzed the recent sales trends in this business?	0–5
10. Do you know the volume and profitability of the competitors?	0–5

11. Is there a single large successful competitor who is highly profitable? 0–10

12. Have you attempted to obtain sales orders, or commitments, or letters of intent from potential customers? 0–15

13. Do other services or products like yours exist? <u>0–5</u>

Idea
Sum

The average score on these 13 questions, on a sampling of several hundred potential entrepreneurs, was 65 out of a possible 75 points.

ITEM #3—HOW ABOUT MONEY?

Points

1. Have you saved enough money to start the business on your own? 0–15

2. Do you know how much money you'll need to get the business started? 0–10

3. How much of your own money can you put into the business versus how much money is needed? Do you need a partner to supply money? 0–15

4. Do you know what sales volume is necessary to break even? 0–7

5. Will it take less than three years before your business reaches the break even sales volume? 0–10

6. Do you know how much credit your suppliers will provide? Do you know the terms of payment in your industry? 0–5

7. What are the normal terms for selling in your industry? 0–3

8. Are you aware of money sources that will help finance your business in the event that you exhaust your initial capital? 0–4

9. Have you talked to a banker about your plans for a new business? 0–3

10. Have you talked to a lawyer about your plans for a new business? 0–3

11. Have you talked to an accountant about your plans for a new business? 0–3

12. Have you found a good location for your business? 0–10

13. Does the location provide expansion possibilities? 0–5

14. Will the new location require extensive lease-hold improvement expenditures? 0–5

15. Have you examined the trade off of buying instead of leasing a facility? 0–5

16. Is the location convenient for parking, buses, and for employees to get to work, and for suppliers and customers? 0–5
17. Have you checked the lease and zoning requirements? 0–3
18. Did you evaluate several locations before making your final selection? 0–3
19. Have you made a scaled layout of your office or work area to study work flow or customer flow? 0–7
20. Are you a good manager of money? 0–15

Money
Sum

The average score on the above 20 money questions, based upon a sampling of several hundred potential entrepreneurs, was 111 out of a possible 136 points.

ITEM #4—HAVE YOU MADE A REAL INVESTIGATION INTO THE POTENTIAL SUCCESS OF YOUR BUSINESS?

Points

1. Have you compared the standard operating ratios for your business with the industry averages, and Dun & Bradstreet? 0–2
2. Have you decided firmly on a single legal form of organization? Have you researched all the alternatives? 0–5
3. Have you written down a statement of what you want to do for your customers, suppliers, and employees, to help them understand the purpose of your business? 0–15
4. Have you answered the difficult question, "What business am I in?" 0–15

Success
Sum

Average score on the above four questions, based upon a sampling of several hundred entrepreneurs, was 25 out of a possible 37 points.

ITEM #5—RISK MANAGEMENT

Points

1. Have you considered the impact on your business of government regulatory agencies like OSHA, Equal Employment Opportunity Employment, etc.? 0–3
2. Have you made allowances for unpredictable expenses resulting from uninsured risks, such as bad debts, or shoplifting, or fire? 0–5

3. Do you know the kind of insurance that you should purchase? Should you purchase product liability insurance?   0–4
4. Have you determined for which hazards you should provide insurance?   0–5

     Risk
     Sum

The average score on the above four questions, based upon a sampling of several hundred entrepreneurs, was 15 out of a possible 17 points.

ITEM #6—EMPLOYEE RELATION AND PURCHASING

     Points

1. Have you hired your first employee? Does the employee have the requisite skills to grow on the job as well as do the job in the initial phases?   0–10
2. Have you prepared a general wage structure and does it compare favorably with prevailing wage rates?   0–7
3. Are your working conditions desirable?   0–10
4. If you plan to employ your friends and relatives, are you sure the family will not get in the way of the business?   0–10
5. Are you planning an employee incentive program?   0–3
6. If so, is it your program or their program?   0–7
7. Have you evaluated alternative sources of supply?   0–7
8. Have you carefully analyzed the pros and cons of each source of supply? Each vendor? And not made friends with a single salesman or vendor and thereby chosen to buy from that vendor on a friendship basis?   0–5
9. Have you investigated other sources of supply, not available locally, but maybe through direct mail? Cooperative purchasing? Overseas pricing?   0–5

     People
     Sum

Average score—43 out of a possible 64 points.

ITEM #7—ADVERTISING AND SALES PROMOTION

     Points

1. Do you have copies of your competitors' advertisements for the last twelve months?   0–5
2. Do you understand how much your competitors are spending on each advertisement and percentage of sales?   0–5

3. Have you defined your customer? Do you know how and   0–15
    why your customer buys?
4. Have you determined the media, or message, which will   0–7
    influence your customers' buying habits?
5. Do you know what successful and unsuccessful advertis-   0–7
    ing will be for your business?
6. Have you investigated direct mailing as an alternative?   0–5
7. Do you have a good mailing list?   0–5
8. Have you selected the most promising features and bene-   0–10
    fits of your business to promote?
9. Do you know a list of media, or methods, that is most suit-   0–12
    able for advertising your business?
10. Do you know the cost of these media?   0–5
11. Have you discussed marketing issues which are central to   0–15
    your business with a marketing expert?

Adver-
tising
Sum

Average score—65 out of a possible 89 points.

ITEM #8—PRICING

Points

1. Have you decided to price your product on the basis of   0–15
    the cost of the product or what the competitors charge for
    the product? Shouldn't you price it based upon what the
    market will bear?
2. Have you thought through the advantages of being a price   0–10
    leader or a price follower?
3. Have you considered your competitors' reactions to any   0–7
    of your pricing policies?
4. Have you considered the relative importance of each   0–10
    market segment with different pricing policies?
5. Have you investigated pricing issues to be sure you're not   0–3
    in violation of any of the codes? (Robinson-Patman, etc.)
6. Is your pricing sufficient so that you will make a profit on   0–5
    each of the products you sell?
7. Do you know what your contribution margin is on each   0–4
    product?
8. Has it taken into account your breakeven volume?   0–5
9. Do you anticipate having to raise or lower your price to   0–5
    meet competitors in the future?
10. Do you offer special discounts for special customers? Is   0–3
    this a generally known policy?

11. Have you developed a chart of accounts to classify your expenses? — 0–10

12. Do you know what your largest expense items are? Can you control or reduce these expenses? — 0–10

13. Have you attempted to control these expenses from the very beginning? — 0–10

14. Do you have a flexible expense budget to be able to handle unexpected expenses? — 0–7

Pricing
Sum

Average score—55 total possible socre 89 points.

ITEM #9—MISCELLANEOUS

Points

1. Have you been able to comply with the local town government regulations by filing the appropriate forms with the town? — 0–2

2. Have you done the same for the state and the federal government? — 0–2

3. Have you provided an adequate system of records in order to generate your tax payments and especially your payroll taxes? — 0–3

4. Is your chart of accounts sensible? Are there items that are too large or too small? — 0–2

5. Will you be able to compare your performance with existing standard operating ratios? (D&B) — 0–2

6. Have you obtained a social security number or tax identification number for your business? — 0–2

7. Is your business clear from sales tax exemptions? — 0–2

8. Have you provided for a sense of security about these government issues to all your employees? — 0–2

9. Have you complied with regulations about copyrighting, trademarks, brand names, and trade names? — 0–3

10. Have you figured out whether or not you could make more money working for someone else? — 0–5

11. Are you prepared to invest boundless energy and time in this business venture? — 0–8

12. Does your family and spouse go along with your desire to start a business? — 0–15

13. Do you know how to discover the second product or second location or second feature of your business? — 0–8

14. Have you spoken to the Small Business Adminstration for help? — 0–10

15. Have you secured any of the SBA's pamphlets?   0–3
16. Have you gotten any help from any source? They'd recommend: Score, Ace, Small Business Institute.   0–5

               _____

Misc.
Sum

Average Miscellaneous score 57
Total Miscellaneous possible points 74

Below in the breakdown of this checklist.

	Average Score	Total Possible Score
1. Are you equipped for a business venture—7 questions	28	31
2. How good is your idea—3 questions	65	41
3. How about raising money—20 questions	111	136
4. How about the potential success of your business—4 questions	25	37
5. Risk management—4 questions	15	17
6. Employee skills and purchasing—9 questions	43	64
6. Advertising and sales promotion—11 questions	65	89
8. Pricing—14 questions	55	89
9. Miscellaneous—16 questions	57	74
	463	619

Your   Success   Pricing
Sum   Sum   Sum

BEFORE YOU START

How about you?

Are you the kind of person who can get a business started and make it go? (Before you answer this question, use the worksheet on the next few pages.)   _____

Think about *why* you want to own your own business. Do you want to badly enough to keep you working long hours without knowing how much money you'll end up with?   _____

Have you worked in a business like the one you want to start?   _____

Have you worked for someone else as a foreman or manager? _____

Have you had any business training in school? _____

Have you saved any money? _____

How about the money?

Do you know how much money you will need to get your business started? (Use worksheets 2 and 3 to figure this out.) _____

Have you counted up how much money of your own you can put into the business? _____

Do you know how much credit you can get from your suppliers—the people you will buy from? _____

Do you know where you can borrow the rest of the money you need to start your business? _____

Have you figured out what net income per year you expect to get from the business? Count your salary and your profit on the money you put into the business. _____

Can you live on less than this so that you can use some of it to help your business grow? _____

Have you talked to a banker about your plans? _____

How about a partner?

If you need a partner with money or know-how that you don't have, do you know someone who will fit—someone you can get along with? _____

Do you know the good and bad points about going it alone, having a partner, and incorporating your business? _____

Have you talked to a lawyer about it? _____

How about your customers?

Do most businesses in your community seem to be doing well? _____

Have you tried to find out whether stores like the one you want to open are doing well in your community and in the rest of the country? _____

Do you know what kind of people will want to buy what you plan to sell? _____

What people like that live in the area where you want to
open your store? _____

Do they need a store like yours? _____

If not, have you thought about opening a different kind
of store or going to another neighborhood? _____

WORKSHEET NO. 1

Under each question, check the answer that says what you feel or comes
closest to it. Be honest with yourself.

Are you a self-starter?

I do things on my own. Nobody has to tell me to get going.

If someone gets me started, I keep going all right.

Easy does it, man. I don't put myself out until I have to.

How do you feel about other people?

I like people. I can get along with just about anybody.

I have plenty of friends—I don't need anyone else.

Most people bug me.

Can you lead others?

I can get most people to go along when I start something.

I can give the orders if someone tells me what we should do.

I let someone else get things moving. Then I go along if I feel like it.

Can you take responsibility?

I like to take charge of things and see them through.

I'll take over if I have to, but I'd rather let someone else be
responsible.

There's always some eager beaver around wanting to show how
smart he is. I say let him.

How good an organizer are you?

I like to have a plan before I start. I'm usually the one to get things
lined up when the gangs wants to do something.

I do all right unless things get too goofed up. Then I cop out.

You get all set and then something comes along and blows the whole bag. So I just take things as they come.

How good a worker are you?

I can keep going as long as I need to. I don't mind working hard for something I want.

I'll work hard for a while, but when I've had enough, that's it, man!

I can't see that hard work gets you anywhere.

CAN YOU MAKE DECISIONS?

I can make up my mind in a hurry if I have to. It usually turns out okay, too.

I can if I have plenty of time. If I have to make up my mind fast, I think later I should have decided the other way.

I don't like to be the one who has to decide things. I'd probably blow it.

CAN PEOPLE TRUST WHAT YOU SAY?

You bet they can. I don't say things I don't mean.

I try to be on the level most of the time, but sometimes I just say what's easiest.

What's the sweat if the other fellow doesn't know the difference?

CAN YOU STICK WITH IT?

If I make up my mind to do something, I don't let *anything* stop me.

I usually finish what I start—if it doesn't get fouled up.

If it doesn't go right away, I turn off. Why beat your brains out?

HOW GOOD IS YOUR HEALTH?

Man, I never run down!

I have enough energy for most things I want to do.

I run out of juice sooner than most of my friends seem to.

Now count the checks you made. How many checks are there beside the *first* answer to each question? How many checks are there beside the *second* answer to each question? How many checks are there beside the *third* answer to each question?

If most of your checks are beside the first answers, you probably have what it takes to run a business. If not, you're likely to have more trouble than you can handle by yourself. Better find a partner who is strong on the points you're weak on. If many checks are beside the third answer, not even a good partner will be able to shore you up.

GETTING STARTED

YOUR BUILDING

Have you found a good building for your store? _____

Will you have enough room when your business gets bigger? _____

Can you fix the building the way you want it without spending too much money? _____

Can people get to it easily from parking spaces, bus stops, or their homes? _____

Have you had a lawyer check the lease and zoning? _____

EQUIPMENT AND SUPPLIES

Do you know just what equipment and supplies you need and how much they will cost? (Worksheet 3 on page 136 and the lists you made for it should show this.) _____

Can you save money by buying secondhand equipment? _____

YOUR MERCHANDISE

Have you decided what things you will sell? _____

Do you know how much or how many of each you will buy to open your store with? _____

Have you found suppliers who will sell you what you need at a good price? _____

Have you compared the prices and credit terms of different suppliers? _____

YOUR RECORDS

Have you planned a system of records that will keep track of your income and expenses, what you owe other people, and what other people owe you? _____

Have you worked out a way to keep tract of your inventory so that you will always have enough on hand for your customers but not more than you can sell? _____

Have you figured out how to keep your payroll records and take care of tax reports and payments? _____

Do you know what financial statements you should prepare? _____

Do you know how to use these financial statements? _____

Do you know an accountant who will help you with your records and financial statements? _____

YOUR STORE AND THE LAW

Do you know what licenses and permits you need? _____

Do you know what business laws you have to obey? _____

Do you know a lawyer you can go to for advice and for help with legal papers? _____

PROTECTING YOUR STORE

Have you made plans for protecting your store against thefts of all kinds—shoplifting, robbery, burglary, employee stealing? _____

Have you talked with an insurance agent about what kinds of insurance you need? _____

BUYING A BUSINESS SOMEONE ELSE HAS STARTED

Have you made a list of what you like and don't like about buying a business someone else has started? _____

Are you sure you know the real reason why the owner wants to sell the business? _____

Have you compared the cost of buying the business with the cost of starting a new business? _____

Is the stock up to date and in good condition? _____

Is the building in good condition? _____

Will the owner of the building transfer the lease to you? _____

Have you talked with other businesspersons in the area to see what they think of the business? _____

Have you talked with the company's suppliers? _____

Have you talked with a lawyer about it? _____

MAKING IT GO

ADVERTISING

Have you decided how you will advertise? (Newspapers—posters—handbills—radio—by mail?) _____

Do you know where to get help with your ads? _____

Have you watched what other stores do to get people to buy? _____

THE PRICES YOU CHARGE

Do you know how to figure what you should charge for each item you sell? _____

Do you know what other stores like yours charge? _____

BUYING

Do you have a plan for finding out what your customers want? _____

Will your plan for keeping track of your inventory tell you when it is time to order more and how much to order?
Do you plan to buy most of your stock from a few suppliers rather than a little from many, so that those you buy from will help you succeed? _____

SELLING

Have you decided whether you will have salesclerks or selfservice? _____

Do you know how to get customers to buy? _____

Have you thought about why you like to buy from some _____ salespersons and others turn you off?

YOUR EMPLOYEES

If you need to hire someone to help you, do you know where to look? _____

Do you know what kind of person you need? _____

Do you know how much to pay? _____

Do you have a plan for training your employees? _____

CREDIT FOR YOUR CUSTOMERS

Have you decided whether to let your customers buy on credit? _____

Do you know the good and bad points about joining a credit-card plan? _____

Can you tell a deadbeat from a good credit customer? _____

A FEW EXTRA QUESTIONS

Have you figured out whether you could make more money working for someone else? _____

Does your family go along with your plan to start a business of your own? _____

Do you know where to find out about new ideas and new products? _____

Do you have a work plan for yourself and your employees? _____

Have you gone to the nearest Small Business Administration office for help with your plans? _____

If you have answered all these questions carefully, you've done some hard work and serious thinking. That's good. But you have probably found some things you still need to know more about or do something about.

Do all you can for yourself, but don't hesitate to ask for help from people who can tell you what you need to know. Remember, running a business takes guts! You've got to be able to decide what you need and then go after it. *Good luck!*

WORKSHEET NO. 2

ESTIMATED MONTHLY EXPENSES

Item	Your estimate of monthly expenses based on sales of $_____ per year *Column 1*	Your estimate of how much cash you need to start your business (See column 3) *Column 2*	What to put in column 2 (These figures are typical for one kind of business. You will have to decide how many months to allow for in your business.) *Column 3*
Salary of owner-manager	$	$	2 times column 1
All other salaries and wages			3 times column 1
Rent			3 times column 1
Advertising			3 times column 1
Delivery expense			3 times column 1
Supplies			3 times column 1
Telephone and telegraph			3 times column 1
Other utilities			3 times column 1
Insurance			Payment required by insurance company
Taxes, including Social Security			4 times column 1
Interest			3 times column 1
Maintenance			3 times column 1
Legal and other professional fees			3 times column 1
Miscellaneous			3 times column 1
STARTING COSTS YOU ONLY HAVE TO PAY ONCE			Leave column 2 blank
Fixtures and equipment			Fill in worksheet 3 on page and put the total here
Decorating and remodeling			Talk it over with a contractor
Installation of fixtures and equipment			Talk to suppliers from who you buy these
Starting inventory			Suppliers will probably help you estimate this
Deposits with public utilities			Find out from utilities companies

			Description
Legal and other professional fees			Lawyer, accountant and so on
Licenses and permits			Find out from city offices what you have to have
Advertising and promotion for opening			Estimate what you'll use
Accounts receivable			What you need to buy more stock until credit customers pay
Cash			For unexpected expenses or losses, special purchases, etc.
Other			Make a separate list and enter total
TOTAL ESTIMATED CASH YOU NEED TO START WITH			Add up all the numbers in Column 2

WORKSHEET NO. 3—LIST OF FURNITURE, FIXTURES, AND EQUIPMENT

Leave out or add items to suit your business. Use separate sheets to list exactly what you need for each of the items below.	If you plan to pay cash in full, enter the full amount below and in the last column.	If you are going to pay by installments, fill out the columns below. Enter in the last column your downpayment plus at least one installment.			Estimate of the cash you need for furniture, fixtures, and equipment
		Price	Downpayment	Amount of each installment	
Counters	$	$	$	$	$
Storage shelves, cabinets					
Display stands, shelves, tables					
Cash register					
Safe					
Window display fixtures					
Special lighting					
Delivery equipment if needed					
TOTAL FURNITURE, FIXTURES, AND EQUIPMENT (Enter this figure also in worksheet 2 under "Starting Costs You Only Have to Pay Once.")					$

APPENDIX B

INFORMATION QUESTIONNAIRE

This questionnaire is to be used as background for the development of a business plan.

1. What is the present name of the company?
2. Is the company a corporation, partnership, or sole proprietorship?
3. If the company is a corporation, please set forth the date and the state of incorporation.
4. Please furnish the names of the persons who formed the company.
5. Was the company originally organized as a corporation, partnership, or sole proprietorship?
6. Please furnish the names of the initial shareholders and/or providers of funds (debt and equity) of the company. Supply dates of each sale of securities, number of shares issued, and the consideration received for the shares. If no cash consideration was received, indicate the dollar value ascribed to each consideration.
7. Please describe the nature of the company's business. Has the nature of the company's business changed or evolved since its inception? Is it intended to place future emphasis on different areas?
8. Does the company conduct business under names other than its own? If so, please set forth the names and places where they are used.
9. Does the company utilize any trademarks or tradenames? If so, submit copies.
10. What geographical area does the company serve? Are there any limitations on what markets can be reached, *e.g.,* freight, duties, service, maintenance, patent licenses, tariffs, government regulation, etc.? Does the company intend to enlarge its present areas of distribution or service?
11. Please describe the major products or services of the company.

12. In which states and/or countries other than its state of incorporation is the company licensed or qualified to do business?

13. Please furnish a listing plus a physical description of all offices, plants, laboratories, warehouses, stores, outlets, studios, or other facilities (include size of plot, square footage of enclosed space, etc.).

14. Please describe the method or methods of distribution and sales. If any contractual arrangements are involved, please describe and/or furnish copies.

15. Please list and describe to the degree relevant, all patents, technical information, trademarks, franchises, copyrights, patent and technical information, licenses owned and/or used.

16. Please furnish a detailed five-year breakdown of sales, earnings, income, or losses of the company's major divisions, departments, and product categories. Give the percentage of total income or loss attributed to each.

17. Please furnish a detailed breakdown of major suppliers of raw materials, goods, etc. Give their names, addresses, and volume of purchases. Are other sources readily available or is the company dependent to any degree on any one supplier? What would result if the product or products of said supplier or suppliers were no longer readily procurable? Does the company have any long term contracts with its suppliers?

18. If the company utilizes the services of subcontractor and/or processors of its products or components of subassemblies, please describe the work done and the availability of other subcontractors or processors. Does the company have any long term contracts with such persons?

19. Furnish a three-year record of names, addresses, and volume of purchases of major customers or outlets for the company's products or services. The prospectus or offering circular will list names of customers who account for more than 10 percent of the company's business. Could this in any way be deleterious to the company?

20. Please furnish names of the company's major competitors; describe the nature and area of their competition—is it direct or indirect? What is the company's approximate rank in the industry? Are there numerous competitors? What is the degree of competition? Can new companies readily enter the field? Do the company's competitors possess greater financial resources? Are they longer established and better recognized?

21. Please furnish a complete list of all officers and/or directors plus the following data:

a. Age
b. Education
c. Title and function—responsibilities
d. Length of service with company
e. Posts held and functions performed for company prior to present post
f. Compensation
g. Past business associations and posts held
h. Special distinctions
i. Other directorates or present business affiliations

22. Please furnish a copy of all stock option plans.
23. Please furnish a copy of or describe any bonus and profit-sharing plans.
24. Please furnish copies of or describe any other employee fringe benefits.
25. Please furnish copies of any pension plan.
26. Please state the total number of employees, full and part time, the major categories of employees and number within each. If the company is to any degree dependent on technology or other expertise, please give details, *e.g.*, number of Ph.D.s, M.A.s, engineers, technicians, medical personnel, etc.
27. Are your employees represented by one or more unions? Please list each union by name or number. Please furnish copies of the union contracts.
28. Please furnish a general description of labor relations, past strikes, handling of grievances, etc. Has the company experienced any difficulties in obtaining qualified personnel? Has the company had any problems with respect to personnel turnover?
29. Please describe all acquisitions of other companies, assets, personnel, etc., made by the company, or any intended acquisitions. Please furnish copies of all acquisitions agreements.
30. Please describe any major dispositions of subsidiaries, divisions, assets, equipment, plants, etc., made by the company.
31. Has any officer, director, or major shareholder ever (a) had any difficulties of any nature with the Securities and Exchange Commission, the National Association of Securities Dealers, or any state securities commission or agency, (b) been convicted of a felony, or (c) been under indictment, investigation, or threatened by the SEC, NASD, a state commission, or public agency with prosecution for violation of a state or federal statute? Has any such person ever been adjudicated a bankrupt?
    If the answer to any of the questions is in the affirmative, please describe the circumstances in detail.

32. Has the company made (a) any private placements of its equity or debt securities, or (b) any public sale of its equity or debt securities? If so, please furnish complete details including copies of documents used in the placement and/or sale.

33. Furnish a specimen copy of all outstanding and authorized equity and debt securities.

34. Furnish the following data regarding the distribution of the company's voting stock:

    a. classes of stock and number of shares of each outstanding;
    b. total number of shareholders plus list of shareholders;
    c. names, residence addresses and shareholders of ten largest shareholders of each class;
    d. relationships of major shareholders to each other or to the officers and directors of the company; and
    e. details of any voting trust agreements, shareholders agreements or other arrangements to vote stock jointly.

35. Are there any options to purchase stock or other securities or warrants outstanding other than employees' stock option plans? If so, please furnish copies or describe such plan.

36. Does the company have any long term or short term debt, secured or unsecured, or has the company guaranteed such debt on behalf of others? Please furnish copies of the documents creating the debt or guarantee, or describe the debt or guarantee.

37. Please furnish detailed audited statements for the last five years if available.

38. Please furnish interim statements covering the period subsequent to the last audited financial statement.

39. Please furnish comparative figures of earning and net worth for five years.

40. Please furnish an explanation of any and all abnormal, nonrecurring or unusual items in earnings statements or balance sheets.

41. Please furnish a statement of cash flow if materially different from statement of net earnings.

42. Please furnish a statement as to any contingent or possible liabilities not shown on balance sheet. Please include guarantees, warranties, litigation, etc.

43. With respect to the company's inventories, please state (a) major categories, (b) method used in valuation, LIFO, FIFO, other, and (c) control systems. If your "inventories" are distinctive in any fashion, *e.g.*, film libraries, promotional displays, etc., please state how they are handled on your books.

44. What is the company's policy regarding depreciation, depletion, and amortization? Which items are capitalized and which expensed? Are there any deferred write-offs?

45. Are your company's methods of accounting similar to the rest of the industry? If not, please describe the differences and the reason for such differences.

46. Please state the status of federal and state tax examinations. When was your last examination, and are there any open questions?

47. Please describe all bank relationships and credit lines. Are factors involved?

48. Please describe any pending or threatened claims and litigation, by identifying the parties, the amount involved, the names of involved and please furnish copies of all documents with respect thereto.

49. Please describe all insurance coverages, *e.g.*, plant, equipment, properties, work interruption, key employees, other.

50. Please describe your company's projection of sales and earnings for the next three years, including explanations with respect to any increase or decrease.

51. Please furnish lists of all real estate owned by the company, including, without limitation, the following: (a) the improvements on the property, (b) the assessed valuation and amount of current real estate taxes, (c) any mortgages, including amount, rate of interest and due date, (d) any liens or encumbrances, and (e) the estimated present value.

52. Please furnish a list of all real estate leased by the company, including, without limitation, the following: (a) the amount of space (b) the rent-fixed and contingent, (c) the term of lease, (d) the renewal options, (e) the purchase options, (f) the minimum annual gross rentals, and (g) the minimum total gross rental obligation to expiration of all leases in force.

53. Please list all equipment leased by the company if aggregate annual rentals exceed $5,000 or if the company is dependent on the equipment. If any other property is leased at a sizeable aggregate annual rental, please furnish details of the lease, including without limitation the terms, options to renew and/or purchase, etc.

54. Please describe all depreciable property owned by the company including, without limitation, the following: (a) the original cost to company, (b) the depreciation to date, in addition to a statement as to the method employed, (c) the remaining cost, and (d) the aging of items listed (remaining depreciable life).

55. Please furnish copies of all brochures, catalogues, mailers, publi-

city releases, newspaper or magazine articles, literature and the like distributed by the company or concerning the company, its products, personnel, or services.

56. Please describe the company's research and development activities.

57. Please give a complete description of any unusual contracts relating to the company, its business, products, or services.

58. Please describe exactly how the net proceeds (after underwriting commission and all expenses) are to be used by the company.

59. Please describe the company's plans for expansion or growth.

60. Please set forth any information not previously disclosed in your answers that an investor would use in making a decision as to whether he or she should invest in the company.

61. Please furnish copies of the following:
    a. Certificate of Incorporation and all amendments.
    b. By-laws and all amendments.
    c. Employee agreements, if any.

APPENDIX C

Suggested Outline of a Business Plan

Cover Sheet: Name of business, names of principals, address and phone number of business

Statement of Purpose

Table of Contents

I. The Business
   - A. Description of Business
   - B. Market
   - C. Competition
   - D. Location of Business
   - E. Management
   - F. Personnel
   - G. Application and Expected Effect of Loan (if needed)
   - H. Summary

II. Financial Data
   - A. Sources and Applications of Funding
   - B. Capital Equipment List
   - C. Balance Sheet
   - D. Breakeven Analysis
   - E. Income Projections (Profit and Loss Statements)
       1. Three-year summary
       2. Detail by month for first year
       3. Detail by quarter for second and third years
       4. Notes of explanation
   - F. Pro-Forma Cash Flow
       1. Detail by month for first year
       2. Detail by quarter for second and third years
       3. Notes of explanation
   - G. Deviation Analysis

H. Historical Financial Reports for Existing Business
   1. Balance sheets for past three years
   2. Income statements for past three years
   3. Tax returns

III. Supporting Documents: Personal résumés, personal financial requirements and statements, cost of living budget, credit reports, letters of reference, job descriptions, letters of intent, copies of leases, contracts, legal documents, and anything else of relevance to the plan.

APPENDIX D

SAMPLE BUSINESS PLANS

The introductions and tables of contents of these business plans are included not as examples of either effective or ineffective business plans, but rather to acquaint the reader with several actual business plans. These were chosen more for their representation of various types of plans. They are all actual plans, disguised where needed, especially as relates to geographic location, financial information, and individual identities, which may account for some but not all of the inconsistencies, errors, and omissions.

BRIOX TECHNOLOGY, INC.

This is an interesting story—one with a good ending. It began when my brother, John Anthony Mancuso, acting as a salesman for a valve company, in upstate New York called on Briox Technologies. He mentioned my interest in small business to the Briox entrepreneur, David Gessner. As can be observed from the résumés in the business plan, Gessner was the holder of a technical master's degree, and, as such, he elected to attend an interesting three-day workshop sponsored by the Institute of New Enterprise Development (INED) in Belmont, Massachusetts. This agency specializes in helping new entrepreneurs get started. For a small fee, Gessner attended a weekend "how to write a business plan" seminar which was held in Salt Lake City, Utah. Hence, Gessner was fairly well versed in the construction of a business plan. Moreover, as will be evident in a moment, he possessed a deep and burning desire to start, finance, and manage a small business of his own. John Mancuso suggested that he show the business plan to me.

Gessner and I met; I was impressed with him and his business, and I introduced him to a Minority Enterprise Small Business Investment Company (MESBIC). Gessner cleverly constructed the business plan to highlight the minority employment aspect of his business. The plan, as attached, was financed by several friends and relatives (angels) and by the Worcester Cooperation Council, Inc. (WCCI). The business moved to Worcester, and Gessner began to operate the medical oxygen company.

This is where the story becomes interesting. It took only a few months to use up all of the original investment. During that time the company was unable to perfect the oxygenerator that was to make oxygen from water. The idea was good—even great—but the technology was only fair—maybe poor. Within six months of the private placement, the business was bust, Al Stubman was fired, and Gessner was all alone with no money, no sales, and no product. A more sensible man would have known when to quit, and would have gone in search of a job. Instead, he sought part-time employment, did some consulting (he assisted in a small business course at WPI), and collected unemployment. The last of these actions—collecting unemployment—was the most emotional and most rewarding experience of all. Gessner collected for over one year, and these funds provided the main sustenance for his family.

With the addition of hindsight, these unemployment checks were a vital motivation to keep him going: They supplied the nourishment for the next year or so. If a person who contemplates going into a small business has never collected an unemployment check, may I recommend that he visit his unemployment office. The sign over the door will read "Employment Office" but everyone calls it the "Unemployment Office." It's a very dehumanizing process. Go see for yourself, if you haven't already.

During these never-ending months of product development, Gessner continued to improve his radical new invention, the oxygenerator. Finally, after two years of trying, he decided to shift horses.

Just as Ed Land of Polaroid was initially interested in building a business around polarized glass (supposedly for the windshields and headlights of automobiles), Dave Gessner began his business with the wrong initial product. Gessner soon improved upon the existing and proven technology pioneered by the competitors—making oxygen by filtering air. He developed a brochure, attracted new investors, acquired a new partner/investor, and began again. In the past few years, after 4 years, he now leads a profitable company with annual sales in the $10 million range.

I said that starting a business and succeeding at it requires perseverance and motivation—sometimes bordering on obsession. Gessner proves my points.

AMERICAN LASER, INC.

This is not an untypical story. In fact, it's recurring quite frequently. Although this story is disguised, it is true. These two fellows bought a business when their employer decided to go out of the business. And, best of all, they succeeded. This may become an even more common practice in the future.

In fact, the largest employer in the entire state of Vermont, an asbestos mine, experienced a similar transaction. After years of poor financial management, the parent company announced plans to close its doors. The people were going to lose their jobs, and the closing of the business was a statewide concern. The good news is what happened. The employees banded together, obtained financing from the state and bought the company. Naturally, as with many of these stories, the elected president was the former foreman of the maintenance division. After one year under employee ownership, all the stockholders were able to have their entire initial investment returned. In the subsequent years, the business had demonstrated excellent profitability.

The same is true in the case of American Laser. As a division of the larger parent company, it consistently lost in excess of $1 million per year. This is devastating, given the size of the sales of the division. When these two people took over the company, they had only marginal management experience. The business plan was written in module form. This allowed the entrepreneurs to package the appropriate modules in order to maximize the appeal. The plan is a good one. However, in fact, the list of customers in the plan failed to materialize in the first year. In other words, *none* of the customers listed in the report purchased products during the first year the firm was in business.

The plan failed to raise venture money. However, it did *not* fail to launch the business. Moreover, the business is extremely successful; and in the fifth year after the start of this business, the firm was sold to another business for $1 million.

After discussing the appeal of this new business with several venture sources, the founders were extremely dejected. They found the terms and conditions of any new money to be terribly limiting. Subsequently, they walked into a bank and pleaded their case with an unusual, creative, and friendly banker. Within a half an hour, the banker advanced them a personal, unsecured loan to launch their business. I was there and I saw it happen—an unusual event if I ever saw one. Earlier in this book I said, "Pick a banker, not a bank." Later on the same page, I said. "A good banker can be a venture capitalist in disguise." This one was more than that: He became an admired friend. He received all of the loan back and kept the new growing company in town. An interesting story.

PERSPECTIVES, INC.

This is an excellent business plan. It is well written; the entrepreneur is successful; the idea is superior. However, the plan never raised any money: It was a failure.

It was shown to many investors, probably more than it should have been, but it was always a bridesmaid. One of the common criticisms of the plan was the inability to test the idea on a small scale. One of the investors claimed that the plan was too large an investment prior to any measurable level of success being obtainable. There was considerable negotiating about the viability of a regional publication for the senior citizens, say, in Florida. But on a regional scale, it was much less appealing financially. So the idea died.

However, as with most good ideas, it only died for this entrepreneur. Publishing, like many industries, is a special and private business, and John O'Mara had very little publishing experience. But another entrepreneur with a different business plan, totally unrelated to this venture, launched a very similar product. The data obtained by the grapevine claims that the business is now a solid financial success.

John O'Mara gained a great deal of experience in developing this business plan—so much so, in fact, that he wrote another one. Soon, he left the secure arms of his large company employer in order to launch a new business called the Computer Security Institute. This venture provided newsletters, information, and seminars for larger firms interested in protecting confidential information stored in computers. I'm told that the venture is extremely successful because the initial membership fee alone, from my outside vantage point, certainly must help cover some overhead. The advantage of having customers send money in advance (membership fees) is an interesting method of financing an entrepreneurial venture.

IN-LINE TECHNOLOGY

The plan presented here is a shortened version of the actual document used to finance In-Line Technology. The actual document was about four times longer. It contained numerous photos and product descriptions. The financing was successful. The firm was able to raise the funds stated in the prospectus. The funds were supplied by friends and relatives, and the final $50 thousand was provided by an extremely successful and well-known New York venture capitalist. The venture capitalist, because of his reputation, was able to negotiate an extra bonus for investing in this young but promising business. The two founders were extremely reluctant to give extra compensation to the venture sources, but they finally decided to go along.

The new money transfusion helped, and the firm began to grow. The venture source forced the additional services of a paid-for management consultant to work several days per month at In-Line Technology. This was not part of the private placement agreement but the after-the-placement verbal persuasion was sufficient. In other words, the original private placement legal document did not specifically require In-Line to accept outside consulting advice. The legal agreement men for private placements of this type and size are usually secondary to verbal agreements. In fact, the business improved based on this consulting advice.

In-Line never made money. Occasionally, it had a few months of profit but never any sustained or significant profits. It always seemed to almost make a profit in the following few years, but it never became very successful. Finally, the venture capitalist grew restless and introduced In-Line Technology to a larger firm on the West Coast—Applied Materials, Inc. The firms were merged in January of 1976, and the investors in this business plan realized a 3:1 gain. Hence, the firm raised money and performed at an unprofitable level, yet the investors and stockholders still made a profit. This is seldom the case, and without the assistance of the New York venture capitalist, the firm would still be struggling. The venture placement was determined at a breakfast meeting in New York. This was the only meeting the venture source had with the firm. He never visited the plant.

About nine months after the merger, one of the two founders was fired and the other was made a consultant. In other words, they were both eased out of the business. This partnership of Gene St. Onge and Hank Bok works well and they have just launched a new business. Based upon the funds gained from the sale of In-Line Technology, the two men have started another small business, Hydro-tech. This firm is entering the interesting area of hydroponics, which is a form of scientific farming. This business calls for year around growing of tomatoes, cucumbers, and lettuce in greenhouses. The success of this newest business is still undetermined. It's interesting to recall some of the early comments that the likelihood of starting a new business is increased if you have previous experience in starting businesses. Many entrepreneurs will start five to six businesses in a lifetime.

B.L.T.

The reader of this business plan must be careful not to let recent events such as the energy crisis cloud the proper reading of the document. This plan was written in 1969. It followed very closely on the heels of a successful public stock offering for Robo-Wash, a competitor. The plan was written by three extremely talented men who spent most of their careers on Wall Street in New York. While none of the three founders had any experience in either the gas station or car wash fields, they knew their way around Wall Street. They were experts at raising money.

The business plan is extremely simple. It is not terribly exciting to read. The strongest point is the level of management achievement of the three principals. This was enough for this start-up business to raise in excess of $1,000,000 from a handful of venture capitalists. The money was raised over several placements, and the firm experienced continual delays and postponements in building and operating the gas station/car wash combination. The business began in fine style with a prototype gas station/car wash operating profitably in southern Connecticut. However, this was the only profitable business enterprise with B.L.T. The business as a whole never made money. The firm lost the $10 million of investment plus a good deal of bank debt. The reasons for failures were manyfold. However, the business plan, as simple as it was, was sufficient just as it was, to raise over $1 million.

IN-LINE TECHNOLOGIES, INC.
High Technology Investment

CONTENTS

I.   INTRODUCTION

The electronics industry today still offers great potential to the entrepreneur for the creation of sizeable, profitable business ventures
especially in the areas of <u>proprietary</u> product marketing.   This is true
for several reasons.   First and foremost, of course, is the fact that the
dynamic state-of-the-art technology existing in the electronics industry
today affords a greater ease of market entry for the innovator.   New,
unique, and different approaches to the solution of old problems are
welcomed, and are, in fact, a requirement for a successful company
engaged in the marketing of proprietary products.

For such companies the rate of growth and, of course, the rate of
profitability are limited primarily by the financial structure and support
of the organization, assuming that dynamic leadership, superior marketing capability, and exceptional technical talent are available.   With a
proper financial base the growth pattern of such organization in today's
growing and expanding electronics market is highly probable.

The purpose of this business plan is to present in significant detail a
plan whereby an organization fitting the above pattern can make a substantial impact on the proprietary product market in a short period of
time with a minimum of the type of entrepreneurial risk usually found
to be an integral part of such plans.   The minimization of these risks
comes about because of the following basic facts:

1.   In-Line Technology, Inc. is a thriving organization that
     exists and will provide the vehicle for this plan.
2.   In-Line Technology has already designed and manufactured
     90% of its fiscal year 1974 product line and is in the process
     of beginning its initial phases of marketing production tested
     and customer proved equipment.
3.   In-Line Technology is supplying equipment to a rapidly
     expanding market for semiconductors that is forecasted to be
     greater than $2 billion by 1976, *almost a factor of 2 greater
     than the 1971 total in just the United States alone.
4.   In-Line Technology can accurately control and predict first
     year's bookings and shipments (with adequate financing) due to
     management's combined experience of over thirty years of
     marketing and engineering in the photo-chemical processing
     field.

---

*Market information from "Electronics' 1973 forecast of Electronics
Markets.

In-Line Founders are in Tune with Photoprocessing Trend

A company that started as a part-time effort some 18 months ago has recently become its founders' sole business concern, and indeed, they appear in a good position to profit from semiconductor manufacturers' growing enthusiasm for automating their photoprocessing operations.

While Hendrik F. Bok and Eugene R. St. Onge worked together in the Systems division of EPEC Industries Inc., New Bedford, Mass., they saw the need for systems that could automatically handle cleaning, drying, etching, and developing. "There are a lot of different systems available," notes Bok, "but you have to buy the etcher from one company, the coater from another. To form a complete line of equipment, a plant manager needs to buy four or five makes of equipment that aren't always compatible."

The two men joined forces to make specialized turnkey photoprocessing systems, and In-Line Technology Inc. was born in Assonet, Mass. By now, In-Line has emerged from a custom-equipment phase with a number of standard items, including cleaners, coaters, dryers, developers, etchers, wet strippers, and plasma strippers, all of which are interfaced for either manual or automatic loading.

Cutting loose. During In-Line's first year, Bok and St. Onge kept their jobs at EPEC, but last October they were able to buy out EPEC'S Spray division and devote full time to In-Line, of which they are sole owners. Sales this year may reach $1 million.

Bok thinks part of their success is a result of "the imagination to come up with something new," but part of it is traceable to their backgrounds also. Bok, 47, founded his first company in 1954 in his native Netherlands. (He still speaks with a Dutch accent.) It made spray coaters, and in 1958 he brought the process with him to the U.S. where three years later he founded another company with expertise based on the same process. Joining EPEC in 1967 as a vice president, he gained experience in coating and first started to build integrated systems including sprayers, dryers, exposure equipment, and developers.

While Bok considers himself a "concept" engineer, St. Onge, 36, is a process engineer. One need they see is for better yields, and they believe their automatic production lines, which include automatic wafer handling, can help. Since wafers and plates are untouched throughout production, and the line is so timed that clean plates don't have to wait before being coated, dirt caused pinholes and other faults are cut down.

LASER WELDING AND DRILLING
Employee Ownership
of High Technology Business

CONTENTS

1.0 NOTICE OF INTENTION

In making this preliminary proposal to ALI, there are many statements of the intentions of Albert D. Castro and William Lock forming a business. It should be noted:

1. This is only a preliminary document, serving as a basis of discussion only. In no way will either Mr. Castro or Mr. Lock be held to any statement, commitment, etc., without their specific signed intention to do so.

2. American Laser Corp. has full knowledge of our intention. However, there is no agreement yet between ALI with either Mr. Lock or Mr. Castro in regards to this business.

3. Estimates of completion in the glass laser field, potential sales volume, marketing plans, etc., are all only those of Mr. Lock and Mr. Castro and although they believe them to be as accurate and reliable as possible, no guarantee to their validity is implied.

2.0 SUMMARY

We, Albert D. Castro and William H. Lock are making a pre-liminary proposal to American Laser Corporation that it sell to us its complete glass laser business. For this portion of what was American Laser line of laser equipment, we are offering $85,000. We propose to form a company within the area of Phoenix that will profit from the substantial investment that ALI has made to develop their laser products. Our marketing/selling plans are basically to retain two sales representatives from ALI's national organization, to concentrate our own sales efforts in the west coast area, and to promote these products through continued effort in applications engineering.

We plan our organization to be a small, conservative one (6 - 7 people for the first six months) but one whose sales growth should be 50% per year. A study of the market for our products and the competition indicates to us that the product line we desire is one characterized by its high quality, its reliability, and its sales appeal. To finance this company, we have been able to raise $25,000 between us, and our proposal to ALI is that we pay them $40,000 cash and that they accept a $45,000, three-year note from us for the rest of the payment. For this consideration, we agree that ALI's note will be the senior debt of our company. We will form our company with Albert D. Castro as president (and a 60% owner) and William H. Lock as vice president (and a 40% owner). Sales projections indicate a sales volume of $203,000 in 1974 and $332,000 in 1975. We expect to "break even" approximately two years after start of business. A preliminary cash-flow analysis indicates to us that we need at least $50,000 from some loaner.

BLT CORPORATION
Car Wash/Gas Station Combination

THE B.L.T. COMPANY

PARTICIPATION IN A TECHNOLOGICAL AND
MERCHANDISING REVOLUTION

THE AUTOMOBILE SERVICE INDUSTRY IS IN THE EARLY
STAGE OF A TECHNOLOGICAL AND MERCHANDISING REVOLU-
TION. THE COMBINATION OF TWO ESSENTIAL AUTOMOTIVE
NEEDS--CAR WASHING AND GASOLINE--HAS PRODUCED A
HIGHLY PROMOTABLE AND EXTREMELY PROFITABLE SERVICE.

TECHNOLOGICAL REVOLUTION

The technological revolution is the result of the development and
perfection of a new generation of car wash equipment. This equipment
is highly automated and inexpensive to operate and maintain.

MERCHANDISING REVOLUTION

The merchandising revolution is the result of combining the purchase of gasoline with the car washing function. This combination has
created a new and highly promotable service which offers the consumer
distinct economic and convenience benefits previously unavailable.

PROFITABILITY

The profitability of the modern gas pumping-car wash unit is
based upon the following fundamental business principles: Low labor,
high gross margins, and minimal inventory and accounts receivable.

THE B.L.T. COMPANY CONCEPT

The B.L.T. Company was organized to capitalize on the technological and merchandising revolution and the fundamental business
advantages outlined above. The B.L.T. Company intends to multiply
the profitability of an individual car wash and gas pumping-car wash
unit through the establishment of a national chain of wholly owned and
franchised installations.

Each wholly owned car wash unit is expected to generate between $25,000 and $40,000 pre tax annual earnings on an investment of approximately $50,000. Each franchised unit is expected to generate initial income from the sale of equipment of between $5,000 and $10,000, plus continuing income of between $3,000 - $6,000 annually.

Each wholly owned gas pumping-car wash unit is expected to generate between $50,000 and $70,000 pre tax annual earnings on an initial investment of about $65,000. Each franchised gas pumping-car wash unit is expected to generate initial income from the sale of equipment of between $7,000 and $12,000, plus continuing income of between $5,000 - $7,000 annually.

BRIOX TECHNOLOGIES
Medical Oxygen Generator

MEDICAL OXYGEN GENERATOR

FOR HOMECARE PATIENTS

BUSINESS PLAN

SEPTEMBER, 1974

Briox Technologies, Inc.
65 Tainter Street
Worcester, Massachusetts 01610

617/757-7474

163

CONTENTS

SUMMARY

Briox Technologies, Inc. is a company in the Biomedical Equipment field which is responding to the needs of homecare service businesses and hospitals. The company was founded in September 1973 by David M. Gessner with the commitment of his personal funds. WCCI Capital Corporation of Worcester, Massachusetts, and several individuals have provided additional seed financing.

The Product

The first product is a home oxygen generating system, the OXY-GENERATOR, to replace expensive-to-deliver high pressure cylinders currently in use for the treatment of Chronic Obstructive Pulmonary Disease (COPD). The company has completed a full-scale prototype which was complete and operating on April 9, 1974.

Field Evaluation

Five demonstrator OXY-GENERATORS are being built for laboratory and field evaluation. At the recent national meeting of the American Thoracic Society in Cincinnati six board certified pulmonary specialists expressed interest in conducting field evaluations with their patients.

The Market

The total market size for home oxygen generating systems is 66,000 and is growing at an annual compounded rate of $7\frac{1}{2}\%$. The company will capture at least 6% of this market by 1978 with annual sales of 5,000 units @ $2100 yielding revenues of $10.5 million with a net profit greater than 15% of sales.

Production

OXY-GENERATORS will be produced by assembly of commercial components and subcontracted subassemblies. The primary subassembly will be provided under exclusive license by TELEDYNE ISOTOPES. As the company grows the investment in manufacturing facilities will be increased in order to reduce costs and to increase capability and flexibility.

Distribution

OXY-GENERATORS will be sold to existing Respiratory Therapy Equipment Dealers who will rent them to COPD patients for use in the home. Dealer reaction to the product is positive. The company will trade exclusive distributorships within a territory for firm order commitments.

Financing Required

The company needs $100,000 to fund the development and implementation of a manufacturing plan to produce 20 units/month. Management proposes to issue an additional 25,000 shares which will bring the total issued to 85,000. Twenty thousand shares will be sold in private placement at $5.00 per share. Financial arrangements should be complete by October 31, 1974.

"PERSPECTIVE"
Senior Citizens' Magazine

CONTENTS

SUMMARY OF BUSINESS PLAN

A MULTI-SERVICE corporation will be established dedicated to serving the needs of 30 million Americans in the 50 to 65 age group -- a group that commands the largest discretionary purchasing power in the U.S.

The initial service will be the quarterly paid-subscription magazine, PERSPECTIVE. The editorial objectives of this specialized publication will be to put the middle years in their proper context -- to show why and how they can be an exciting, challenging and independent time of life. Retirement planning will also receive a great deal of attention, with special emphasis on financial planning. In all cases the approach will be of a practical "how to" nature, attempting to establish a deep seated rapport between staff and reader.

Advertising acceptance will be promoted by offering a comprehensive readership profile package. By utilizing its computer expertise, the corporation plans to generate in-depth psychographic profiles (i.e., life style, beliefs, attitudes, etc.). The decision to offer psychographics was confirmed by the corporation's recent survey which indicated that advertising executives of consumer oriented companies were looking to supplement the demographics which they felt did not fully describe their target markets. Psychographic data will fill this void. However, standard demographic descriptions including age, sex, income and education will be included also.

The attraction of advertising is further enhanced by the absence of media directed solely to middle agers. For those advertisers selling to middle agers, there is no cost-effective magazine alternative available. The only publication addressing itself solely to middle agers is a non-profit organization -- one that does not accept advertising.

Advertising will be solicited from a variety of national firms such as health/life insurance companies, airlines, pharmaceutical firms, investment counseling services, land development organizations, travel/leisure groups, book clubs, and home study.

After eighteen months, PERSPECTIVE will switch to bi-monthly publication while retaining the $6 annual subscription price.

Circulation objectives are:

        500,000 subscribers at the end of 1st year
        700,000 subscribers at the end of 2nd year
        850,000 subscribers at the end of 3rd year
        950,000 subscribers at the end of 4th year
      1,000,000 subscribers at the end of 5th year

Another key innovation will be the guarantee to Charter subscribers that their subscription rate of $6 will NEVER be increased provided that they subscribe on a continuing basis. It is expected that this offer will have an extremely positive effect on subscription sales. Analysis has shown that this will be an economically feasible offer.

Once PERSPECTIVE has identified and cultivated a customer base, the corporation plans to expand its capabilities by offering additional services to its subscribers. Regular communications via the editorial pages will facilitate the promotion of services currently in demand by middle-aged citizens. Among these are mail order pharmaceuticals, group insurance programs, group travel, book clubs and investment counseling.

A two stage financing package is planned. The initial phase will require $60,000 to test readership acceptance. Once proven, $1,500,000 will be secured to launch operations and expansion.

The corporation plans to be profitable within two years. After five years a $1,500,000 profit (after taxes) is expected on revenues of $13,000,000.

APPENDIX E

GLOSSARY

Acid Test Ratio Cash plus those other assets that can be used *immediately* converted to cash should equal or exceed current liabilities. The formula used to determine the ratio is as follows:

$$\frac{\text{Cash plus Receivables (net) plus Marketable Securities}}{\text{Current Liabilities}}$$

The acid test ratio is one of the most important credit barometers used by lending institutions, as it indicates the abilities of a business enterprise to meet its current obligations.

Aging Receivables A scheduling of accounts receivable according to the length of time they have been outstanding. This shows which accounts are not being paid in a timely manner and may reveal any difficulty in collecting long overdue receivables. This may also be an important indicator of developing cash flow problems.

Amortization To liquidate on an installment basis; the process of gradually paying off a liability over a period of time, *i.e., a mortgage is amortized by periodically paying off part of the face amount of the mortgage.*

Assets The valuable resources, or properties and property rights owned by an individual or business enterprise.

Balance Sheet An itemized statement which lists the total assets and the total liabilities of a given business to portray its net worth at a given moment in time.

Breakeven Analysis A method used to determine the point at which the business will neither make a profit nor incur a loss. That point is expressed in either the total dollars of revenue exactly offset by total expenses (fixed and variable); or in total units of production, the cost of which exactly equals the income derived by their sale.

Capital Equipment Equipment that you use to manufacture a product, provide a service, or use to sell, store, and deliver merchandise. Such equipment will not be sold in the normal course of business, but will be used and worn out or be consumed over time as you do business.

Cash Flow   The actual movement of cash within a business: cash inflow minus cash outflow. A term used to designate the reported net income of a corporation plus amounts charged off for depreciation, depletion, amortization, and extraordinary charges to reserves, which are bookkeeping deductions and not actually paid out in cash. Used to offer a better indication of the ability of a firm to meet its own obligations and to pay dividends rather than with the conventional net income figure.

Cash Position   See *Liquidity*.

Corporation   An artificial legal entity created by government grant and endowed with certain powers, a voluntary organization of persons, either actual individuals or legal entities, legally bound to form a business enterprise.

Current Assets   Cash or other items that will normally be turned into cash within one year, and assets that will be used up in the operations of a firm within one year.

Current Liabilities   Amounts owed that will ordinarily be paid by a firm within one year. Such items include accounts payable, wages payable, taxes payable, the current portion of a long-term debt, and interest and dividends payable.

Current Ratio   A ratio of a firm's current assets to its current liabilities. The current ratio includes the value of inventories which have not yet been sold, so it is not the best evaluation of the current status of the firm. The acid test ratio, covering the most liquid of current assets, provides a better evaluation.

Deal   A proposal for financing business creation or expansion; a series of transactions and preparation of documents in order to obtain funds for business expansion or creation.

Depreciation   A reduction in the value of fixed assets. The most important causes of depreciation are wear and tear, the effect of the elements, and gradual obsolescence that makes it unprofitable to continue using some assets until they have been exhausted. The purpose of the *bookkeeping charge for depreciation* is to write off the original cost of an asset (less expected salvage value) by equitably distributing charges against operations over its entire useful life.

Entrepreneur   An innovator of a business enterprise who recognizes opportunities to introduce a new product, a new production process, or an improved organization, and who raises the necessary money, assembles the factors of production, and organizes an operation to exploit the opportunity.

Equity The monetary value of a property or business that exceeds the claims and/or liens against it by others.

Illiquid See *Liquidity.*

Liquidity A term used to describe the solvency of a business, and which has special reference to the degree of readiness in which assets can be converted into cash without a loss. Also called *cash position.* If a firm's current assets cannot be converted into cash to meet current liabilities, the firm is said to be *illiquid.*

Long-Term Liabilities These are liabilities (expenses) that will not mature within the next year.

Market The number of people and their total spending (actual or potential) for your product line within the geographic limits of your distribution ability. The *Market Share* is the percentage of your sales compared to the sales of your competitors in total for a particular product line.

Net Worth The owner's equity in a given business represented by the excess of the total assets over the total amounts owing to outside creditors (total liabilities) at a given moment in time. Also, the net worth of an individual as determined by deducting the amount of all his personal liabilities from the total value of his personal assets.

Partnership A legal relationship created by the voluntary association of two or more persons to carry on as co-owners of a business for profit; a type of business organization in which two or more persons agree on the amount of their contributions (capital and effort) and on the distribution of profits, if any.

Pro Forma A projection or estimate of what may result in the future from actions in the present. A pro forma financial statement is one that shows how the actual operations of the business will turn out if certain assumptions are realized.

Profit The excess of the selling price over all costs and expenses incurred in making the sale. Also, the reward to the entrepreneur for the risks assumed by him in the establishment, operation, and management of a given enterprise or undertaking.

Sole Proprietorship or Proprietorship A type of business organization in which one individual owns the business. Legally, the owner *is* the business and personal assets are typically exposed to liabilities of the business.

Sub-Chapter S Corporation or Tax Option Corporation A corporation that elected under Sub-Chapter S of the IRS Tax Code (by unanimous consent of its shareholders) not to pay any corporate tax on its income and, instead, to have the shareholders pay taxes on it, even though it is not distributed. Shareholders of a tax option corporation are also entitled to deduct, on the individual returns, their shares of any net operating loss sustained by the corporation, subject to limitations in the tax code. In many respects, Sub-Chapter S permits a corporation to behave for tax purposes as a proprietorship or partnership.

Take-Over   The acquisition of one company by another company.

Target Market   The *specific* individuals, distinguished by socio-economic, demographic, and/or interest characteristics, who are the most likely potential customers for the goods and/or services of a business.

Working Capital, Net   The excess of current assets over current liabilities. These excess current assets are available for carrying on business operations.

APPENDIX F

SAMPLE PARTNERSHIP AGREEMENT AND CORPORATE CHECKLIST

A note on the sample Partnership Agreement and Corporate Checklist. These forms have been made available to by General Business Services, Inc. of Rockville, MD. GBS is a nationwide company providing tax and business counseling services to small businesses. We have modified the forms slightly. To obtain originals, ask your GBS representative for GBS form 8418: Partnership Agreement, or GBS form 8438: Corporate Checklist.

SAMPLE PARTNERSHIP AGREEMENT

Agreement made _____ , 19___ , between _____ of _____ , City

of _____ , County of _____ , State of _____ , and

_____ of _____ (address), City of _____ ,

County of _____ , State of _____ , hereinafter referred to as partners.

ITEM ONE

NAME, PURPOSE, AND DOMICILE

The name of the partnership shall be _____ . The partnership shall be conducted for the purposes

of _____ . The principal place of business shall be at

_____ unless relocated by majority consent of the partners.

ITEM TWO

DURATION OF AGREEMENT

The term of this agreement shall be for _____ years, commencing on _____ , 19___ , and

terminating on _____ , 19__ , unless sooner terminated by mutual consent of the parties or by operation
of the provisions of this agreement.

ITEM THREE

CONTRIBUTION

Each partner shall contribute _____ Dollars ($_____) on or before _____ ,
19   to be used by the partnership to establish its capital position. Any additional contribution required of partners shall only
be determined and established in accordance with Item Seventeen.

ITEM FOUR

BOOKS AND RECORDS

Books of accounts shall be maintained by the partners, and proper entries made therein of all sales, purchases, receipts, payments, transactions, and property of the partnership, and the books of accounts and all records of the partnership shall be retained at the principal place of business as specified in Item One herein. Each partner shall have free access at all times to all books and records maintained relative to the partnership business.

ITEM FIVE   DIVISION OF PROFITS AND LOSSES

Each partner shall be entitled to _____ percent (_____ %) of the net profits of the business and all losses occurring in the course of the business shall be borne in the same proportion, unless the losses are occasioned by the wilful neglect or default, and not mere mistake or error, of any of the partners, in which case the loss so incurred shall be made good by the

partner through whose neglect or default the losses shall arise. Distribution of profits shall be made on the _____ day

of _____ each year.

ITEM SIX

PERFORMANCE

Each partner shall apply all of his experience, training, and ability in discharging his assigned functions in the partnership and in the performance of all work that may be necessary or advantageous to further business interests of the partnership.

175

ITEM SEVEN

BUSINESS EXPENSES

The rent of the buildings where the partnership business shall be carried on, and the cost of repairs and alterations, all rates, taxes, payments for insurance, and other expenses in respect to the buildings used by the partnership, and the wages for all persons employed by the partnership are all to become payable on the account of the partnership. All losses incurred shall be paid out of the capital of the partnership or the profits arising from the partnership business, or, if both shall be deficient, by the partners on a pro rata basis, in proportion to their original contributions.

ITEM EIGHT

ACCOUNTING

The fiscal year of the partnership shall be from_____ to_____ of each year. On the

_____ day of_____ , commencing in 19__, and on the_____ day

of_____ in each succeeding year, a general accounting shall be made and taken by the partners of all sales, purchases, receipts, payments, and transactions of the partnership during the preceding fiscal year, and of all the capital property and current liabilities of the partnership. The general accounting shall be written in the partnership account books and signed in each book by each partner immediately after it is completed. After the signature of each partner is entered, each partner shall keep one of the books and shall be bound by every account, except that if any manifest error is

found therein by any partner and shown to the other partners within_____ months after the error shall have been noted by all of them, the error shall be rectified.

ITEM NINE

SEPARATE DEBTS

No partner shall enter into any bond or become surety, security, bail or co-signer for any person, partnership or corporation, or knowingly condone anything whereby the partnership property may be attached or be taken in execution, without the written consent of the other partners.

Each partner shall punctually pay his separate debts and indemnify the other partners and the capital and property of the partnership against his separate debts and all expenses relating thereto.

ITEM TEN

AUTHORITY

No partner shall buy any goods or articles into any contract exceeding the value of_____ Dollars ($_____) without the prior consent in writing of the other partners; or the other partners shall have the option to take the goods or accept the contract on account of the partnership or let the goods remain the sole property of the partner who shall have obligated himself.

ITEM ELEVEN

EMPLOYEE MANAGEMENT

No partner shall hire or dismiss any person in the employment of the partnership without the consent of the other partners, except in cases of gross misconduct by the employee.

ITEM TWELVE

SALARY

No partner shall receive any salary from the partnership, and the only compensation to be paid shall be as provided in Items Five and Fourteen herein.

ITEM THIRTEEN

DEATH OF PARTNER

In the event of the death of one partner, the legal representative of the deceased partner shall remain as a partner in the firm, except that the exercising of the right on the part of the representative of the deceased partner shall not continue for a period

in excess of _____ months, even though under the terms hereof a greater period of time is provided before the termination of this agreement. The original rights of the partners herein shall accrue to their heirs, executors, or assigns.

ITEM FOURTEEN

ADVANCE DRAWS

Each partner shall be at liberty to draw out of the business in anticipation of the expected profits any sums that may be mutually agreed on, and the sums are to be drawn only after there has been entered in the books of the partnership the terms of agreement, giving the date, the amount to be drawn by the respective partners, the time at which the sums shall be drawn, and any other conditions or matters mutually agreed on. The signatures of each partner shall be affixed thereon. The total sum of the advance draw for each partner shall be deducted from the sum that partner is entitled to under the distribution of profits as provided for in Item Five of this agreement.

ITEM FIFTEEN

RETIREMENT

In the event any partner shall desire to retire from the partnership, he shall give _____ months' notice in writing to

the other partners and the continuing partners shall pay to the retiring partner at the termination of the _____ months' notice the value of the interest of the retiring partner in the partnership. The value shall be determined by a closing of the books and a rendition of the appropriate profit and loss, trial balance, and balance sheet statements. All disputes arising therefrom shall be determined as provided in Item Eighteen.

ITEM SIXTEEN

RIGHTS OF CONTINUING PARTNERS

On the retirement of any partner, the continuing partners shall be at liberty, if they so desire, to retain all trade names designating the firm name used, and each of the partners shall sign and execute assignments, instruments, or papers that shall be reasonably required for effectuating an amicable retirement.

ITEM SEVENTEEN

ADDITIONAL CONTRIBUTIONS

The partners shall not have to contribute any additional capital to the partnership to that required under Item Three herein, except as follows: (1) each partner shall be required to contribute a proportionate share in additional contributions if the fiscal year closes with an insufficiency in the capital account of profits of the partnership to meet current expenses, or (2) the

capital account falls below _____ Dollars ($_____) for a period of

_____ months.

ITEM EIGHTEEN

ARBITRATION

If any differences shall arise between or among partners as to their rights or liabilities under this agreement, or under any instrument made in furtherance of the partnership business, the difference shall be determined and the instrument shall be

settled by _____ , acting as arbitrator, and his decision shall be final as to the contents and interpretations of the instrument and as to the proper mode of carrying the provision into effect.

ITEM NINETEEN

RELEASE OF DEBTS

No partner shall compound, release, or discharge any debt that shall be due or owing to the partnership, without receiving the full amount thereof, unless that partner obtains the prior written consent of the other partners to the discharge of the indebtedness.

ITEM TWENTY

ADDITIONS, ALTERATIONS, OR MODIFICATIONS

Where it shall appear to the partners that this agreement, or any terms and conditions contained herein, are in any way ineffective or deficient, or not expressed as originally intended, and any alteration or addition shall be deemed necessary, the partners will enter into, execute, and perform all further deeds and instruments as their counsel shall advise. Any addition, alteration, or modification shall be in writing, and no oral agreement shall be effective.

In witness whereof, the parties have executed this agreement on _____ the day and year first above written.

Courtesy of General Business Service, Inc.

CORPORATE CHECKLIST

A. The formation of a corporation constitutes the formation of a separate legal entity under state law. It is essential that the services of a competent local attorney be obtained to help the client file the Articles of Incorporation and meet the terms of the state law.

B. Below is a sample election for the corporation to be treated as a Section 1244 small business corporation. This is included so that the client may have it available to discuss with his attorney.

C. Following is a list of steps that will be necessary for a new corporation. It should not be deemed to be all inclusive. It is not intended to be used as substitution to the client of a competent attorney.

1. Incorporators -- Have a meeting of the incorporators and determine the following:

   a. The corporate name
   b. The classes and number of shares to authorize
   c. Business purpose for which the corporation is formed
   d. Initial capital needed
   e. Determine the directors
   f. Location of business
   g. Determine corporate officers and salaries
   h. Check on thin incorporation

2. Determine Start-Up Date -- If the corporation is to take over a going business, a start-up date should be set at some time in the future, so that all steps can be taken without unnecessary haste.

3. Corporate Name -- Check at once with the Secretary of State to see if the corporate name is available.

4. Notify the following:
   a. Insurance Company -- have policies changed. May also be necessary to increase coverage.
   b. Creditors -- inform all creditors of former business.
   c. Customers -- inform all customers of former business.
   d. State and local authorities -- such as state unemployment and disability department and county assessor.

5. Transfer of Assets and Liabilities -- If the corporation is to take over a going business, determine what assets and liabilities are to be turned over to the corporation, and shares or notes to be issued in exchange. Does it qualify as a tax-free exchange under IRC Sec. 3.

6. Banks -- Select bank or banks and furnish resolution authorizing who is to sign checks and negotiate loans.

7. Identification Number -- File application for an Identification No., Federal Form SS-4.

8. Workmen's Compensation -- File for coverage.

9. Unemployment Insurance -- File for coverage.

10. Special Licenses -- Check on transfer of new license such as food, drug, cigarette, liquor, etc.

11. Final Returns -- If the new corporation is taking over a going business,

file Sales Tax, FICA Tax, Unemployment Tax and Workmen's Compensation final returns for the old business after the corporation takes over the operation of the new business.

12. Federal Unemployment -- Determine if final Form 940, Employer's Annual Federal Unemployment Tax return is to be filed on old business.

13. Sales Tax -- Obtain a new sales tax vendor's license on the first day of business. Do not use any tax stamps purchased by the former business or do not use the plate from the former business.

14. Tax Elections:

a. Election under Subchapter S -- Determine if the corporation is going to elect to be taxed as a partnership under Subchapter S. If so, prepare and file Form 2553, Election by Small Business Corporation, within thirty days after the first day of fiscal year or date new corporation commences to "do business."

b. Section 1244 Stock -- If corporation is eligible, issue stock in accordance with a written plan included in the minutes.

c. Year Ending -- Determine the date the corporation's year will end.

d. Accounting -- Determine the method of accounting the corporation will use.

SAMPLE PLAN FOR SEC. 1244 STOCK OFFER   *(for inclusion in minutes)*

This Corporation is a small business corporation as defined in Sec. 1244(c)(2) of the Internal Revenue Code of 1954.

The Board of Directors wishes to offer for sale and issue shares of its common stock authorized by its Certificate of Incorporation; and

That the offer, sale and issue of such shares be carried out in such a manner that, in the hands of qualified shareholders, such shares will receive the benefits of Sec. 1244 of the Internal Revenue Code of 1954; and

Whereas, there is not now outstanding any offering, or portion thereof, of this Corporation to sell or issue any of its stock; and

*Now, therefore, be it resolved, that the President of this Corporation and such other officers as he may designate be, and hereby are, authorized and directed to offer for sale and to sell and to issue up to   shares of the common stock in the total amount of $ * at $ per share payable in cash or other property** during the period from the date hereof to   ** or to the date when this Corporation shall make a subsequent offering of any stock, whichever shall first occur.*

*   Total amount subject to limitations.
** Stock issued for stock or securities may not qualify.
***This period must not be more than two years from the date of the plan.

Courtesy of General Business Service, Inc.

APPENDIX G

BLANK FORMS FOR PROJECTION OF FINANCIAL STATEMENTS

INDICATE FACTORS USED
IN PREPARING PROJECTION

1. Average receivable collection period in days _____
2. Inventory Turnover in Days _____
3. Trade Payable Turnover in Days _____
4. % Federal Tax to Profits before Tax   % _____
5. Depreciation per Year $ _____
6. Total Officers' or Partners' Compensation
   per month $ _____

SUGGESTIONS FOR PREPARATION
OF PROJECTION

Other Estimates needed for each period of the Projection are underlined below.

Blank lines in Projection are to accommodate unusual items of significance.

References to the Divisions of the Projection are abbreviated as follows:

Profit and Loss Statement	is PL
Cash Projection Receipts	is CR
Cash Projection Disbursements	is CD
Balance Sheet Assets	is BA
Balance Sheet Liabilities	is BL

In the first column, record the actual PROFIT AND LOSS STATEMENT and BALANCE SHEET of date immediately prior to projection period.

In each subsequent column covering a projection period (month, quarter, etc.):

1. Enter on date line, projection period covered and ending date thereof.

2. Complete PL, recording NET SALES, less all discounts and allowances; showing costs and expenses as indicated. *Compute NET PROFIT OR LOSS.

3. Record in CD on lines indicated, PL entries for DIRECT LABOR. OTHER MF'G EXPENSE, SALES, GENERAL and ADMINISTRATIVE EXPENSE and OTHER EXPENSE, less depreciation expense included therein. Record in CR, OTHER INCOME (PL).

4. Combine FIXED ASSETS (per prior column BA) and fixed asset additions, subtract depreciation expense and enter result in FIXED ASSETS (BA). Record cost of fixed asset additions in CD.

5. Combine INCOME TAX PROVISION (PL) with INCOME TAXES (per prior column BL), subtract payment of income tax and record result as INCOME TAXES (BL). Record income tax payment in CD.

6. Combine NET PROFIT or LOSS (PL) with SURPLUS or NET WORTH (per prior column BL),

subtract DIVIDENDS OR WITHDRAWALS, record result as SURPLUS or NET WORTH (BL). Record DIVIDENDS or WITHDRAWALS in CD.

7. Record CASH (per prior column BA) as CASH BALANCE (opening) (CR).

8. Combine RECEIVABLES (per prior column BA) with NET SALES (PL), allocate resulting total between RECEIVABLE COLLECTIONS (CR) and RECEIVABLES (BA) per average collection period (Factor 1 above).

9. Combine TRADE PAYABLES (per prior column BL), with cost of material purchased (less discounts), allocate resulting total between TRADE PAYABLES (CD) and TRADE PAYABLES (BL) per turnover of payables (Factor 3 above).

10. Combine INVENTORY (per prior column BA), cost of materials purchased (less discounts) and DIRECT LABOR and OTHER M'FG EXPENSE (PL), subtract COST OF GOODS SOLD (PL), record result in INVENTORY (BA).

11. Review all items in prior column Balance Sheet (except CASH and NOTES PAYABLE—BANKS) for which no entries have been made in present period BALANCE SHEET. If there is no change in these items, transfer to present period BALANCE SHEET. If items are changed, reflect changes through CR or CD. Carry deferred charges (BA) and accruals (BL) without change.

12. Foot CASH PROJECTION: If cash deficiency indicated, enter amount to adjust in BANK LOAN PROCEEDS (CR); Combine this adjustment with NOTES PAYABLE—BANKS (per prior column BL) and enter as NOTES PAYABLE—BANKS (BL); if excessive cash is indicated, and NOTES PAYABLE—BANKS (per prior column BL) appears, provide BANK LOAN REPAYMENT (CD); reduce NOTES PAYABLE—BANKS (per prior column BL) by this provision, entering result as NOTES PAYABLE—BANKS (BL). Refoot CASH PROJECTION and enter resulting CASH BALANCE (closing) as CASH (BA).

13. Foot and balance BALANCE SHEET.

*For Manufacturer projecting substantial increases or decreases in inventory during projection period.
Enter as title on Line No. 5 (PL).
"INCREASE OR DECREASE IN WORK IN PROCESS FINISHED INVENTORIES"—record increase in red, decrease in black.

ACTUAL   PROJECTIONS

				ACTUAL				PROJECTIONS			
SPREAD IN HUNDREDS ☐ DATE											
SPREAD IN THOUSANDS ☐ PERIOD											
P	1	NET SALES			1						
R	2	Less: Materials Used			2						
O	3	Direct Labor			3						
F	4	Other Manufacturing Expense			4						
I	5				5						
T	6	COST OF GOODS SOLD			6						
	7	GROSS PROFIT			7						
	8	Less: Sales Expense			8						
and	9	General and Administrative Expense			9						
	10				10						
L	11	OPERATING PROFIT			11						
O	12	Less: Other Expense or Income (Net)			12						
S	13	Income Tax Provision			13						
S	14				14						
	15	NET PROFIT			15						
	16	CASH BALANCE (Opening)			16						
	17	Plus RECEIPTS: Receivable Collections			17						
C	18				18						
A	19				19						
S	20	Bank Loan Proceeds			20						
H	21	Total			21						
	22	Less: DISBURSEMENTS: Trade Payables			22						
	23	Direct Labor			23						
P	24	Other M'fg Expense			24						
R	25	Sales, Gen'l and Adm. Exp.			25						
O	26	Fixed Asset Additions			26						
J	27	Income Taxes			27						
E	28				28						
C	29	Dividends or Withdrawals			29						
T	30				30						
I	31	Bank Loan Repayment			31						
O	32	Total			32						
N	33	CASH BALANCE (Closing)			33						
	34	ASSETS: Cash			34						
	35	Marketable Securities			35						
	36	Receivables (Net)			36						
	37	Inventory (Net)			37						
	38				38						
	39	CURRENT ASSETS			39						
	40	Fixed Assets (Net)			40						
	41				41						
	42				42						
	43				43						
B	44	Deferred Charges			44						
A	45	TOTAL ASSETS			45						
L	46	LIABILITIES: Notes Payable—Banks			46						
A	47	Trade Payables			47						
N	48	Income Tax			48						
C	49				49						
E	50				50						
	51	Accruals			51						
	52	CURRENT LIABILITIES			52						
S	53				53						
H	54				54						
E	55				55						
E	56	CAPITAL STOCK Net Worth for			56						
T	57	SURPLUS Partnership or Individual			57						
	58	TOTAL LIABILITIES AND NET WORTH			58						
	59	WORKING CAPITAL			59						

APPENDIX H

ACTUAL BUSINESS PLANS

1. **GUY MAINILLA INDUSTRIES**

2. **MARRONE ENTERPRISES, INC./
   THE NORTH WORKS RESTAURANT**

3. **THE NEBUR COMPUTER CORP***

*Certain facts in this business plan have been altered to protect the confidential nature of the business. However, the essence of the business plan remains intact.

GUY MAINELLA INDUSTRIES, INC.

BUSINESS PLAN
February 1981

CONTENTS

Summary of Business Plan

Guy Mainella Industries, Inc., 55 Lake Street, Nashua, New Hampshire was incorporated under the laws of N.H. April 1, 1979. GMI, Inc. is wholly owned by Guy Mainella, who serves as President, Treasurer, and Chairman of the Board. The corporation succeeds Solar Energy Enterprises (SEE), a company formed by Mainella in April, 1977 to research and develop solar products. As of this date, SEE and GMI, Inc. have expended nearly $250,000 to develop the Advanced Solar Collector (ASC), which is currently in production.

The ASC is a low-cost, long-life flat plate solar water heating panel for domestic and small commercial applications. The ASC, developed by Mainella with engineering consultation, represents a significant breakthrough in the solar field. The ASC reverses a trend toward high-technology, high-cost collectors. GMI, Inc. is marketing the lightweight (less than two pounds per square foot) ASC, which features the Automatic Manifold (Pat. Pend.), for a recommended installed price of $1650. Tax credits can reduce that cost to under $700.

GMI, Inc. has been able to market a solar system of simple, yet sturdy design. Our ASC is unsurpassed in cost effectiveness. It can be installed by the homeowner, opening a vast new market, *i.e.* the do-it-yourself market. Further, the ASC produces more BTUs per dollar per year than any collector ever marketed in the U.S.

GMI, Inc. seeks to raise $250,000 for 35 percent of the Corporation's stock for operating capital, marketing ($100,000), and inventory.

GMI, Inc. expects 1981 revenues to total $1.3 million with a year-end profit, after taxes, of $170,000. In 1982, the Corp. expects to more than double revenues to $3.0 million.

The Product

The ASC is a flat plate solar water heating panel designed to preheat water for domestic and commercial applications. The ASC will heat potable water (not anti-freeze) thus eliminating the need for a costly heat exchanger. The ASC weighs 58 pounds (2½ times less than many collectors) yet it's rugged and efficient. Its light weight means that for the first time in the solar industry, a customer can buy the GMI system and install it himself eliminating, if he chooses, costly professional assistance. However, even with installation help, the ASC costs less to install than any mass produced solar panel ever offered in the U.S.

The ASC is an active collector; it requires a small circulating pump to move water from a storage tank through the panels. The ASC heats water by circulating approximately one-half gallon of water from a basement storage tank through each panel during sunlight hours. (see brochure)

Each panel features a specially extruded rubber absorber mat made of Nordel hydrocarbon rubber (EPDM). (see brochure) The ASC mat is a Serpentine pattern 4.4" wide by 76' long, covering an area of about 27.5 square feet. Each piece of mat is adhered to a 4 × 8 feet sheet of Thermax rigid insulation, type TF610 with an R value of 7.2/in.

The absorber mat represents a significant cost reduction over heavier copper and/or aluminum absorbers. It is also impervious to damage from freezing. Thus, the mat when combined with our Automatic Manifold, makes it possible to heat potable water in any climate without resorting to anti-freezes, drain-down, or drain-back systems.

The ASC also features 3-M Company's remarkable Flexigard 7410 polyester and acrylic film. Used as a glazing instead of glass or plastic, Flexigard gives the ASC a durable, yet lightweight and inexpensive single glazing. Flexigard 7410 has weathered for ten years in Florida without yellowing or loss in transmissivity. GMI, Inc. is the only collector manufacturer in the country to successfully mount 3-M's Flexigard to a large collector panel using our newly developed fabric-stretching process for which we may seek a patent.

The ASC is encased in a .070 extruded aluminum frame, designed to our specifications by New Jersey Aluminum Co. The panel manufacturing process is typical of the industry, requiring adhesives, corner keys, washers and rivets—all commonly available from several suppliers.

The manufacturing process, while it does not lend itself to mass production techniques, is not involved or difficult and can be done by reasonably skilled individuals working for slightly above the minimum wage.

The end result is a new breed of solar collector: light, durable, handsome, efficient, yet the most affordable and, quite simply, the most cost effective solar water heater ever mass produced in America.

Suppliers

GMI, Inc. presently buys the absorber mat (SolaRoll) from Bio-Energy Systems, Inc. of Ellenville, NY. A second source does exist for this product.

3-M Co., St. Paul, MN manufactures the Flexigard glazing; there are similar, but not as thoroughly tested products. All other components are shelf items, available from a variety of sources.

Components

The ASC relies on two major advances in technology: our Automatic Manifold (Pat. Pend.), and our one-of-a-kind method of applying the Flexigard under tension to our panel frame.

The Automatic Manifold (see brochure) was invented by Mainella. It is a nonmechanical means of reducing water flow through a shortened manifold during sunlight hours (while the collector is working), while at night it permits a small amount of storage tank water to circulate only through the manifold.

The circulation is limited because the unprotected absorber mat is permitted to freeze before the insulated manifold reaches a temperature of about 40° F. At that time, the circulator receives a signal from a sensor on the manifold and pumps about one-half gallon of water through the inlet pipes, to the Automatic Manifold and back to the storage tank. The pump shuts off until the manifold temperatures once again drop to about 40° F.

This unique invention is the heart of the ASC. Because of it, no anti-freeze is required, no solenoid valves, and no drain back system is ever needed. It makes it possible to heat potable water in any climate with no risk of freeze damage.

The method of applying the glazing is proprietary. It represents such an advance in the state-of-the-art that the 3-M company, which was allowed to see the system in operation, has agreed to display our solar panels at energy shows in Boston, St. Louis, Miami and other shows to be determined—at no cost to GMI, Inc. The marketing advantage of 3-M's support to our company is obvious.

It is worth noting that GMI, Inc. is able to mount the Flexigard 7410 to a 30 square foot panel tighter than any of the biggest names in the solar industry, *e.g.* Grumman, Revere, Reynolds, SolaRoll, etc.

Cost to Manufacture

The ASC is currently being manufactured at a cost of $4.045 per square foot, materials only. These costs are based on a finished panel of 45" × 97" with an effective net absorber area of 27.5 square feet and a gross area of 30.6 ft^2.

In addition, two man-hours are required to build an ASC. It is our belief that once high volume production begins, the ASC will require a total labor cost of approximately $7.50. However, figures in the attached financial plan are based on an average labor cost of $10/unit.

ASC materials Cost—2/1/81	
76' SolaRoll (Absorber Mat) @ .71/ft	$53.96
36 sq/ft Flexigard @ .40/ft/sq	$14.40
1.5 qts Plio-Nail Adhesive @ $3.50/qt	$ 4.50
Alum frame	$16.00
Thermax Insulation 32 sq ft @ .36/ft/sq	$11.52
Thermo-ply @ $4.50/sheet (4 × 8')	$ 4.50
Copper Manifold (complete)	$ 7.50
3M Y9460 Adhesive	$ 1.73
Alum Tape 2.5" × 24'	$ .90
Corner Keys (8)	$ .50
2-12-20 grommets	$ .25
1-3-5 grommet	$ .05
16-rivets	$ .50
½-sensor (Note: every other panel has sensor)	$ 1.85

2-¾″ × 4′ Square Alum Tube $ 3.20
                                        Total Materials $121.36
                                        Price per square foot $ 4.045

The ASC presently requires two man hours to build. Estimated labor cost in full production is $9 per collector (two men at $4.50/hr).

        Add Labor Cost $ 9.00
        Total Materials & Labor $130.36
        Total Price per square foot $ 4.345

Wholesale Cost

GMI, Inc. is making all sales based on the attached trade price list. In addition, GMI, Inc. has recently instituted a Co-op Advertising Rebate of 2 percent and has agreed to pre-pay freight charges, the cost of which has been absorbed in a price increase of $10 per panel and $20 for the Rheem storage tank. The option exists for local purchasers to pick up systems at the factory in Nashua.

The GMI System

GMI, Inc. manufactures only the ASC and the special bracket used to mount the panel on rooftops. However, we also market the GMI System, which consists of: two ASCs, a Rheem Solaraide storage tank, a Grundfos Circulator, an Independent Energy C-30 controller, or an Independent Energy C-100 controller, two sensors, and a rooftop insulation package that will make it even easier for the consumer to mount the Advanced Solar Collector.

Drawbacks

The ASC represents a bold step in the solar industry. We have actually simplified solar technology (making it less expensive) by using recently developed components (the absorber mat and Flexigard) and by our own innovations such as the Automatic Manifold and the method for applying the Flexigard.

However, solar energy does not enjoy the confidence of the American people or widespread acceptance within the traditional marketing channels, *e.g.* plumbing and heating dealers.

The greatest drawback to the success of GMI, Inc. is the difficulty of establishing a broad-based, multichannel network of solar dealers. Recent developments, however, strongly indicate that drawback is being overcome because of the interest of such previously cynical dealers as Plywood Ranch, Brewsters, Grossman's, Lechmeres, Abundant Life,

Mass Hardware Home Centers, Channel Lumber and a broad cross section of Building Material Centers, as evidenced by their interest at the recent NE Lumbermen's Show (Boston, Jan. '81) and our recent success in establishing some of these outlets as dealers. (See below)

Additionally, GMI, Inc. must overcome the public skepticism concerning polyester/acrylic glazing materials and the basic concept of a solar panel that so overwhelmingly contradicts everything previously believed about solar panels, *i.e.*: very expensive, glass-covered, anti-freeze panels that weigh 120 pounds or more and cost upwards of $3,000 (*Industry Ave.*, 1979).

Our confidence that these problems will disappear in the face of surging energy costs has been buoyed by our recent marketing successes.

Existing Solar Products

There are currently more than 100 companies manufacturing solar water heating systems. Virtually all of them employ standard flat plate technology, conventional components, and have been little changed in recent years. They fall into two broad categories: copper absorber mats that require either anti-freeze or drain down valves to protect them from freezing. As stated, our ASC has an absorber mat that freezes without damage and an automatic manifold that protects the manifold and inlet/outlet pipes from freezing.

Units made by competition cannot be installed by the consumer because of their weight, complexity and high cost. As such, they have no real chance of gaining acceptance from mass retailers. The major manufacturers, with heavy financial commitments to product development, inventory, and marketing, are not in a position to simplify their equipment. Instead, flat plate collectors have actually become heavier, harder to handle and, of course, more expensive. Our ASC reverses that trend And, because of that we are already enjoying an excellent response from the targeted market area: mass retailers, home building centers, and stove dealers.

The Market

The solar market in the United States stood at $280,000,000 annually for 1979, the last year for which figures are available. The Department of Energy reports an annual growth over the last five years of between 20 and 30 percent. Evidence of that is contained in industry-wide sales figures for 1977 of $200 million and 1978 of $240 million.

Recent published sales figures (*Solar Age Magazine*) indicate more than 12 million square feet of low and medium temperature flat plate collectors were sold during 1980. That is up from about 10 million square feet in 1978.

The solar industry sales leader, all with more than 200,000 square feet sold each from 1977 are, not necessarily in order, Sunstream (Grumman), Revere, Daystar and Libby-Owens-Ford. (Daystar, owned by Exxon, is in the process of being sold and may, in fact, be shut down if it cannot be sold. Daystar systems sold for an average of $4,000, installed, during 1980.)

GMI, Inc. has set a modest first year sales goal of 94,000 square feet of solar collectors. This is less than .6 percent of industry sales for 1979. We also expect, based on early reaction to our design and system cost effectiveness, to show sharply higher sales figures for our second year.

This anticipation is based on several factors:

a. Skyrocketing energy costs across the country, especially for oil, gas, and electricity in the Northeast.
b. No available solar equipment produces more MBTUs for less cost than our ASC. (see brochure)
c. No mass-produced solar heating system can be installed by the consumer for less money than the ASC.
d. The very positive response from mass retailers to our concept of low cost, reasonable performance, and ease of installation—exactly what they require to make solar a high volume business.

Below are some typical examples of how solar water heating equipment is priced in the New England area.

New England Energy Alternatives, Inc., Stoughton, MA offers a 40 square foot system for $3200, installed. They use either Sunworks or Libby-Owens-Ford collectors that weigh about 120 pounds each.

A plumbing contractor in Nashua, NH offers a 60 square foot State solar system for $2400, without installation. (This dealer has since switched to GMI, Inc's. ASC system.)

The acceptage average cost of a domestic solar water heating system in the U.S. in 1980 was $3200, installed, before federal and/or state tax credits. These systems, typically, are 40 square feet. The GMI system is 60 square feet, but produces about the same number of BTUs per year.

The price comparison looks like this:

GMI		*Ave. Solar System*
$1650	Installed	$3200
$ 660	Less 40% Federal Tax Credit	$1280
$ 990	Total After Federal Tax Credit	$1920
$16.50	Price Per Square Foot	$ 48
($990 ÷ 60 ft²)		($1920 ÷ 40 ft²)

If each system produces approximately 7.2 MBTUs per year, the cost per million BTUs per year would be:

> *GMI*   *Ave. Solar System*
> $137.50 ($990 ÷ 7.2 MBTUs) $266.6 ($1920 ÷ 7.2 MBTUs)

it should also be pointed out that in states such as Massachusetts, Rhode Island, and many others very lucrative state tax credits further reduce the net cost of solar systems to the consumer. For example: In Massachusetts, which has a 35 percent tax credit, the GMI System would only cost $643.50! ($990 − 35%). Not all states have such extravagant credits, but many are quite good. Rhode Island, for example, is about the same as Massachusetts.

Most solar systems today are sold on the basic of alleged "efficiency" expressed in percentage points, *e.g.* 65, 70, 75 percent for very efficient flat plate collectors. Consumers, however, cannot be expected to understand the complicated formulas used to compute collector efficiency. Cognizant of that, GMI, Inc. markets our system on the basis of Millions of BTUs per Dollar per Year (MBTUs/$/Yr). Our figure of $137.50 (see above) is unsurpassed in the industry. Moreover, this figure when applied to average savings (see brochure) makes simple sense for the consumer, without hyperbole or technical language.

The ASC panels (two) will yield approximately 7.2 MBTUs per year in a typical Massachusetts situation. Other collectors will yield more . . . sometimes 20 percent. But, they also cost *twice* as much or more and the total savings will not be twice as much. The GMI system makes sense because it is cost effective. The consumer is far more likely to spend $643.50 (in Mass.) to save half his water heating costs than he would be to spend twice as much (or more) to save 60 percent of his water heating costs.

And, our optimism is buoyed by the fact that Exxon Corp. has chosen to divest itself of Daystar because it could sell only 5,000 collectors in 1979 nationwide. Daystar is perhaps the finest collector made in America, but its $4200 average installed cost was out of reach for 99 percent of the people. The GMI system is within reach of the mass market where we are already enjoying success.

Marketing Strategy

GMI, Inc. is underselling every existing solar system now in the marketplace in the U.S. Very simply, all collectors marketed through traditional channels (plumbing & heating dealers) are Cadillacs with a price tag to match. GMI is offering an extremely cost-effective durable, lightweight collector to a public that has resisted (correctly, we believe) the heavy and expensive solar equipment offered to date. GMI seeks the market wooed and won by BIC, Volkswagon, and a few others who offered a simple, sturdy, low-cost product of excellent quality. GMI, Inc. is on the verge of a major success in this effort because we can market our system through dealers never before tapped by the solar industry.

GMI, Inc. has already established as dealers several major building materials centers who previously rejected bids from other solar collector manufacturers. (see dealer list below)

The panel was very well received by this industry at the recent NE Retail Lumbermen's trade show in Boston. Without exception we have been able to arrange meetings with these retailers. This has never happened before in the solar industry. Mass retailers simply have not been comfortable with the $3200 solar system previously offered. Our DIY (Do-it-Yourself) system appeals to the building materials industry, which expects to do 3.2 billion dollars in volume during 1981.

GMI, Inc. is offering this system (two panels, storage tank, controller, circulator, sensors, mounting brackets, and roof protection set) for a landed cost of $969.95. Retail prices vary, but are currently running between $1200 (Mass. Hardware, Abundant Life, Atlas Industries, Ayer) and a proposed $1400 (Plywood Ranch). GMI does not have distributors. We sell factory direct to dealers, offering the same discount schedule to everyone.

The company is represented in NE by the R.F. Snyder Co., Needham Heights, MA, 617-444-2500. Retained January 12 on 10 percent commission, R.F. Snyder has already signed up several dealers.

The company is engaged in talks with the following mass retailers concerning the handing of our solar system.

> *Lechemere Sales,* Boston—scheduled to open energy stores in 3rd Quarter, 1981 in all locations, but indicates they will show our panels during 2nd quarter in at least one store.
>
> *Somerville Lumber*—a major Massachusetts building center likely to add panels in March.
>
> *F. W. Webb Co.*—major wholesaler to plumbing industry, now franchising a new concept called "The Plumbery" in NE area. Meeting arranged for February 19ths. Buyer is Robert Myers "very interested" in GMI's solar system.
>
> *Abundant Life/Comforter*—Nation's 3rd largest stove manufacturer with 1,200 dealers is weighing our proposal to handle our panels in all their locations. Several meetings since last November culminated in presentation to their 19 U.S. and European distributors January 16. We were well received; no decision yet.

Talks have been initiated with, among others, Channel Lumber, Cotter and Co. (True/Value), American Hardware (Servistar), Nickerson Lumber (10 centers on Cape Cod), Friend Building Centers (Boston), Fischer Stove Co. (same proposal pending as with Abundant Life/Comforter), and potential dealers in St. Louis, the state of Kentucky, Sacramento, and several New England locations.

The Advanced Solar Collector was available, as of February 9, 1981, at the following locations:

Brewsters, Wilmington, MA
Frank Cataldo, Buyer 617-658-6720
Non-working demonstration on display

Mass Hardware Home Center, Waltham, MA
Mike Tramontozzi, Buyer 617-893-6711
Working demonstration on display

Plywood Ranch, Braintree, MA (& Nashua, NH)
George Bacigalaupo 617-848-6464

Northboro Lumber Co., Northboro, MA
Lee Proctor, Partner 617-752-4222
Working demonstration on display

Atlas Industries, Ayer, MA
Walter Coutu, President 617-893-4200

Masi Plumbing & Heating, Nashua, NH
Robert Boisvert, Owner 603-889-2331
Working demonstration on display

Peter-Sun Solar, Hollis, NH
Chuck Petersen, President 603-465-2777

Kalwall Corp., Manchester, NH
Scott Keller, President 603-668-8186

State Lumber Co., Saxonville, MA
George Geralomo, Buyer 617-877-5430

Abundant Life, Liberty Tree Mall, Danvers, MA
Craig Wolcott, Owner 617-777-0312

GMI, Inc. is being helped immeasurably by our unique association with the 3-M Company, St. Paul, MN. Because GMI, Inc. is the only solar panel manufacturer in the world to successfully bond 3-M's Flexigard 7410 Film to a solar panel, the 3-M Company has agreed to show our panel at energy shows, home shows and other expositions across the country—at no cost to GMI, Inc. The panel has been shown in Boston, St. Louis, and will be in Miami in March—other shows to be determined. 3-M has further agreed to carte blanche use of their name in our literature and has agreed to distribute our brochure where appropriate to potential dealers, including a spring, 1981 mailing to 8,000 U.S. building material centers.

GMI, Inc. has tested several other marketing possibilities. A mailing of 650 pieces to known solar dealers in New England in November, 1980 was unsuccessful. It convinced management that our unique, low-cost system would enjoy ultimate success in the mass market and the response to date from building material centers proves the point.

We are talking with JS&A, a leading marketing firm, about direct mailing.

We continue to handle inquiries from plumbing contractors, but are not actively pursuing this relatively stagnant market.

The GMI system will be mentioned in a forthcoming issue of *Solar Age Magazine,* the largest circulation solar magazine on the market. Further, we have been promised future publicity in the May or June issue, which will feature an update on flat plate technology. Stories also are expected later in February in the *Nashua Telegraph, Boston Globe* and other smaller newspapers, including the *Lawrence Eagle-Tribune.* Mainella is also trying to set up TV appearances during the Home Show in March.

In summary, the marketing strategy is concentrated on the major mass retailers—the precise market never before penetrated by the solar industry because they could not offer a product that made economic sense.

Since January 1st we have had uninterrupted success in talking to these retailers. Not a single home center has turned us down; appointments, often hard to get with buyers, have been set up within days. Example: R. F. Snyder waited three months for an appointment with Lechmere's buyer on another product. GMI was given an appointment for one week after the first call.

The NE Lumbermen's show confirmed our suspicions: GMI, Inc. has the right solar product at the right time. We have identified the right market and now we intend to vigorously exploit the first mass retailing ever of domestic solar water heating equipment, the ASC from GMI, Inc.

Marketing Plan

GMI, Inc. will spend $100,000 to advertise our solar panels in the New England area beginning April 1st, 1981. The campaign will be primarily via radio, utilizing Mainella's experience and name recognition factor in that medium.

The thrust of this campaign will be to introduce GMI's low-cost, lightweight panels to skeptical public that heretofore has resisted the high cost of solar water heating. The radio campaign, augmented by some print media ads and anticipated feature stories, will also serve to solicit new dealers as well as lead customers to those dealers already handling our systems.

The radio spots (see enclosed) will be 30 and 60 seconds long. The initial campaign will be a "blitz" of 100 30- and 60-second spots on four or five radio stations per week for the month of April. These spots will be placed almost exclusively in the A.M. & P.M. drive times, excepting an attempt to place some ads in early season Red Sox games. This initial flight will cost $50,000. (see breakdown) The remaining $50,000 will be used for a support campaign during May and June and then another concentrated campaign in September, when people once again begin to worry about fuel bills. The May-June campaign, costing about $10,000, will be designed to support dealer print ads as they are scheduled—a reinforcement campaign.

Radio has been selected as the primary means of advertising because:

1. It is relatively inexpensive compared to newspaper and especially TV;
2. GMI, Inc. allows 2 percent to dealers for co-op ads and they use print almost exclusively; thus, for the outset radio fullfils its classic role as re-enforcement;
3. Mainella is most familiar with radio; his name is still recognized by radio listeners and the medium gives the best opportunity for Mainella to convince the listener/purchaser that solar finally makes sense;
4. Radio does not require the very expensive production costs associated with TV;
5. Radio ads are easily changed; even during the course of a campaign, spots can be updated, rewritten, dropped or added;
6. In spring, radio represents an opportunity to reach an audience even while many are working outdoors, traveling, etc.

The April radio campaign will utilize the following stations, subject to some revision based on availability:

WHDH, Boston, Jess Cain Show (A.M.) and A.M./P.M. Newscasts	$10,000
WBZ, Boston, A.M. & P.M. Newscasts, weekdays only	$10,000
WEEI-AM, Weekday, Saturday and Sunday A.M. drive only	$ 5,000
WROR-FM, A.M.-P.M. drive and Joe Martell Saturday Night Oldies Show	$ 3,000
WITS-AM, if available early season Red Sox game adjacencies on segments carried by full network	$ 4,000
WEEI-FM, ROS, except A.M. drive	$ 5,000
WCOZ-FM, Light schedules, probably ROS	$ 2,000
WBCN-FM, Light schedules, probably ROS	$ 2,000
WSSH-FM, Light schedules, probably ROS	$ 2,000
TOTAL	$43,000

The remaining $7,000 of this April radio budget will be held for schedules to coincide with seminars and for possible inclusion during Celtics and/or Bruins play-off games.

GMI will buy at least one newscast in A.M. and/or P.M. drive time on each WHDH, WBZ and WEEI AM. Other buys as noted will be drive time, but not newscasts.

Coordinated with the radio campaign will be the following:

1. In-store seminars at various dealers that will advertise in print. Mainella will apear at these throughout the year, duplicating several seminars already done, *e.g.,* Mass Hardware and Abundant Life;
2. Publicity releases to the mass media in the NE states, soliciting "freebies," interviews, etc., including TV coverage of a seminar or solar demonstration;
3. Encouragement to dealers to place print and/or other ads to coordinate with the radio campaign or, to augment the radio campaign with ads during April, May and June;
4. An attempt to place Mainella on TV magazine, talk, and other shows to showcase his solar system;
5. Mailing of a photo and brief puff piece to trade journals, magazines, in-house organs, and the like in an attempt to gain additional free publicity for the system.

In addition, GMI, Inc. has already put into motion the following steps:

1. We have offered to dropship, for $325 ea., one of our solar collectors to any and all of the 2,000+ True Value Hardware franchies across the country in an attempt to get Cotter & Co. (True Value) to test the solar market on a national basis;
2. The same offer has been made to American Hardware (ServiStar, 3700 dealers) and to Abundant Life (Comforter Stoves, 1200 U.S. dealers); in all cases, the offers remain on the table and under active consideration;
3. GMI, Inc. is also talking with Vermont Castings, another major manufacturer with an extensive dealer network (actual number uncertain);
4. We met with Larry Griffin of Lechmere Sales, February 3 to discuss placement of our panels in all seven Lechmere stores—the first time Lechmere's has ever met with a solar collector manufacturer. Lechmere will open multi-million dollar Energy Centers in the third quarter of 1981. We fully expect our panels to be highlighted;
5. Meetings are scheduled within the month with the owners/managers

of 1,800 condos and apartments in Rhode Island, New Hampshire and Massachusetts about conversion of some or all of their buildings to solar water heating. A similar meeting was held with David Prolman, the NH owner of more than 20 duplexes and fourplexes who has asked for an estimate to add solar to one 12 family unit on a possible prelude to a major solar conversion;

6. GMI, Inc. will introduce our system to the general public at the New England Home Show, March 7–15;
7. We are also participating in Solar Seminars in New Hampshire during the months of February and March;
8. Taking advantage of the president's notoriety in the area, Guy Mainella has and will continue to conduct seminars at dealers for his solar panel. Brewsters will advertise a seminar for February 24 in the Boston Globe and Herald;
9. We are negotiating with a national representative to introduce our system to other major building material chains such as Payless Cashways, Lindsley's, O'Malley's, Scotty's and Moore's, among a dozen or so others.
10. We have already sent illustrative brochures to 18 building material centers in the south and west, representing more than 100 outlets in a dozen states; these inquiries are being followed up from the factory, but realistically it will require in-person follow-ups and a demonstration of the marketability of the collector in the New England area where the initial thrust is being made.

In summary, the marketing plan has been conceived to make as big a splash as possible with a reasonable expenditure. A month-long radio campaign amounts to saturation advertising—the biggest regional campaign ever launched in an attempt to sell low-cost solar water heating systems in this area.

GMI, Inc., with demonstration systems working, inventory on hand and collectors on display at some mass merchandisers, is prepared to make an all-out effort to launch what we feel is the only reasonable (*i.e.*, economical) solar unit on the market. Our reception from people heretofore disinterested in solar confirms our confidence that our product will sell. And, the Marketing Plan outlined above is designed to the job.

Product Testing

The ASC has passed the TIPSE test program at Desert Sunshine Exposure Testing Lab (DSET) in Phoenix, Arizona. The ASC was also successfully tested at the University of Connecticut in March-April of 1980. A synopsis of the testing is attached.

We will submit another panel to the University of Connecticut (U-

Conn) for testing this spring because slight changes in our manufacturing process hint that our panel will be somewhat more efficient than the original collector tested at both U-Conn and DSET.

Manufacturing Facilities

GMI, Inc. leases approximately 8,800 square feet of manufacturing and office space on the first floor at 55 Lake Street, Nashua, NH, paying $1760 per month for rent, utilities and taxes. The lease is month to month.

Personnel

GMI, Inc. employs one Production Supervisor ($15,000 per year). Future hires are projected in the financial plan. A part-time bookkeeper was added January 25, 1981 at $11 per hour for approximately 4–5 hours per month.

Research and Development

GMI, Inc. during 1982 will add to the management team a full time director of R & D. A budget appropriation of $25,000 has been made.

The ASC represents, in our belief, the most advanced flat plate collector available in terms of simplicity, durability, ease of installation, low maintenance and MBTUs per dollar per year. GMI President, Guy Mainella, conducted the research that lead to the ASC. Mainella will also be the holder of the patent expected to be issued for his automatic manifold. Further, Mainella developed the pioneering technology for mounting 3-M's Flexigard to the solar frame. A patent application for that technology is being considered.

It is, however, anticipated that Mainella's duties as president will not permit him to remain as fully abreast of developing technology as in the past. That responsibility will fall to the director of R & D.

In the interim, Mainella remains keenly aware of the continued research into a new glazing film (Thermofilm Corp., Palo Alto, CA). GMI, Inc. has written assurances we will have early access to the film that promises to be a better heat trap than Flexigard and will therefore improve collector efficiency.

Mainella has already held preliminary discussions with shrink packers (the techniques used to heat thin films on packages) concerning his ideas for applying the same basic technology to glazing a thinner, less expensive solar collector.

In addition, Mainella has had built and tested new manifold prototypes of Teflon and Polypropylene. They hold promise of dramatically reducing the cost of the collector manifold, *e.g.* from $7.50 each to .75 each.

In total, GMI, Inc. is well served by its inquisitive president and the pre-emminent consultants retained by the company for engineering and technical advise. (see listing below)

Production

GMI, Inc. has produced 4080 square feet (136 panels) of solar collectors. Our expectation is to produce about 94,000 square feet during 1981, representing 3,145 panels with a wholesale value of $896,325. (3145 × $285). Anticipating we will sell virtually the entire production, GMI, Inc. projects a healthy profit. In the *2nd* year, we expect to produce nearly 200,000 square feet with total revenues of $3.0 million.

Other Revenue Sources

The GMI System includes a storage tank, sensors, controller, brackets and circulator, which we buy from other vendors. These components represent revenues of approximately $400 per system or $600,000 in 1981.

Use of Proceeds

GMI, Inc. has earmarked $100,000 for our marketing program. Another $125,000 will be used for operating capital, inventory, hiring additional employees to increase production and for manufacturing equipment, including small tools, power saw, drill press, and a second table for stretching and mounting the glazing to the collector frame.

The remaining $25,000 will be used for R&D and for cash reserves.

Management

Guy Mainella, Corporation President, is a self-taught solar businessman. Mainella was a well-known Boston, Massachusetts radio and television personality until his retirement in October, 1978 to devote full-time to his business. Mainella hosted "Calling All Sports" on WBZ for seven years, broadcast Celtics games on TV and radio, wrote a newspaper column for the *Boston Globe*; his broadcasting career spanned twenty-two years in Milwaukee, Chicago, and Boston.

Mainella formed Solar Energy Enterprises in April, 1977 to research passive and active solar systems. After rejecting all available systems as too expensive, Mainella has designed and seeks to patent the unique ASC.

Mainella was educated at public and private schools in Milwaukee,

Wisconsin. He graduated from Greendale High School in June, 1956 and attended Marquette University in Milwaukee.

He has lectured on broadcasting, sports, and sports/business at Boston University, Holy Cross, Bentley College, WIP, Graham Junior College, and several others.

Mainella is married to Carole and has three children—a son, Scott, a freshman at UNH Wittimore School of Business, and daughters, Lisa (14) and Lauri (13). Mainella is in excellent health, enjoys tennis, swimming, cross country skiing, photography, and reading as hobbies.

Consultants

GMI, Inc. has supported the innovative research and design effort by Mainella by retention of the most respected technical consultants in the Solar Energy Business. We will continue this practice, as noted elsewhere.

Total Environmental Action (TEA), Harrisville, NH has consulted to Mainella's companies since their formation. TEA was founded and is headed by Bruce Anderson (MIT), author of the *Solar Home Book* and an internationally known authority on solar energy. TEA regularly consults to the federal government, assists in drawing up guidelines for solar equipment, and has worked closely with Mainella in developing the ASC for production. TEA's evaluation of the ASC has prompted Vice President Charles Micheal to write to GMI, Inc., in part ". . . you have the potential to produce an *extremely* cost-effective product . . . many people feel that significant advances in collector design and reductions in manufacturing costs can only come about through the introduction of new materials, such as you are doing."

Professor Timothy Johnson, MIT School of Architecture, an internationally known solar design expert, also consults to GMI, Inc. Johnson has done computer simulation on passive designs, offered technical advice on the ASC and will be retained to augment the analysis of test data, adding prestige to our sales and marketing programs.

David B. Fite, Corporate Financial Manager, Digital Equipment Corp., is financial consultant to GMI, Inc. Fite holds a BSBA and MBA degree, is a member of the National Association of Accountants and joined Digital in 1974 after serving as treasurer of Ty-Data for four years.

Dr. William Shurcliff, former Harvard Professor, an internationally recognized authority on solar energy; adviser to the government, author of several volumes on solar heated buildings, solar inventions and solar applications, Shurcliff has consulted to GMI, Inc. on new solar materials.

Corporate Officers
President, Secretary & Treasurer   Guy Mainella

Directors

Chairman	Guy Mainella
Member	Joseph R. Mancuso, New York City

Mancuso is an internationally known Business Consultant (Harvard); author (*How to Start, Finance & Manage Your Own Small Business, Fun & Guts*, and many others), founded the Center for Entrepreneurial Management (New York City), a director of several companies, former WPI professor and businessman.

Member	Carole J. Mainella (Mrs. Guy)

Other Key Personnel

Gerald R. Prunier, attorney (Prunier Mazerolle & Frasca), Nashua, N.H. A widely known and respected attorney, Prunier is counsel to some of Nashua's finest companies, yet has been carefully selected because of his ability and willingness to devote time to a small company. (603) 889-4200

Feeley & Driscoll, Certified Public Accountants, Two Wellman Ave., Nashua and 133 State Street, Boston. Partner Dan Driscoll and his staff have provided the attached financial plan and the enclosed financial statement. (603) 889-0444

The Nashua Trust Co., Main Street, Nashua, NH 03060 is the corporation's bank. Mark Leonardi, Vice President. (603) 882-2755

THE FINANCIAL PLAN

The following notations will be of assistance in reading the Financial Plan:

1. The Plan assumes no additional infusion of capital;
2. Accounts Receivable are aged 45 days;
3. Sales Commission paid to Man. Rep, is figured at 8%, assuming not all sales will be made by him;
4. Interest only is being paid on SBA Loan until 6/81;
5. System selling price is $975 in 2nd year; $1,000 in 3rd year;
6. A provision is made for a $210,000 Advertising budget in 1982 and for $500,000 in 1983;
7. Interest in 2nd year has been doubled, assuming a larger loan;
8. 3rd year SG & A assumes $36,000 salary for a Gen. Sales Mgr.;
9. ASC costs assumed to be $110 for 2nd year, expecting lower prices because of larger quantity purchases of raw goods;

10. ASC costs increased to $120 in 3rd year to reflect likely increases in component costs;
11. Cost of "Other Goods" is $350 in 3rd year;
12. No seasonal adjustment is made for sales, expecting national sales by end of 1st year;
13. The Financial Plan shows a maximum deficit of $185,197 in the 7th month of the 1st year.

Questions & Answers regarding GMI's Advanced Solar Collector (ASC)

Question: Will **3M**'s Flexigard film break if struck by a tree, meteor, baseball or all of the above?

Answer: It would not support either an elephant or a human being. However, it is very strong and very durable; if pierced, it can be easily and inexpensively patched. Please note the **3M** Fact Sheet. (A baseball would bounce off).

Question: All other solar water heaters are so expensive. Why is the GMI System so inexpensive?

Answer: GMI, Inc. is a small, growing progressive company with low overhead and bright ideas. We've made solar simple, therefore less expensive. We've patented the unique Automatic Manifold which eliminates heat exchangers and anti-freeze from solar systems. We've made our ASC light, so you can install it yourself and have also taken the "high technology" of "proper" tilt, perfect location, etc. out of the solar picture. We also want to stay in the solar business longer than Exxon.

Question: Is solar water heating equipment really a good buy if it only saves me 45% or so of my hot water heating bill?

Answer: How important is a 45% savings on anything to you? Compare your water heating costs from recent months to a couple years ago. Frighten yourself by speculating on what they will be a couple years from now. Consider this: if you invest $1,000 today in a GMI solar system, your annual return will be around $150 (or more, depending on variables); if you put $1,000 in a savings account, you might earn $65 (less income tax, of course). The government pays you 40% of the cost of a solar water heater.

Question: The ASC sounds good, but what happens if the power fails for a prolonged period and the pipes to my collectors freeze?

Answer: Nothing, if it's installed properly. Qest Polybutylene piping on the inlet and outlet connections will absorb the expansion of frozen water and will not be damaged. (We're sure; we tested it thoroughly.) Remember, GMI guarantees our collector, but we're unable to insure against calamities like prolonged power failures. By the way, did you know the average power failure in New Hampshire during 1979 lasted 63 minutes? You couldn't freeze a glass of water in that time!

Question: What about maintenance? Does this collector take care of itself?

Answer: Better than most other things you own. We'd like you to inspect the little marvel once or twice a year to make sure there was no meteor damage, lifting of the tape or damage to the insulation into the building. You could wash the glazing if you're careful and persnickity, but why bother? Unless your house is enveloped in smog, the rain will clean the ASC nicely. If you do wash it, please don't use steel wool.

M

Guy Mainella
Industries, Inc.
SOLAR COLLECTORS

55 Lake Street
Nashua N.H. 03060
Tel (603) 889-0246

3M 7410 Flexigard Protective Film
BRAND

- **What is "FLEXIGARD" Film?**
  It is a composite of Polyester and Acrylic.

- **Scratching of Film:**
  Film is not scratch resistant, because of inherent and unique surface properties. The film is essentially self-cleaning, and should not require washing. However, if cleaning does become necessary, the use of a soft cloth and water is recommended.

- **Transmission:**
  89 percent

- **Thermal Expansion, Sagging:**
  Heat will not cause film to sag or expand. Sagging will occur if film is not pulled tight or properly installed.

- **Stagnation:**
  Neither performance nor quality of film has been affected during cap off/shutdown stagnation tests.

- **Cold Cracking:**
  This is an oriented film composite and is not subject to cold cracking.

- **UV Exposure:**
  In actual use test, mounted on an air wash collector, no sign of deterioration was observed. Film continues to look exceedingly good after a one year period. The exposed face of "FLEXIGARD" Film has shown exceptional stability to weathering over a 15 year period.

- **Life Expectancy of Film:**
  Minimum of 10 years.

- **Repairing or Patching Film:**
  Use 3M 465 double coated adhesive tape and "FLEXIGARD" Film for repairing or patching.

- **Load Strength:**
  The ability of the film to bear a load is generally greater than that of the fastening method.

3M *FLEXIGARD 7410 is used exclusively on all GMI, Inc. Advanced Solar Collectors.*

EPDM Elastomer — The Material that Lasts

GMI's Advanced Solar Collectors feature the EPDM Rubber Absorber Mat exclusively

GMI uses the durable, Ethylene Propylene (EPDM) Rubber because of its combination of superior ozone, heat and ultra-violet resistance. In addition, our absorber mats made of this material possess very good low temperature properties.

EPDM shows remarkable durability even after 10 years exposure to sunlight in Florida. EPDM has a long life even when exposed to temperature variations as great as minus -75°F. to intermittent temperatures of 350°F.

GMI's tough, natural black formulation, exclusively for solar applications, will give years of dependable service . . . in freezing weather and even under stagnation temperature conditions in hot weather. EPDM — Another GMI System Component that LASTS!

Guy Mainella
Industries. Inc.
SOLAR COLLECTORS

55 Lake Street,
Nashua, N.H. 03060
Tel. (603) 889-0246

Solar Energy Economics for the Consumer (c)

Guy Mainella Industries, Inc., manufacturer of the new, lightweight Advanced Solar Collector with the Automatic Manifold* has simplified solar water heating. We have also simplified the job of comparing solar equipment.

Do you want to know the essentials? How much will the system cost, installed? How much water will it heat? How much money will you save? How does the GMI, Inc. System compare to other solar water heaters?

The Table below tells the story. It compares GMI's System with two other solar water heating systems. **GMI's System produces more millions of Btus per dollar per year than any other solar water heating system you can buy**. And, even though a few collectors are more efficient, they cost hundreds of dollars more to produce about the same number of Btus. That's because the GMI System costs less per square foot, installed, so the yield in Btus is virtually the same. And, of course, the cost per year per millions of Btus is far lower for our System.

	GMI's ASC	System "X"	System "Y"
Btus per year	7,190,000	7,490,000	7,000,000
Installed Cost	$990	$1650	$2100
Square Feet (net)	54.8	37.4	40
Cost per MBtus/yr	$138	$220	$300

(Compute cost per MBtus/yr by dividing installed cost by Btus per year)

(Table above assumes the following: Blue Hills, MA weather data; collector storage of 15 Btus/ft^2/°F; 45 degree tilt; 60 gallons of hot water per day.)

The Table tells the story. GMI's ASC costs $138 per million Btus per year; no other system comes close.

There's an easy way to estimate your actual dollar savings with an ASC System from GMI, Inc. But, don't be fooled. No one can predict for certain how much money you will save. It depends on how much hot water you use, when you use it, how hot it is, how much sun shines; these variables determine exactly how much money you save. But, here's my honest estimate:

If an average household of four persons uses 16,000,000 Btus per year for heating water and the 60 square foot GMI System provides 7,190,000 Btus, you will save 44.9% of the energy required to heat your water. If you spend $400 per year for electricity, oil or gas you could save 44.9% of $400 or $179.60 in the first year. Your savings will increase, of course, as energy costs increase.

That's the GMI story. We manufacture a high quality, low-cost, lightweight solar collector which is, very simply, the best collector value.

*Patent Pending

206

February, 1981

GMI, Inc. Trade Price List

Item Number	Product	Quantity	Price
100-ES	Advanced Solar Collector with Sensor	6 - Up	$290
100-E	Advanced Solar Collector - no Sensor	6 - Up	$280
200	Independent Energy C-30 Controller	Each	$55
500	Grundfos Circulator with ¾" Iso Valves	Each	$85
600	Rheem Solaraide 66 Gal. Elec. Water Heater	Each	$205
800	GMI Mounting Brackets, set of 12	Set	$30
900	Roof Protection Package 4-#13 PVC End Caps & 4-#13 PVC 90s	Set	$15
901	Watts A540 ¾-inch T & P Relief Valve	Each	$9.95

(All Items above required for typical Domestic Solar Water Heating System)

Options to Above

300	Independent Energy C-100 Controller	Each	$185
700	Rheem Solaraide 82 Gal. Elec. Water Heater	Each	$215
902	Rheem Solaraide 120 Gal. Elec. Water Heater	Each	$325
100-ES	Advanced Solar Collector with Sensor	1 - 5	$325
100-E	Advanced Solar Collector - no Sensor	1 - 5	$315
903	GMI Brochures	100	$20

Prices, products and specifications subject to change without notice.
Terms: Orders prepaid in full without prior credit arrangements.
Shipping: All prices include freight within 100 miles of Nashua, N.H.

Guy Mainella
Industries. Inc.
SOLAR COLLECTORS

55 Lake Street
Nashua N H 03060

Tel (603) 889-0246

Guy Mainville Industries.

PREPARED BY

	1 Jan.	2 Feb.	3 March	4 April	5 May
INCOME STATEMENT					
Net sales	7209	9071	13606	34015	9070
Cost of goods sold	5556	6025	9036	22591	6024
Gross profit	1673	3046	4570	11424	3046
SG & A expenses	8844	6994	58720	14814	1600
Interest expenses	2586	2586	2586	2586	258
Net income [loss]	[9757]	[6534]	[56736]	[5976]	1187
CASH FLOW STATEMENT					
Cash receipts:					
receipts on sales		270	4229	9071	1360
Total cash receipts		270	4229	9071	1360
Cash disbursements:					
Payments on trade	3986	8529	12828	15601	226?
Expenses:					
Direct labor	540	720	810	810	157
Overhead	2210	2210	5555	2155	223
S G & A	5569	7239	11290	58271	137?
Interest	2586	2586	2586	2586	258
Repayment of debt					
Fixed asset additions		6000			
Total cash disb.	14831	27284	33019	79423	9272
Increase [decrease]	[14831]	[27014]	[28790]	[70352]	[291?]
Cash balance-beginning	38620	23789	[3225]	[32015]	[10236]
Cash balance-ending	23789	[3225]	[32015]	[102367]	[1315]

208

	June	July	Aug.	Sept.	Oct.	Nov.	Dec.	Year Total
	6	7	8	9	10	11	12	13
	136061	158738	181415	181415	181415	170077	170077	1330826
	90365	105425	120486	120486	120486	112956	112956	883611
	45696	53313	60927	60927	60929	57121	57121	447215
	13064	13289	55146	14488	14338	13101	13931	244057
	2586	2556	2523	2492	2462	2431	2399	30379
	30046	36968	3260	43949	44129	40789	40771	172779
	34015	90707	136061	158738	181415	181415	181415	790943
	34015	90707	136061	158738	181415	181415	181415	790912
	52434	77134	91001	110936	123072	110936	107037	734114
	2250	2700	3600	4500	3600	3600	3600	28305
	4237	1662	4362	1962	4512	2112	7212	40620
	15809	12269	15136	54043	16533	13308	13695	237367
	2586	2556	2523	2412	3462	2431	2399	30379
	2252	2282	2315	2346	2376	2407	2439	16417
								6000
	79568	98803	118927	176279	152605	135294	136332	1095202
	[45553]	[8096]	17134	[7541]	28810	46121	45033	[104260]
	[131848]	[177101]	[185197]	[168063]	[185604]	[156794]	[110673]	35620
	[177101]	[185197]	[168063]	[185604]	[156794]	[110673]	[65640]	[65640]

	Jan.	Feb.	March	April	May
					INCOME PROJEC
Net sales	168188	257887	257887	257887	25788.
Cost of goods sold	112166	171988	171988	171988	17198
Gross profit	56062	85899	85899	85899	8589
S.G. & A expenses	25000	25000	25000	40000	65000
Interest expense	5000	5000	5000	5000	500
Net income [loss]	26022	55899	55899	40899	1589

	Jan.	Feb.	March	April	May
					INCOME PROJE
Net sales	455000	455000	455000	455000	45500
Cost of goods sold	310880	310880	310880	310880	31088
Gross profit	144120	144120	144120	144120	14412
S.G. & A expenses	45000	45000	73250	73250	7375
Interest expense	5000	5000	5000	5000	500
Net income	94120	94120	65370	65370	6557

6	7	8	9	10	11	12	13
June	July	Aug.	Sept.	Oct.	Nov.	Dec.	Year Total
BY MONTH FOR YEAR ENDING 12/31/82							
257887	257887	257887	257887	257887	257887	257887	3004945
171988	171988	171988	171988	171988	171988	171988	2004034
85899	85899	85899	85899	85899	85899	85899	1000914
40000	25000	25000	40000	40000	25000	15000	390000
5000	5000	5000	5000	5000	5000	5000	60000
40899	55899	55899	40899	40899	55899	65899	550911
June	July	Aug.	Sept.	Oct.	Nov.	Dec.	Year Total
BY MONTH FOR YEAR ENDING 12/31/83							
455000	455000	455000	455000	455000	455000	455000	5460000
310880	310880	310880	310880	310880	310880	310880	3730560
144120	144120	144120	144120	144120	144120	144120	1729440
73750	30000	30000	73750	73750	73750	73750	740000
5000	5000	5000	5000	5000	5000	5000	60000
65370	109120	109120	65370	65370	65370	65370	929440

	1	2	3	4	5
	Jan.	Feb.	March	April	May
ASSETS					
Current assets:					
Cash	23789	[3225]	[32015]	[102367]	[315
Accounts receivable	7499	13300	22677	47621	1247
Inventories	43065	51765	60465	62640	590
Other current assets	950	950	950	950	9
Total current assets:	72303	62790	52077	8844	531
Property and equipment					
Equipment	7049	11049	11049	11049	110
Household imp.	772	2772	2772	2772	27
Motor vehicle	5874	5874	5874	5874	58
	13695	19695	19695	19695	196
Less accumulated dep.	2191	2366	2941	3316	36
	11504	17129	16754	16379	16
Other assets					
Deposits	2010	2010	2010	2010	20
Organization	484	472	460	448	4
	2494	2482	2470	2458	24
	86301	82401	71301	21681	715
LIABILITIES AND STOCKHOLDER'S EQUITY					
Current liabilities					
Notes payable-current	18187	18187	18187	18187	181
Accounts payable	14288	16922	62558	24914	569
Other current liabilities	2214	2214	2214	2214	22
Total current liabilities	34689	37323	82959	45315	773
Long term debt:					
Notes payable	183269	183269	183269	183269	183
Stockholder's equity:					
Common stock	10156	10156	10156	10156	10
Retained earnings	[141813]	[148347]	[205083]	[211059]	[199
[deficit]	[131657]	[138191]	[194927]	[200903]	[189
	86301	82401	71301	27681	715

	7	8	9	10	11	12	13
June	July	Aug.	Sept.	Oct.	Nov.	Dec.	
[177101]	[185197]	[168063]	[185604]	[156794]	[110673]	[65640]	
226768	294799	340153	362830	362830	351492	340154	
51765	14515	44515	59015	51015	62640	6626	
950	950	950	950	950	950	950	
102382	155067	217555	237191	266001	304401	341729	
11049	11049	11049	11049	11041	11049	11049	
2772	2772	2772	2772	2772	2772	2772	
5874	5874	5874	5874	5874	5874	5874	
19695	19695	19695	19695	19695	19695	19695	
4066	4441	4816	0191	5566	5741	6316	
15621	15254	14879	14504	14129	13754	13379	
2010	2010	2010	2010	2010	2010	2010	
424	412	400	388	376	364	352	
2434	2422	2410	2398	2386	2374	2362	
120445	172743	237844	254093	283516	320537	352470	
18187	18187	18187	18187	18187	18187	18187	
78014	95626	156782	134428	121098	120737	119338	
2214	2214	2214	2214	2214	2214	2214	
98415	116027	177183	154829	141499	141138	139739	
181017	118735	176420	174074	171698	169291	166852	
10156	10156	10156	10156	10156	10156	10156	
[69143]	[32473]	[128915]	[84966]	[40837]	[48]	40723	
[58987]	[122019]	[118759]	[74810]	[30681]	10108	50879	
120445	172743	234844	254093	282516	330537	357470	

PREPARED BY

	Jan.	Feb.	March	April	May
SALES:					
ASC units	9	20	30	75	20
ASC dollars	2565	5700	8550	21375	5700
Other sales dollars	1664	4160	6839	15548	415⁀
Gross sales	4229	9860	14789	36973	985⁀
Commissions	—	789	1183	2958	788
Net sales	4229	9071	13606	34015	907⁀
COST OF GOODS SOLD:					
ASC materials	1097	2438	3657	9142	2437
ASC labor	81	180	270	675	180
ASC overhead	130	287	430	1076	286
Total ASC costs	1308	2905	4357	10893	290⁀
Cost of other sales	1248	3120	4679	11698	311⁀
Total cost of goods sold	2556	6025	9036	22591	602⁀

	June	July	Aug.	Sept.	Oct.	Nov.	Dec.	Year Total
			6	7	8	9	10	11	12	13

June	July	Aug.	Sept.	Oct.	Nov.	Dec.	Year Total
300	350	400	400	400	375	375	2934
86500	99750	114000	114000	114000	106875	106875	836190
62392	72791	83190	83190	83190	77991	77991	609991
147892	172541	197190	17110	177190	184866	184866	1446181
11831	13803	15775	15775	15775	14789	14789	115355
136061	158738	181415	181415	181415	170077	170077	1330826
36567	42661	48756	48756	48756	45709	45709	357626
2700	3150	3600	3600	3600	3375	3325	26406
4304	5021	5738	5738	5738	5379	5379	42089
43571	50832	58094	58094	58094	54463	54463	426121
46794	59593	62392	62392	62392	58493	58493	452490
70365	105425	120486	120486	120486	112956	112956	883611

PREPARED BY

		1 Jan.	2 Feb.	3 March	4 April	5 May
1	ASC					
3	Production units	60	80	90	90	175
5,6	Material cost $121.36 per unit	7281	9708	10922	10922	21238
8,9	Labor cost $9 per unit	540	720	810	810	1575
14	Material requirements	7281	9708	10922	10922	21238
17	Payments on material 30 days	2955	7281	9708	10922	10922
23	Other than ASC					
25	Requirements	1248	3120	4679	11698	3119
27	Payments on	1031	1248	3120	4679	11698
32,33	Total payments on material	3986	8529	12828	15601	22620
36,37	Finished units in inventory end of month	174	234	294	309	28

216

6 June	7 July	8 Aug.	9 Sept.	10 Oct.	11 Nov.	12 Dec.	13 Year Total
250	300	400	500	400	400	400	3145
30340	36408	48544	60680	48544	48544	48544	381675
2250	2700	3600	4500	3600	3600	3600	28305
30340	36408	48544	60680	48544	48544	48544	381675
21238	30340	36408	48544	60680	48544	48544	336086
46794	54593	62392	62392	62392	58493	58493	451470
31196	46794	54593	62392	62392	62392	58493	400028
52434	77134	91001	110936	123072	110936	107037	736114
234	184	184	284	284	309	334	

		1 Jan.	2 Feb.	3 March	4 April	5 May
1	ACCRUAL BASIS:					
2	Rent	1760	1760	1760	1760	1760
3	Supplies	300	400	450	450	875
4	Depreciation	375	375	375	375	375
5	Utilities	300	300	400	100	5c
6	Payroll taxes	114	114	114	183	25.
7	Insurance	36	36	56	112	168
8						
9	Total overhead expenses					
10	accrual basis	2885	2985	3155	2980	3481
11						
12						
13						
14						
15						
16	CASH BASIS:					
17	Rent	1760	1760	1760	1760	176c
	Supplies			3225		
19	Depreciation					
20	Utilities	300	300	400	100	5c
21	Payroll taxes	114	114	114	183	25.
22	Insurance	36	36	56	112	16t
23						
24	Total overhead expenses					
25	cash basis	2210	2210	5555	2155	223
26						
27						
28						
29						
30						
31						
32						
33						
34						
35						
36						

6 June	7 July	8 Aug.	9 Sept.	10 Oct.	11 Nov.	12 Dec.	13 Year Total
1266	1266	1266	1266	1266	1266	1266	17662
1250	1500	2000	2500	2000	2000	2000	15725
375	375	375	375	375	375	375	4500
50	50	50	150	200	300	400	2350
253	322	322	322	322	322	322	2963
168	224	224	224	224	224	224	1920
3362	3737	4237	4837	4387	4487	4587	45620

June	July	Aug.	Sept.	Oct.	Nov.	Dec.	Year Total
1266	1266	1266	1266	1266	1266	1266	17662
2500		2500		2500		5000	15725
							—
50	50	50	150	200	300	400	2350
253	322	322	322	322	322	322	2963
168	224	224	224	224	224	224	1920
4237	1862	4362	1962	4512	2112	7212	40620

	1 Jan.	2 Feb.	3 March	4 April	5 May
ACCRUAL BASIS:					
Advertising	580	500	50300	5500	5500
Research & Development	2000	500			
Officer's salary	3200	3200	3200	3200	3200
Office salaries	350	60	475	475	475
Office supplies	100	200	1500	600	150
Auto expense	300	350	350	1000	400
Prof. fees	580	580	580	580	580
Telephone	350	350	300	300	300
Postage	150	200	300	200	150
Payroll taxes	199	199	225	225	241
Insurance	175	175	175	175	175
Freight			525	1313	3500
Other salary	710	530	440	1196	1187
Miscellaneous	150	150	150	150	150
	8844	6994	58720	14814	16008
CASH BASIS:					
Advertising			2500	50000	5500
Research & Development		2000	500		
Officer's salary	3200	3200	3200	3200	3200
Office salaries	350	60	475	475	475
Office supplies	100	200	1500	600	160
Auto expense	300	350	350	1000	400
Prof. fees			500	500	110
Telephone	350	350	300	300	300
Postage	150	200	300	200	150
Payroll taxes	199	199	225	225	241
Insurance			800		600
Freight				525	131
Other salaries	710	530	440	1196	118
Miscellaneous	150	150	150	150	150
Total S.G. & A expense	5509	7239	11240	58271	1372

220

| | 7 | 8 | 9 | 10 | 11 | 12 | 13 |
June	July	Aug.	Sept.	Oct.	Nov.	Dec.	Year Total
500	500	40500	500	500	500	500	106080
							2500
3200	3500	3500	3500	4000	4000	4000	41700
700	700	700	700	700	700	700	6735
150	150	150	150	150	150	150	3500
400	400	1500	1000	400	400	400	16900
580	580	580	580	580	580	580	6960
300	300	300	300	300	300	300	3700
150	150	350	150	100	100	150	2150
241	241	241	283	283	283	283	2944
175	175	175	175	175	175	175	2100
5250	6125	7000	7000	7000	6563	6563	50839
1268	818						6149
150	150	150	150	150	150	150	150
13064	13789	55146	14488	14338	13901	13951	244057
5500	500	2000	40000	500	500	500	107500
							2500
3200	3500	3500	3500	4000	4000	4000	41700
700	700	700	700	700	700	700	6735
160	150	150	150	150	150	150	3500
400	400	1300	1000	400	400	400	6900
250	110	110	110	3000	225	500	5115
300	300	300	300	300	300	300	3700
150	150	350	150	100	100	150	2150
241	241	241	283	283	283	283	2944
			700				2100
3500	5250	6125	7000	7000	7000	6562	44274
1268	818						6149
150	150	150	150	150	150	150	1800
15809	12269	15126	54043	16583	13808	13695	837369

FINANCIAL PROPOSAL FOR
MARRONE ENTERPRISES, INC.

Statement of Purpose

The goal of Marrone Enterprise, Inc. is to take advantage of the current trend of people eating out of the home by establishing a series of moderately priced Pub/Restaurants.

In starting the first unit, Marrone Enterprises, Inc. is seeking a loan of $100,000 to be used toward the purchase of equipment and inventory, maintain sufficient cash reserves and provide adequate working capital to successfully develop a significant consumer following. This sum, together with the $40,000 equity investment of the principals, will be sufficient to finance transition through the growing phase so that the business can operate as an on-going, profitable enterprise.

Table of Contents

General Description

Marrone Enterprises, Inc. will be a Pub/Restaurant offering a unique warm atmosphere, a sandwich and seafood menu, large drinks (an effect created by special glassware), and quality service. Mr. Marrone's past experience has shown that sales will run approximately 55 percent to 45 percent liquor to food, making profits strong due to the large mark-up employed in liquor sales.

Due to its location in a busy commercial/industrial area, just outside downtown Worcester, Marrone Enterprises, Inc. will derive most of its luncheon and cocktail hour (4 P.M.–6 P.M.) business from this business community. During the week nights (Monday through Thursday) from 7 P.M. until midnight, inexpensive food "specials" will be offered to create business volume.

Marrone Enterprises, Inc. will be moderate in size seating approximately one-hundred fifty (150) people. Entertainment would consist of a high-quality system of background music. It would also feature a long bar seating twenty (20) people, as well as a long stand up rail area surrounding the bar. Food and drink would be served at both.

The design would utilize the natural beauty of the building's bricks and beams with barnboard pine being used for partitions and walls. Hanging plants, mirrors and natural wood furniture would highlight the decor.

Marrone Enterprises, Inc. will begin business in October, 1979. Operational hours will be Monday through Saturday from 11:30 A.M. until midnight daily. Because of the unique, warm atmosphere, light, moderately priced menu, large drinks, polite efficient service, proven management, and accessible location, the business will draw not only from its immediate environment, but from further locales as well.

The Market

The market that Marrone Enterprises, Inc. will attract is the immediate business community and shoppers during the lunch and supper hours and the moviegoers, shoppers, and people out for a light meal or drink in the evenings.

The number of people who work within walking distance of the restaurant is in excess of two thousand (2,000). This figure does not include the hundreds of salesmen, customers, and clients that visit these businesses daily. For the people not located in the immediate vicinity, there is ample parking (93 spaces) directly across from the restaurant as well as on-street parking. The only present alternative eating spot to those within walking distance is a local diner seating less than seveny-five (75) people. According to the latest M.D.P.W. Traffic Survey, approximately 29,500 cars pass by the location daily.

The evening market will come from the downtown shoppers and moviegoers and the people from the immediate towns.

Marrone Enterprises, Inc. plans to attract this mrket by combining quality food, beverage and service, with moderate prices, easy accessibility and relaxed atmosphere. Volume is the key to the success of the operation. Marrone Enterprises, Inc. will offer a competitively priced bigger drink and during week nights will offer a very attractively priced food special. These specials will not be as profitable as other menu items but will stimulate business in normally slower periods creating the volume necessary to justify price.

The Location

The proposed location for the first unit of Marrone Enterprises, Inc. is located at 106 Grove Street in Worcester, Massachusetts. The building is an old brick, four-story structure recently designated a historical monument by the Massachusetts Historical Society. Parker Apartment Complex, Inc. has recently purchased the building and is presently renovating for the purpose of retail or office space.

The precise location of 106 Grove Street is on the second floor (street level) and is approximately 4,639 square feet. Marrone Enterprises is renting the property as is (lease copy in appendix) and will be responsible for renovation. A construction chart is available in appendix.

Grove Street is a heavily traveled (29,500 cars daily) access route into downtown Worcester. The area consists almost exclusively of commercial and industrial concerns. There are over two-thousand (2,000) employees within walking distance, as well as hundreds of visiting salesmen, customers, and clients.

The most positive aspects of the Grove Street location are its accessibility and parking. Grove Street is easily accessible to all parts of the city as well as the suburbs. The map enclosed in the appendix illustrates the accessibility and gives the 1977 traffic counts. Parking, a valuable commodity, is also readily available to the location (see parking map in appendix). During the day (until 5 P.M.), parking is provided (in the lease) directly across the street for 93 cars. On-street parking is also available. After 5 P.M., there are three (3) large parking lots (500 spots) also available.

The Competition

Marrone Enterprises, Inc. is unique in that it is not a full menu restaurant and not a lounge but a business that falls between the two. Due to this fact, there is little direct competition in the area.

1. *"Maxwell Silverman's Toolhouse"*—located at Lincoln Square offers a sandwich menu at lunch and full dinners and dancing in the evening. Direct competition would be during lunch. Maxwell's is a fine operation doing very well. Its strength lies in its beautiful decor, good management, and lack of quality competition. The bar area is lacking in warmth and does not encourage people to come in and relax with drinks, an area in which Marrone Enterprises, Inc. will be strong. Because Maxwell's is considered one of the few, if not only, nice spots in the downtown area, people would enjoy a moderately priced alternative, especially the businessmen's drinking crowd.
2. *"Shannon's II"*—located on Highland Street has recently been

converted from Curley's. It offers a luncheon and dinner menu. Food is mediocre but is priced moderately. Management is not strong due mostly to lack of individual ownership. However, it does enjoy a very limited bar business.

3. *"Nick's Grille"*—located at Drury Square features a sandwich menu at lunch and dinners in the evening. Once a highly successful operation, it has tailed off noticably in the last five years. Lack of interest by owner and increased competition may be the reasons.

4. *"Pickwicks"*—located just off Main Street in Worcester is very similar to Marrone Enterprises, Inc. It is very successful to date but relies heavily on the theater crowd next door and caters to the young adults. The food is good, although the menu is a bit vegetarian and is weak in the production of beverages. Parking is available by garage only.

The Management

Marrone Enterprises, Inc. recognizes the importance of a sound managerial team and therefore has organized the following structure. Operational Management: Joe Marrone and Ed Marrone—Organization and Advisory Management: Thomas Sullivan, Esq. and Timothy J. Harrington, C.P.A.—Overall Consulting and Advisory Management: Board of Directors.

Joe Marrone (personal résumé in rear of this section) brings to Marrone Enterprises a lifetime of restaurant experience. Joe's father owned and operated the Wachusett Country Club located in West Boylston, Massachusetts. As Joe grew up, he performed every imaginable job necessary to the running of the club. After graduating from college, Joe became a full time assistant manager to his father, assisting him in the banquet, bar, and restaurant ends of the business. After the death of his father and subsequent sale of the business, Joe became associated with the Piccadilly Pub in Westboro, Massachusetts. Joe began as a bartender and within nine months was promoted to manager. It was at the Piccadilly where Joe became interested in the concept being undertaken by Marrone Enterprises. The Piccadilly operation consisted of a restored brick and beam structure featuring a good drink, weeknight food specials, and a sandwich menu. Joe's job as manager included; hiring and firing of all personnel, ordering of all food and liquor, inventory control and analysis and power of attorney. The Piccadilly operation seated one hundred ten (110) people and when Joe left to manage Holden Hills, average weekly sales were in excess of $10,000.

At Holden Hills Country Club, Joe's responsibilities as general manager included direct control of golf operation, including pro-shop and greens departments; banquet operation, both food and liquor; restaurant operation, both food and liquor ordering; inventory and control and analysis; hiring and firing of all personnel; and all advertising and promotion. At the time Joe took over the job as manager, the downstairs restaurant at the Club had been closed down. Joe converted it from a dining operation to a pub/styled operation similar to Piccadilly's and by August, weekly sales reached a high of $7,400. This fact convinced Joe of the marketability of the pub concept.

Ed Marrone, like Joe, grew up and participated in the operation of the Wachusett Country Club. Ed eventually struck out on his own and became a food salesman, selling directly to restaurants. Because of the scope of Joe's duties at Holden Hills, he recruited Ed to assume the job of manager of the pub operation at the club. Ed's duties as manager included inventory control and analysis, hiring and firing of personnel, and ordering of all food and beverage. Ed is currently manager of Shannon's I, a restaurant in Auburn, Massachusetts and is in charge of the entire operation.

Ed's duties at Marrone Enterprises will be those of head bartender and assistant manager. His job will include assisting in inventory control and analysis, hiring and firing of personnel, and ordering food and liquor. Ed will be directly responsible to Joe with all other employees responsible to Joe and Ed.

Salaries will consist of $400.00 per week for Joe and $225.00 for Ed, whose salary will be supplemented by bartending tips, which are expected to be between $120–$200 weekly.

Assisting Joe and Ed in operational and organizational aspects at the business will be Timothy J. Harrington, C.P.A. and Thomas Sullivan, Esq. Mr. Harrington has been a practicing Certified Public Accountant for seven (7) years and has a number of area restaurants as accounts. Mr. Sullivan has been practicing law for six (6 years) and also runs an independent insurance company making him a valuable advisor.

To assist Marrone Enterprises, Inc. in overall direction and expansion, a Board of Directors has been formed and a list of members and their background can be found in the appendix.

Personnel

The personnel in a service oriented business can be critical factors in the eventual success or failure of the business. Being acutely aware of this fact, Mr. Marrone has had many years of experience in the hiring of the type of personnel needed for Marrone Enterprises, Inc. As a matter of fact, many of his former employees at the Piccadilly and Holden Hills are anxious to assist him in this new venture giving him a nucleus of well-trained experienced help.

The majority of employees needed by Marrone Enterprises, Inc. will be part-time. Today's economy forces most people to work a second, part-time job and, therefore, there is an abundance of potential employees. Because of the part-time help and salaries, benefits and overtime can be kept to a bare minimum.

Attached is an employee work schedule for the different phases of business.

Summary

Marrone Enterprises, Inc. is being formed for the purpose of establishing a series of restaurant/pubs featuring a unique warm atmosphere, a limited sandwich/seafood menu, large drinks, and quality service. The over-sized drinks, moderately priced food menu, and the weeknight food "specials" will result in a large volume of business. Experience has shown that sales will run approximately 55 percent liquor to 45 percent food, making the sales profitable due to the large mark-up employed in liquor sales.

The restaurant will be open from 11:30 A.M. until 1:00 A.M. Monday through Saturday. Food will be served from 11:30 A.M. until midnight.

Careful analysis of the potential market shows an unfilled demand for a restaurant/pub operation. There is a particularly sharp demand for a luncheon and after work cocktail hour. There are over two thousand (2,000) business people within walking distance and the only alternative to the proposed new restaurant/pub is a local diner. There is also a definite void in the area for a restaurant that shoppers and theatre goers can visit, before or after their excursions, for a light sandwich and drinks. This is a void that Marrone Enterprises, Inc. seeks to fill. Prices, $1.25–$4.95, will be moderate. Marrone Enterprises will attract business initially through an advertising and promotional campaign, reputation and the owner's following, and eventually word of mouth.

The only direct competition will come from the following restaurants during lunches. The Chadwick Diner, located inside the surrounding industrial complex, caters more to the blue collar worker rather than the white collar that Marrone Enterprises will cater to. Maxwell's located in Lincoln Square, caters to business people but is too expensive for most to visit with any frequency. Nick's Grille located at Chadwick Square, a popular luncheon spot mainly because it is the only one in the area, is presently in the process of being sold. In the evenings, the only direct competition would be Pickwick's Pub located on Main Street in downtown Worcester. Pickwick's format is quite similar and is presently undergoing expansion because demand is so great. Marrone Enterprises will secure its share of the market by offering an attractive, comfortable atmosphere, moderate more affordable prices, and greater dollar value.

The location of Marrone Enterprises' first unit is one of its strongest assets. it is situated in an area with a heavy concentration of industry and commerce. One half mile to the left is downtown Worcester and soon to be new Civic Center. One half mile to the right is the Gold Star Boulevard Industrial Complex, as well as numerous commercial businesses and shopping areas. The D.P.W.'s most recent surveys indicate that approximately 29,500 cars pass directly in front of the location daily. The building, a designated historical monument, will not only help create the atmosphere for the restaurant with its natural brick and beams, but is also being renovated for the purpose of being an office-retail complex. Parking is extremely ample with 93 spots plus on-street parking available before 5 P.M. and over 500 spots available after 5 P.M.

Management will also be a strong suit of Marrone Enterprises. Joe Marrone will be the manager and brings with him a lifetime of restaurant experience. Joe's family owned the Wachusett Country Club in West Boylston and Joe learned all facets of the business while growing up and eventually assisting in the running of the business. From there Joe helped start and managed for five (5) years the Piccadilly Pub in Westboro, an enormously successful restaurant/pub very similar to the intended operations of Marrone Enterprises. Joe then left the Piccadilly for the challenge of becoming general manager of the Holden Hills Country Club in Holden, Massachusetts. Joe was very successful in turning around what had been a negative business. One of the major factors in the turnaround of that business was the Pub Room Restaurant he created in the downstairs dining area of the club.

Assisting Joe in the running of Marrone Enterprises will be his brother Ed Marrone. Ed, like Joe, grew up working at the Wachusett Country Club and after a stint as a food salesman managed the pub operations for Joe at Holden Hills.

The management team of Marrone Enterprises will also consist of Timothy J. Harrington, C.P.A., an experienced restaurant accountant, and Thomas Sullivan, Esq. and insurance broker who will assist in legal and insurance matters. In order to give objective analysis and to assist with business and expansion planning, Marrone Enterprises has formed a Board of Directors, made up of local businessmen with varied but related business backgrounds.

The majority of the personnel at Marrone Enterprises will be primarily part-time. The personnel needs will be dictated by business volume. Joe Marrone will be bringing in many of his former employees from the Piccadilly and Holden Hills, giving him a strong nucleus of well trained, dedicated employees.

EMPLOYEE NEEDS FOR BUSINESS START UP
SIX DAY WEEK

Position	Hours		Cost	Total
		DAY SHIFT		
Cook	10 a.m.– 4 p.m.	$3.50	$3.50	$126.00
Dishwasher	10 a.m.– 2 p.m.		2.90	69.00
Waitress	11 a.m.– 5 p.m.		1.74	62.64
Waitress	11 a.m.– 3 p.m.		1.74	41.76
Bartender	11 a.m.– 4 p.m.		3.00	90.00
Manager	9 a.m.–11 p.m.		Salary	400.00
		NIGHT SHIFT		
Cook	5 p.m.–12 p.m.		$3.50	$147.00
Dishwasher	7 p.m.–11 p.m.		2.90	69.60
Waitress	5 p.m.–11 p.m.		1.74	62.62
Waitress	7 p.m.– 1 a.m.		1.74	62.64
Bartender	4 p.m.– 1 a.m.		Salary	225.00
				$1356.28

EMPLOYEE NEEDS FOR INTERMEDIATE BUSINESS
SIX DAY WEEK

Position	Hours	Cost	Total
		DAY SHIFT	
Cook	9 a.m.–5 p.m.	$3.50	$168.00
Dishwasher	9 a.m.–3 p.m.	2.90	104.40
Waitress	11 a.m.–5 p.m.	1.74	62.64
Waitress	11 a.m.–3 p.m.	1.74	41.76
Waitress	11 a.m.–3 p.m.	1.74	41.76
Bartender	11 a.m.–4 p.m.	3.00	90.00
Manager	9 a.m.–	Salary	400.00
		NIGHT SHIFT	
Cook	5 p.m.–12 p.m.	3.50	147.00
Dishwasher	7 p.m.– 1 a.m.	2.90	104.40
Waitress	5 p.m.–11 p.m.	1.74	62.64
Waitress	7 p.m.– 1 a.m.	1.74	62.64
Waitress	7 p.m.– 1 a.m.	1.74	62.64
Bartender	4 p.m.– 1 a.m.	Salary	225.00
			$1572.88

EMPLOYEES FOR PEAK BUSINESS
SIX DAY WEEK

Position	Hours	Cost	Total
		DAY SHIFT	
Cook	9 a.m.–5 p.m.	$3.50	$168.00
Asst. cook	11 a.m.–2 p.m.	3.00	54.00
Dishwasher	9 a.m.–5 p.m.	2.90	99.20
Waitress	11 a.m.–5 p.m.	1.74	62.64
Waitress	11 a.m.–5 p.m.	1.74	62.64
Waitress	11 a.m.–3 p.m.	1.74	41.76
Bartender	11 a.m.–6 p.m.	3.00	126.00
Manager	9 a.m.–	Salary	400.00
		NIGHT SHIFT	
Cook	5 p.m.–12 p.m.	3.50	147.00
Asst. cook	7 p.m.–11 p.m.	3.00	48.00
Dishwasher	5 p.m.– 1 a.m.	2.90	99.20
Waitress	5 p.m.– 1 a.m.	1.74	83.52
Waitress	5 p.m.– 1 a.m.	1.74	83.52
Waitress	5 p.m.–12 p.m.	1.74	73.08
Bartender	6 p.m.– 1 a.m.	Salary	225.00
Manager	8 p.m.– 2 a.m.	Salary	250.00
			$2023.56

MARRONE ENTERPRISES RESTAURANT PROJECTED CASH FLOW

	FIRST YEAR					
	OCTOBER	NOVEMBER	DECEMBER	JANUARY	FEBRUARY	MARCH
Receipts:						
From Operations	$ 12,000	$ 14,000	$ 16,000	$ 18,000	$ 20,000	$ 22,000
Loan Proceeds	100,000	—	—	—	—	—
Contributed Capital	40,000	—	—	—	—	—
Total Cash Available	$152,000	$ 14,000	$ 16,000	$ 18,000	$ 20,000	$ 22,000
Disbursements:						
Purchases, Operating Expenses (Less Depreciation)	11,472	17,044	15,848	19,601	21,233	22,865
Equipment Purchases and Leasehold Improvements	110,000	—	—	—	—	—
Inventory Start-Ups	5,000	—	—	—	—	—
Opening Promotion	2,000	—	—	—	—	—
Prepaid Expenses	2,500	—	—	—	—	—
Deposits on Rent and Utilities	2,000	—	—	—	—	—
Debt Repayment	765	775	785	795	805	815
Total Disbursements	$133,737	$ 17,819	$ 16,633	$ 20,396	$ 22,038	$ 23,680
Cash Flow	$ 18,263	$ (3,819)	$ (633)	$ (2,396)	$ (2,038)	$ 1,680)
Cumulative Cash	$ 18,263	$ 14,444	$ 13,811	$ 11,415	$ 9,377	$ 7,697

232

MARRONE ENTERPRISES RESTAURANT PROJECTED CASH FLOW (Continued)

| | FIRST YEAR | | | | | | |
	APRIL	MAY	JUNE	JULY	AUGUST	SEPTEMBER	TOTALS
Receipts:							
From Operations	$ 24,000	$ 26,000	$ 28,000	$ 30,000	$ 32,000	$ 34,000	$276,000
Loan Proceeds	—	—	—	—	—	—	100,000
Contributed Capital	—	—	—	—	—	—	40,000
	$ 24,000	$ 26,000	$ 28,000	$ 30,000	$ 32,000	$ 34,000	$416,000
Disbursements:							
Purchases, Operating Expenses (Less Depreciation)	23,997	25,629	27,261	28,209	30,105	30,105	273,369
Equipment Purchases and Leasehold Improvements	—	—	—	—	—	—	110,000
Inventory Start-ups	—	—	—	—	—	—	5,000
Opening Promotion	—	—	—	—	—	—	2,000
Prepaid Expenses	—	—	—	—	—	—	2,500
Deposits on Rent and Utilities	—	—	—	—	—	—	2,000
Debt Repayment	825	835	845	855	865	875	9,840
Total Disbursements	$ 24,822	$ 26,464	$ 28,106	$ 29,064	$ 30,970	$ 30,980	$404,709
Cash Flow	$ (822)	$ (464))	$ (106)	$ 936	$ 1,030	$ 3,020	$ 11,291
Cumulative Cash	$ 18,263	$ 6,411	$ 6,305	$ 7,241	$ 8,271	$ 11,291	$ 11,291

MARRONE ENTERPRISES PROJECTED CASH FLOW

	FIRST QUARTER	SECOND YEAR SECOND QUARTER	THIRD QUARTER	FOURTH QUARTER	YEAR TO DATE
Receipts					
From Operations	$105,000	$115,000	$120,000	$125,000	$465,000
Loan Proceeds	—	—	—	—	—
Contributed Capital	—	—	—	—	—
Total Cash Available	$105,000	$115,000	$120,000	$125,000	$465,000
Disbursements					
Purchases and Operating Expenses	95,988	97,496	99,558	103,835	396,877
Equipment Purchases	2,000	—	—	—	2,000
Debt Repayment	2,700	2,800	2,900	3,000	11,400
Total Disbursements	$100,688	$100,296	$102,458	$106,835	$410,277
Cash Flow	$ 4,312	$ 14,704	$ 17,542	$ 18,165	$ 54,723
Cumulative Cash	$ 15,603	$ 30,307	$ 47,849	$ 66,014	

MARRONE ENTERPRISES PROJECTED CASH FLOW

	FIRST QUARTER	THIRD YEAR SECOND QUARTER	THIRD QUARTER	FOURTH QUARTER	YEAR TO DATE
Receipts					
From Operations	$127,500	$130,000	$132,500	$135,000	$525,000
Loan Proceeds	—	—	—	—	—
Contributed Capital					
Total Cash Available	$127,500	$130,000	$132,500	$135,000	$525,000
Disbursements					
Purchases and Operating Expenses	105,760	107,031	108,080	109,127	429,998
Equipment Purchases	5,000	—	—	—	5,000
Debt Repayment	3,150	3,300	3,450	3,600	13,500
Total Disbursements	$113,910	$110,331	$111,530	$112,727	$448,498
Cash Flow	$ 13,590	$ 19,669	$ 20,970	$ 22,273	$ 76,502
Cumulative Cash	$ 79,604	$ 99,273	$120,243	$142,516	

MARRONE ENTERPRISES RESTAURANT PROJECTED INCOME & EXPENSES

		FIRST YEAR					
		OCTOBER	NOVEMBER	DECEMBER	JANUARY	FEBRUARY	MARCH
Income							
Sales—Beverage	55%	$ 6,600	$ 7,700	$ 8,800	$ 9,900	$ 11,000	$ 12,100
Food	45%	5,400	6,300	7,200	8,100	9,000	9,900
Total Sales		12,000	14,000	16,000	18,000	20,000	22,000
Cost of Sales							
Purchases—Beverage	25%	1,650	1,925	2,200	2,475	2,750	3,025
Food	48%	2,592	3,024	3,456	3,888	4,320	4,752
Total Cost of Sales		4,242	4,949	5,656	6,363	7,070	7,777
Gross Profit from Sales	64.65%	7,758	9,051	10,344	11,637	12,930	14,223
Operating Expenses							
Administration		700	700	700	700	700	700
Advertising		800	800	800	800	800	800
Depreciation		833	833	833	833	833	833
Discount on Charge Sales		90	105	120	135	150	165
Employee Benefit		778	798	912	1,026	1,140	1,254
Interest		1,000	990	980	970	960	950
Insurance, Licenses & Fees	4%	480	560	640	720	800	880
Maintenance		200	200	200	200	200	200
Office	2%	240	280	320	360	400	440
Payroll		5,090	5,190	5,760	6,330	6,900	7,470
Rent		1,160	1,160	1,160	1,160	1,160	1,160
Supplies	2.5%	300	350	400	450	500	550
Utilities	3.3%	400	462	528	594	660	726
Promotion		1,000	500	500	500	500	500
Total Operating Expenses		13,071	12,928	13,853	14,778	15,703	16,628
Net Profit (Loss) Before Income Taxes		$ (5,313)	$ (3,877)	$ (3,509)	$ (3,141)	$ (2,733)	$ (2,405)

MARRONE ENTERPRISES RESTAURANT PROJECTED INCOME AND EXPENSES (Continued)

| | | FIRST YEAR | | | | | | TOTAL FOR |
		APRIL	MAY	JUNE	JULY	AUGUST	SEPTEMBER	THE YEAR
Income								
Sales—Beverage	55%	$ 13,200	$ 14,300	$ 15,400	$ 16,500	$ 17,600	$ 18,700	$151,800
Food	45%	10,800	11,700	12,600	13,500	14,400	15,300	124,200
Total Sales		24,000	26,000	28,000	30,000	32,000	34,000	276,000
Cost of Sales								
Purchases—Beverage	25%	3,300	3,575	3,850	4,125	4,400	4,675	37,950
Food	48%	5,184	5,616	6,048	6,480	6,912	7,344	59,616
Total Cost of Sales		8,484	9,191	9,898	10,605	11,312	12,019	97,566
Gross Profit from Sales	64.65%	15,516	16,809	18,102	19,395	20,688	21,981	178,434
Operating Expenses								
Administration		700	700	700	700	700	700	8,400
Advertising		800	800	800	800	800	800	9,600
Depreciation		833	833	833	833	833	833	9,996
Discount on Charge Sales		180	195	210	225	240	255	2,070
Employee Benefit		1,368	1,482	1,596	1,596	1,596	1,596	15,142
Interest		940	930	920	910	900	890	11,340
Insurance, Licenses & Fees	4%	960	1,040	1,120	1,200	1,280	1,360	11,040
Maintenance		200	200	200	200	200	200	2,400
Office	2%	480	520	560	600	640	680	5,520
Payroll		8,040	8,610	9,180	9,180	9,180	9,110	90,110
Rent		1,160	1,160	1,160	1,160	1,160	1,160	13,920
Supplies	2.5%	600	650	700	750	800	850	6,900
Utilities	3.3%	792	858	924	990	1,056	1,122	9,112
Promotion		—	—	—	—	—	—	3,500
Total Operating Expenses		17,053	17,978	18,903	19,144	19,385	19,626	199,050
Net Profit (Loss) Before Income Taxes		$ (1,537)	$ (1,169)	$ (801)	$ 251	$ 1,303	$ 2,355	$ (20,616)

MARRONE ENTERPRISES RESTAURANT PROJECTED INCOME & EXPENSES

		FIRST QUARTER	SECOND YEAR SECOND QUARTER	THIRD QUARTER	FOURTH QUARTER	YEAR TO DATE
Income						
Sales—Beverage	55%	$ 57,750	$ 63,250	$ 66,000	$ 68,750	$255,750
Food	45%	47,250	51,750	54,000	56,250	209,250
Total Sales		105,000	115,000	120,000	125,000	465,000
Cost of Sales						
Purchases—Beverage	25%	14,438	13,813	16,500	16,963	61,714
Food	48%	22,680	24,840	25,920	27,000	100,400
Total Cost of Sales		37,118	38,653	42,420	43,963	162,154
Gross Profit from Sales		67,882	76,347	77,580	81,037	302,846
Operating Expenses						
Administration		2,200	2,200	2,200	2,200	8,800
Advertising		2,500	2,500	2,500	2,500	10,000
Depreciation		2,500	2,500	2,500	2,500	10,000
Discount on Charge Sales		788	863	900	938	3,489
Employee Benefit		5,170	5,170	5,170	5,170	20,680
Interest		2,595	2,495	2,395	2,295	9,780
Insurance, Licenses & Fees 4%		4,200	4,600	4,800	5,000	18,600
Maintenance		650	650	650	650	2,600
Office	2%	2,100	2,300	2,400	2,500	9,300
Payroll		29,450	29,450	29,450	29,450	117,800
Rent		3,480	3,480	3,480	3,480	13,920
Supplies	2.5%	2,625	2,875	3,000	3,125	11,625
Utilities	3.3%	3,465	3,795	3,960	4,125	15,345
Total Operating Expenses		61,723	62,878	63,405	63,933	251,939
*Net Profit Become Income Taxes***		6,159	13,469	14,175	17,104	50,907

MARRONE ENTERPRISES RESTAURANT PROJECTED INCOME AND EXPENSES

THIRD YEAR

	%	FIRST QUARTER	SECOND QUARTER	THIRD QUARTER	FOURTH QUARTER	YEAR TO DATE
Income						
Sales—Beverage	55%	$ 70,125	$ 71,500	$ 72,875	$ 74,250	$288,750
Food	45%	57,375	58,500	59,625	60,750	236,250
Total Sales		127,500	130,000	132,500	135,000	525,000
Cost of Sales						
Purchases—Beverage	25%	17,531	17,875	18,219	18,563	72,188
Food	48%	27,540	28,080	28,620	29,160	113,400
Total Cost of Sales		45,071	45,955	46,839	47,723	185,588
Gross Profit from Sales		82,429	84,045	85,661	87,277	339,412
Operating Expenses						
Administration		2,200	2,200	2,200	2,200	8,800
Advertising		2,600	2,600	2,600	2,800	10,400
Depreciation		2,500	2,500	2,500	2,500	10,000
Discount on Charge Sales		956	975	994	1,013	3,938
Employee Benefit		5,580	5,580	5,580	5,580	22,320
Interest		2,145	1,995	1,845	1,695	7,680
Insurance, Licenses & Fees	4%	5,100	5,200	5,300	5,400	21,000
Maintenance		690	690	690	690	2,760
Office	2%	2,550	2,600	2,650	2,700	10,500
Payroll		29,100	29,100	29,100	29,100	116,400
Rent		3,480	3,480	3,480	3,480	13,920
Supplies	2.5%	3,188	3,250	3,313	3,375	13,126
Utilities	3.3%	4,208	4,290	4,373	4,455	17,326
Total Operating Expenses		64,297	64,460	64,625	64,788	258,170
Net Profit Before Income Taxes*		18,132	19,585	21,036	22,489	81,242

*No provision for income taxes has been made during the first and second year due to the availability of investment tax credit and operating loss carryover. The provision at the end of the third year would be $12,000.

MARRONE ENTERPRISES RESTAURANT
PROJECTED INCOME AND EXPENSES
FOURTH YEAR

Sales		
Beverage 55%		$429,000
Food 45%		351,000
Total Sales		$780,000
Cost of Sales		
Purchases—Beverage 25%		107,250
Food 48%		168,480
Total Cost of Sales		$275,730
Gross Profit from Sales		504,270
Operating Expenses		308,170
Profit Before Income Taxes		$196,100
Income Tax Provision		77,855
Net Income After Taxes		$118,245

MARRONE ENTERPRISES
PROJECTED INCOME AND EXPENSES
FIFTH YEAR

Sales		
Beverage 55%		$445,500
Food 45%		364,500
Total Sales		$810,000
Cost of Sales		
Purchases—Beverage 25%		111,375
Food 48%		174,960
Total Cost of Sales		$286,335
Gross Profit Sales		523,655
Operating Expenses		314,760
Profit Before Income Taxes		$208,905
Income Tax Provision		82,355
Net Income After Taxes		$126,500

MARRONE ENTERPRISES PROJECTED INCOME AND EXPENSES
SIXTH YEAR

Sales		
Beverage 55%		$467,500
Food 45%		382,500
Total Sales		$850,000
Cost of Sales		
Purchases—Beverage 25%		116,875
Food 45%		172,125
Total Cost of Sales		$289,000
Gross Profit Sales		561,000

Operating Expenses	325,760
Profit Before Income Tax Provision	$235,240
Income Tax Provision	105,200
Net Income After Taxes	$130,040

MARRONE ENTERPRISES PROJECTED INCOME AND EXPENSES
SEVENTH YEAR

Sales		
Beverage 55%		$484,000
Food	45%	396,000
Total Sales		$880,000
Cost of Sales		
Purchases—Beverage 25%		121,000
Food	45%	178,200
Total Cost of Sales		$299,200
Gross Profit Sales		580,800
Operating Expenses		332,500
Profit Before Income Taxes		$248,300
Income Tax Provision		112,000
Net Income After Taxes		$136,300

MARRONE ENTERPRISES PROJECTED ONE MONTH BALANCE SHEET

OCTOBER 1979

ASSETS

Cash	$ 18,263	
Inventory	5,000	
Prepaid Expenses	4,500	
Total Current Assets		$ 27,763
Equipment	$110,000	
Accumulated Depreciation	(833)	
Net Equipment		109,167
Deposits		2,000
Total Assets		$138,930

LIABILITIES AND EQUITY

Accounts Payable	$ 5,008	
Note Payable	99,235	
Total Liabilities		$104,243
Contributed Capital	$ 40,000	
Deficit	(5,313)	
		34,687
Total Liabilities and Stockholders' Equity		$138,930

MARRONE ENTERPRISES PROJECTED ONE YEAR BALANCE SHEET

SEPTEMBER 30, 1980

ASSETS

Cash	$ 11,291	
Inventory	5,000	
Prepaid Expenses	4,500	
Total Current Assets		$ 20,791
Equipment	$110,000	
Accumulated Depreciation	(9,996)	
Net Property and Equipment		100,004
Deposits		2,000
Total Assets		$122,795

LIABILITIES AND EQUITY

Accounts Payable	$ 13,251	
Note Payable	90,160	
Total Liabilities		$103,411
Contributed Capital	$ 40,000	
Deficit	(20,616)	
		19,384
Total Liabilities and Stockholders' Equity		$122,795

MARRONE ENTERPRISES PROJECTED TWO YEAR BALANCE SHEET

SEPTEMBER 30, 1981

ASSETS

Cash	$ 66,014	
Inventory	6,000	
Prepaid Expenses	5,000	
Total Current Assets		$77,014
Equipment	$112,000	
Accumulated Depreciation	(19,992)	
Net Equipment		92,008
Deposits		2,000
Total Assets		$171,022

LIABILITIES AND EQUITY

Accounts Payable	$ 21,971	
Notes Payable	78,760	
Total Liabilities		$100,731
Contributed Capital	$ 40,000	
Retained Earnings	30,291	

	70,291
Total Liabilities and Equity	$171,022

MARRONE ENTERPRISES PROJECTED THIRD YEAR BALANCE SHEET

ASSETS

Cash	$142,516	
Inventory	7,500	
Prepaid Expenses	5,000	
Total Current Assets		$155,016
Equipment	$117,000	
Accumulated Depreciation	(29,992)	
Net Equipment		87,008
Deposits		2,000
Total Assets		$244,024

LIABILITIES AND EQUITY

Accounts Payable	$ 27,231	
Accrued Income Taxes	12,000	
Notes Payable	65,260	
Total Liabilities		$104,491
Contributed Capital	$ 40,000	
Retained Earnings	99,533	
		139,533
Total Liabilities and Equity		$244,024

SALES COMPUTATION
Turnover based on 150 seats @ $3.50 per person

		Mon	Tues	Wed	Thurs	Fri	Sat
First Month	Lunch	30%/$160	30%/$160	30%/$160	30%/$160	100%/$525	30%/$160
	Evening	30%/$160	30%/$160	30%/$160	30%/$160	100%/$525	100%/$525
	Weekly Sales=$3015						
		Mon	Tues	Wed	Thurs	Fri	Sat
Fourth Month	Lunch	50%/$260	50%/$260	50%/$260	50%/$260	100%/$525	50%/$260
	Evening	50%/$260	50%/$260	75%/$390	75%/$390	100%/$525	100%/$525
	Weekly Sales=$4185						
		Mon	Tues	Wed	Thurs	Fri	Sat
Eighth Month	Lunch	75%/$390	75%/$390	75%/$390	75%/$390	150%/$790	75%/$390
	Evening	75%/$390	75%/$390	75%/$390	75%/$390	200%/$1050	150%/$790
	Weekly Sales=$6100						
		Mon	Tues	Wed	Thurs	Fri	Sat
Twelfth Month	Lunch	75%/$390	100%/$525	100%/$525	100%/$525	150%/$790	100%/$525
	Evening	100%/$525	100%/$525	150%/$790	150%/$790	200%/$1050	200%/$1050
	Weekly Sales=$8000						

RÉSUMÉ

PERSONAL

Name: Joseph Marrone
Address: Mark Circle—Holden, Massachusetts 01520
Marital Status: Married
Date of Birth: 29 October 1949
Place of Birth: Worcester, Massachusetts

EDUCATION

High School: St. John's High School   1963–1967 (graduated)
Shrewsbury, Massachusetts

College: Worcester Junior College   1967–1969 (A.M. degree)
Worcester, Massachusetts

Biscayne College   1969–1971 (B.A. degree)
North Miami, Florida

EXPERIENCE

Company: Holden Hills Country Club—Holden, Massachusetts
Employed: February 1978 to Present
Title: General Manager
Duties: Responsible for entire operation, inclusive of golf course, greens, banquet and restaurant. Handle all advertising. Responsible for purchase of all food and beverage, inventory control and analyses.

Company: Piccadilly Pub—Westboro, Massachusetts
Employed: July 1973—February 1978
Title: Manager
Duties: Shared responsibility of running the business with the proprietor. He worked days and I worked evenings. Responsible for food and beverage purchases. Responsible for the hiring of personnel and related problems, inventory control and was given power of attorney.

Company: Wachusett Country Club—West Boylston, Massachusetts
Employed: September 1971—March 1972
Title: Assistant Manager
Duties: Acquired basic knowledge and skills of all facets of the restaurant business while assisting the manager, from bartending to ordering as well as gaining experience in inventory control.

Company: Pate's Charcoal Pit—Chatham, Massachusetts
Employed: Summers—1970 and 1971
Title: Waiter
Duties: Waiting on tables, customer contact and maintaining relaxed pleasant atmosphere.

RÉSUMÉ

PERSONAL

Name:	Edward J. Marrone
Address:	5 Oakwood Drive, Sterling Junction, Massachusetts 01565
Marital Status:	Married
Date of Birth:	February 3, 1951
Place of Birth:	Worcester, Massachusetts

EDUCATION

High School: West Boylston Junior-Senior High School
West Boylston, Massachusetts (1965–1969—Graduated)

EXPERIENCE

Company:	Shannon's I—Restaurant, Auburn, Massachusetts
Employed:	June 1, 1979 to present
Title:	Manager
Duties:	Responsible for entire operation. Hiring of personnel and related problems. Responsible for food and beverage purchases, inventory control and analysis.

Company:	Holden Hills Country Club, Holden, Massachusetts
Employed:	April/1978—March, 1979
Title:	Pub Manager
Duties:	Responsible for hiring personnel, purchasing of food and beverage, inventory control and analysis.

CITY OF WORCESTER
OFFICE OF THE
LICENSE COMMISSION
CITY HALL 01608

May 10, 1979

Mr. Joseph M. Marrone, Mgr.
33 Mark Circle
Holden, Ma. 01520

Dear Mr. Marrone: Re: Common Victualer All Alcoholic Bev-
                              erages license at Marrone Enter-
                              prises, Inc., 104-110 Grove St.

      The License Commission unanimously voted today to grant you a

Common Victualer All Alcoholic Beverages license at the above address

subject to approvals from the Building and Health Departments and also

verification of the address.

Very truly yours,

Joseph W. Riordan

Joseph W. Riordan
Chairman
Board of License Commission

bcv

Copy to: Alcoholic Beverages Control Commission
          Richard G. Crotty, Esq.

BOARD OF DIRECTORS

JOSEPH M. MARRONE

Graduate of Biscayne College. Ten years experience in restaurant finance and management. President and Treasurer of Marrone Enterprises, Inc.

ROBERT PIRANI

Graduate Niagra University. B.S. Economics. Master Electrician. President and Treasurer of Joseph G. Pirani Inc., electrical contractors. Gross sales $2–$3 million.

JOHN K. MARRONE

Senior Production Control Specialist for Norton Co. Member American Production and Inventory Control Society, Mass. Real Estate Broker.

ROBERT J. MAHER

Graduate Holy Cross College, B.S. Economics. Masters Degree in Hospital Administration from St. Louis University. Assistant Administrator for St. Vincent's Hospital, Worchester, Mass.

EDWARD H. GRANT

Graduate Dartmouth, Tuck Graduate School of Business. President Edward H. Grant Co., Manufacturers Agents. Gross sales $8 million dollars.

EDWARD J. MARRONE

Secretary and working stockholder of Marrone Enterprises. Three years experience in restaurant sales and management.

CAPITAL EXPENSES

Air Condition/Heating Unit (bid enclosed)	$14,000
Plumbing (bid enclosed)	12,500
Wiring-electrical (bid enclosed)	4,500
Equipment—Kitchen and Bar (breakdown enclosed)	37,764
Glassware, China, Utensils, etc.	5,000
Table and Chairs	10,000

Carpeting	10,000
Outside Awning	1,200
Interior Decor (window shutters, mirrors etc.)	5,000
Office Furniture	3,000
Light Fixtures	2,000
Misc. Expenses and Cost Overruns	5,000
	$110,964

THIS INDENTURE, made this   day of   in the year one thousand
nine hundred and

Lessor, and   Parker Apartment Complex

Lessee

WITNESSETH: That the Lessor doth demise and Lease unto the Lessee the Premises duly described as follows:

Approximately 4639 square feet of space located at 106 Grove Street, Worcester, Massachusetts.

To have and to hold the above described premises for the period of   five (5) years
        Begining the   day of
           A. D., 19   and this lease shall continue in full force and effect thereafter until the
                                    day of
           A. D., 19
          Yielding and Paying as rent, the sum of $13,917   dollars annually, in equal monthly
payments of $1,159.75   dollars in advance, on the 1st   of each and every month   Hereafter,
during said term; the first payment thereof to be made on the   1st   day of   now ensuing.

       The Lessee in addition to the rent hereinbefore mentioned hereby agrees to pay to the Lessor, during the term of this Lease and any extensions or renewals thereof; that portion of any increase in taxes assessed and levied against the building of which the leased premises is a part over the tax assessed for the year   . For the purposes of this Corporation, the Lessee pays only that portion of the increases which the leased premises bears to the total area in the building of which the leased premises is a part. The Lessee further agrees to pay such tax to the Lessor within thirty (30) days after written notice from the Lessor of the amount due. Tax bills shall be sufficient evidence of the amount of said tax and said amounts shall be binding upon all parties for the calculations as described above.

The Lessee shall have the option to extend this lease for a further term of   years by notice in writing ninety (90) days prior to the expiration of the initial term of this lease to the Lessor. All terms of this lease shall remain in full force or effect for such further term, excepting the rent reserved herein, which shall be subject to negotiation by the parties.

No alteration, addition or improvement to the leased premises shall be made by the Lessee without the Lessor's written consent.* Any such alteration, addition or improvement after such consent has been given shall be at the sole expense of the Lessee and at the Lessor's option upon expiration or other sooner termination of this lease shall become the property of the Lessor. It is agreed that such consent shall not be unreasonably withheld.   *excepting those stated in Amendment #.

The Lessee further agrees that all merchandise, furniture, and personal property of any kind and description which is placed on said premises, and belonging to the Lessee during the continuance of this lease, is to be at the risk and hazard of the Lessee and that if the whole or any part thereof shall be destroyed or damaged by fire, water or otherwise, or by the use or abuse of water, or by leaking or bursting pipes, or in any other way or manner, no part of said loss or damage is to be charged to or be borne by the Lessor, except if caused by the Lessor's negligence.

The Lessee, upon paying the basic rent and all additional rent and other charges herein provided for, and performing all the other terms of this lease, shall quietly have and enjoy the leased premises during ther term of this lease, subject however, to the reservations and conditions of this lease.

The Lessee by taking possession of the leased premises shall be conclusive evidence that the Lessee accepts the same "as is" and that the Lessor nor it's agents made no representations, statements, warranties, express or implied, except those specifically set forth in the provisions of this lease.

The Lessor shall furnish at it's sole expense reasonable heat, needed for the operation of a restaurant-tavern operation electricity, water, air conditioning, and janitorial service during the term of this lease extension or renewal thereof. The Lessor shall not be liable for failure to supply such utilities during the term of this lease or any interruption or deficiency thereof, due to any reason beyond the Lessor's control., but Lessor agrees to take any reasonable and prompt action to resume any interruption of service.

The Lessor shall furnish carpeting or other suitable floor covering, for the leased premises and further agrees to maintain and replace same when necessary, due to normal wear and tear.

The Lessor shall provide a parking area for the use of Lessee, his employees and clientele, to be used in common with other tenants and visitors of the building; and further will provide parking lot maintenance and snow removal.

The Lessee shall provide and install such carpet protection or protectors as may be necessary under desks, chairs, office equipment to protect against unnecessary wear and tear, and further the Lessee shall keep the demised premises in a clean and presentable condition at all times at the Lessee's sole expense.

The Lessor shall keep and maintain the common passway and common areas, and that damage or injury to others occurring thereon shall be the responsibility of the Lessor, except where such damage or injury is occasioned by the negligence of the Lessee. The Lessee shall be responsible for injuries and damages occurring within or on the premises herein demised, except where such injury or damage is occasioned by the negligence of the Lessor.

The Lessee, employees, servants or agents shall turn off or disconnect at the termination of the normal working hours, or cessation of work upon the demised premises all of the electric appliances, fixtures, air conditioners, water or other electrical equipment. The Lessor reserves the right to enter into the demised premises for the purpose of disconnecting or turning off the aforesaid; as the Lessee may have failed to act in accordance hereto. However, it is understood and agreed that certain appliances and fixtures necessary to the operation of a restaurant-tavern will remain on and their operation not disturbed.

The Lessee does not have the right to sublet or assign all or part of the demised premises, without express written approval and consent of the Lessor, and the Lessor agrees not to unreasonably withhold said approval.

The lease shall be subject and subordinate to any and all mortgages, deeds of trust and other instruments in the nature of a mortgage, now or at any time hereafter, a lien or liens on the property of which the leased premises are a part and the Lessee shall, when requested, promptly execute and deliver such written instruments as shall be necessary to show the subordination of this lease to said mortgage, deeds of trust or other such instruments in the nature of a mortgage.

The Lessee shall maintain with respect to the leased premises and the property, of which the leased premises are a part, comprehensive public liability insurance in the amount of $100,000   with property damage insurance limits of $25,000   in responsible companies qualified to do business in Massachusetts and in good standing therein insuring the Lessor as well as the Lessee against injury to persons or damage to property as provided.

The Lessee shall not permit any hole to be drilled and made in the stone or brickwork of said building, or erect or place any placard or sign on the outer wall of said building,*and will keep good with glass of the same kind or quality as that which may be broken, all the glass now or hereafter on the premises, unless the same shall be broken by fire, explosion, sonic boom, or other unavoidable casualty, the Lessee hereby acknowledges that the premises are now in good order and the glass now whole, and

*The Lessor agrees that such permission with regard to the drilling of holes and placing of signs shall not be unreasonably withheld in view of a restaurant-tavern opera

shall be at the expiration of the said term, or any extension thereof; the Lessee, employee, agents or servants shall not make or suffer any unlawful, improper, ~~noisy~~ or otherwise offensive use thereof, nor mar, deface, or alter any part of the leased premises; The Lessor, it's agents or servants may during the term of said lease, or any extension thereof, at reasonable times, enter to view said premises and examine the condition thereof, and make necessary repairs, and may show the said premises to others, and at any time within ninety (90) days next before expiration of said term, or extension of said term affix notice of letting; said Lessee, employees, agents and servants shall conform to said reasonable regulations as may from time to time be established by the Lessor, for the general convenience and comfort of the tenents and the welfare of said building; the Lessee at the expiration of said term or any extension thereof shall remove all goods and effects and those of all persons claiming under,   and will personally deliver and yield up to the Lessor the said premises, and all extensions and additions made to or upon the same in good repair, order and condition in all respects, except for reasonable use, wear and tear and damage by fire and other unavoidable casualty excepted, and that any notice from the Lessor relating to the demised premises, or the occupancy thereof, shall be deemed duly served if left at the demised premises addressed to the Lessee.

substantial
PROVIDED ALWAYS, that in the case the said premises, or any substantial part thereof, or the whole or any part of the building, of which they are a part, shall be taken for any street or public use or shall be damaged or destroyed by fire or other unavoidable casualty, or by the action of the City or other authorities, or shall receive any direct or consequential damage for which the Lessor or the Lessee shall be entitled to compensation by reason of anything lawfully done in pursuance of any public authority after the execution herein and before the expiration of said term, then this lease and the said term shall terminate at the election of the Lessor, and such election may be made in case of any such taking, notwithstanding the entire interest of the Lessor may have been divested by said taking, and if it shall not so elect, then in case of any such taking or destruction of, or damage to, the demised premises, rendering the same or any part thereof unfit for use and occupation, a just proportion of the rent herein before reserved according to the nature and extent of the injury sustained by the demised premises, shall be suspended or abated until the demised premises shall have been put in proper condition for use and occupation. 3

PROVIDED ALSO, and these presents are upon this condition, that if the Lessee shall neglect or fail to perform or observe any of the covenants contained in this lease, and on the part of said Lessee to performed and observed, or if said Lessee shall be declared bankrupt or insolvent according to law, or if any assignment shall be made of it's property for the benefit of creditors, then and in any of the said cases (notwithstanding any license or waiver of any prior breach of condition) the Lessor lawfully may immediately or at any time thereafter, and without demand or notice enter into or upon the said premises, or any part thereof in the name of the whole, and repossess the same as of it's former estate and except the Lessee and those claiming through or under it and remove it's effect, ~~(forcibly if necessary)~~ without being deemed guilty of any manner of trespass and without prejudice to any remedies which might otherwise be used for arrears of rent or preceeding breach of covenant and upon entry as aforesaid this lease shall terminate.

And it is agreed that in case of a termination action of the estate hereby created by an entry for breach of the condition herein contained, the Lessee shall indemnify the Lessor or it's heirs, successors or assigns, for all loss or damage which it may during the residue of the term above specified, suffered by reason of such termination, whether through decreased rent of said estate or otherwise; and it is also agreed substantial
that if the leased premises or any part thereof, shall be damaged by fire or other unavoidable casualty, so as to be thereby rendered unfit for use and casualty, so as to be thereby rendered unfit for use and occupation then and in such case the rent hereinbefore reserved, or a just and proportionate part thereof, according to the nature and extent of the injury sustained, shall be abated until the said premises shall have been duly repaired and restored by the Lessor or it's heirs, successors or assigns, or, at the election of the said Lessor or it's legal representatives, this lease may be terminated and ended. 5

It is also understood and agreed that

IN WITNESS WHEREOF, the LESSOR and LESSEE hereunto set their hands and seals.

_____   _____

LESSOR   LESSOR

_____   _____

LESSEE   LESSEE

1. It is agreed, however, that any regulations shall be reasonable and consistent with the customary use and operation of a restaurant-tavern operation.

2. The Lessor agrees to make such election and notification to the Lessee within ninety (90) days after the taking of said casualty loss.

3. In any case where there is no termination of the lease, the Lessor agrees to promptly repair and restore the premises to their former condition.

4. In any case where there is no termination of the lease, the Lessor agrees to promptly repair and restore the premises to their former condition.

5. The Lessor agrees to make such election and notification to the Lessee within ninety (90) days after the taking of said casualty loss.

AMENDMENT #1

FUEL ESCALATOR: The Lessee in addition to the rent hereinbefore mentioned hereby agrees to pay to the Lessor during the term of this Lease and any extensions and renewals thereof; that portion of any increase in the cost of fuel for heating purposes. The Lessee pays only that portion of the increases which the leased premises bears to the total area in the building which the leased premises is a part. Cost of fuel increases will be based as of the cost of fuel as of the beginning date of this Lease; any increases after this date will be so prorated, and hereby agrees to pay such bills within thirty (30) days upon receipt of same.

AMENDMENT #2

OPTION YEARS: The Lessee in addition to the rent hereinbefore mentioned hereby agrees to pay to the Lessor during the first three (3) years of the option years of this Lease which commences at the expiration date of the original term hereof, upon the same covenants and conditions as are contained in this Lease and in addition the Lessee agrees that a cost of living escalator will be applied as an increase in the monthly rental fee; that such fee will be reestablished by the percentage increase as announced by the National Cost of Living Council or its equal with base year being 1979. The Lessee further agrees that during the last two years of the five (5) year option period which commences eight (8) years after the expiration date of the original term hereof, upon the same covenants and conditions as are contained in this Lease excepting the rent reserved herein, which shall be subject to negotiation by the parties, such negotiations shall not be considered unreasonable and shall be relevant to the cost of operation and shall be considered a reasonable return for the space described within this Lease. If the aforementioned negotiation cannot be satisfactorily concluded ninety (90) days before the commencement of the next rental period, then they will submit to arbitration. The Lessor and Lessee agree at the commencement of the nineth (9th) year of the Lease that good faith negotiation will commence with regard to a third five (5) year option period.

AMENDMENT #3

Not to include initial rehabilitation and design for the purpose of this agreement.

1st of 2.

AMENDMENT #4

The Lessor agrees to the following:

a) That the "moat" located adjacent to the premises and
    between it and the sidewalk will either be covered
    or filled;

b) That it will provide and construct any necessary ramps
    in order to conform with City and State regulations
    with respect to the handicapped;

c) Provide evidence that the sprinkler system for the
    location is in good working order;

d) Remove exterior paint and signs from the exterior walls
    in an area outlined by the side walls of Lessee portion
    of the premises and the height of the building within
    that area, and

e) The Lessor agrees that all fixtures that are placed in
    the premises by the Lessee shall remain the property of
    the Lessee to the extent that any such fixtures may be
    removed and the premises remain in the same condition
    at the time of letting.

2nd of 2.

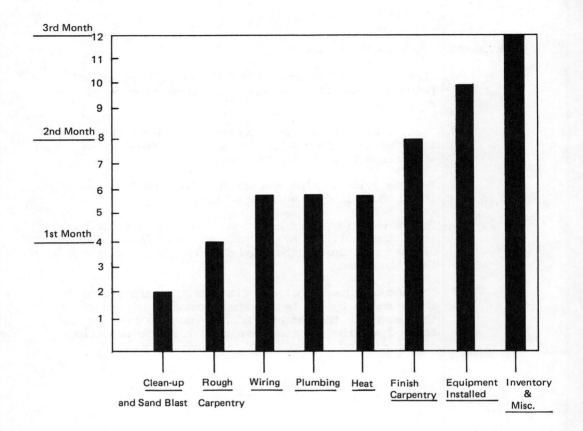

3rd Month

2nd Month

1st Month

Clean-up and Sand Blast   Rough Carpentry   Wiring   Plumbing   Heat   Finish Carpentry   Equipment Installed   Inventory & Misc.

WILLIAM G. WALKER, Sr.

PLUMBING	OIL BURNERS	HEATING
Master Plumber		Master Pipe Fitter
Lic. No. 8830	Lic. No. 12960	Lic. No. 2973
RURAL ROUTE #1		BOX 186 P.A.
TURKEY HILL TRAIL		RUTLAND, MASS. 01543

TEL. 886-4052

NAME Joseph Marone   DATE May 8, 1979

STREET Grove St.   PHONE

CITY Worcester,   STATE Mass.

WE HEREBY SUBMIT SPECIFICATIONS AND ESTIMATES FOR the installation of -

Mens Room - 1 Hanicapped Toilet, 1 Urinal, 2 Lavatories and 1 floor drain.
Womens Room - 1 Handicapped Toilet, 1 Elongated Toilet, 2 Lavatories,
and 1 Floor drain.
Kitchen - 1 2hole Pot Sink, Hookup Dishwasher, Ice Machine and Electric
Hot Water Tank.
Bar - 2 2hole Bar Sinks and hookup 2 Beer cooler drains.
To furnish all pipe and fittings for Drain and Water lines.
No Electrical work.

WE HEREBY PROPOSE TO FURNISH LABOR AND MATERIALS FOR THE SUM OF $12,500.00

Twelve thousand five hundred   DOLLARS WITH PAYMENT TO BE MADE AS FOLLOWS

$4000.00 at start of job, $4000.00 when rough work is complete, $4500.00
upon completion of job.

ALL MATERIAL IS GUARANTEED TO BE AS SPECIFIED. ALL WORK TO BE COMPLETED IN A WORKMANLIKE MAN-
NER ACCORDING TO STANDARD PRACTICES. ANY ALTERATION OR DEVIATION FROM ABOVE SPECIFICATIONS WILL
INVOLVE EXTRA COSTS. OWNER TO CARRY FIRE, TORNADO AND OTHER NECESSARY INSURANCE.

AUTHORIZED SIGNATURE _William G. Walker_

ACCEPTANCE OF PROPOSAL

THE ABOVE PRICES, SPECIFICATIONS AND CONDITIONS ARE SATISFACTORY AND ARE HEREBY ACCEPTED. YOU ARE
AUTHORIZED TO DO THE WORK AS SPECIFIED. PAYMENT WILL BE MADE AS OUTLINED ABOVE.

SIGNATURE

ACCEPTED
DATE May 8, 1979   SIGNATURE

Route 146A ● Eddie Dowling Highway ● North Smithfield, R.I. 02895

──── **(401)● 769-3220**   Prov. Area **(401)● 421-3810** ────

June 7, 1979

Mr. Joseph Maroney
The Pub
Grove St.
Worcester, MA

Dear Mr. Maroney:

We are pleased to quote you on the following:

Item 1	– 1 ea.	30 cubic ft. White Freezer	$ 1050.00
2	– 1 ea.	Convection oven-gas	1895.00
3	– 1 ea.	1000 Watt Microwave Oven	1195.00
4	– 1 ea.	5'x30" s/s Top Work Table	215.00
5	– 1 ea.	40lb. Fryer-Gas	695.00
6	– 1 ea.	3' Char-broiler with stand	1750.00
7	– 1 ea.	3 Section hot food table	350.00
8	– 1 ea.	2'x30" Bread Cabinet	445.00
9	– 1 ea.	6 Burner Range with 1 Oven	940.00
10	– 1 ea.	4' Sand unit-12 pans	1350.00
11	– 1 ea.	11'-0"x3'-6"x2'-0 High s/s hood with filters-installed	2800.00
12	– 1 ea.	2 Door refrigerator-top mount	2350.00
13	– 1 ea.	Wall mount exhaust fan 2 speed with damper and switch-installed	1050.00
14	–	14'-8"x12" Dbc. s/s Overshelf with (2) 4' Heat lamps	1050.00

Food service equipment and supplies

258

Item 15 – 1 ea.	14'-8"x15" s/s Tray rest with wire shelving under	$ 695.00
16 – 1 ea.	12" Slicer-manual	1250.00
17 – 2 ea.	6'x30" s/s Top Work Table	460.00
18 – 1 ea.	300lb. Ice machine on 540lb. storage bin	2150.00
19 – 1 ea.	21"x54" 3 Comp. pot sink with 18x21 drainboard and faucet	490.00
20 – 1 ea.	Undercounter dishwasher with chloritizer- No s/s panels	1165.00
21 – 1 ea.	10' s/s Landing table with backsplash, pre-rinse sink and spray and 4' rack shelf	1350.00
22 – 1 ea.	5 Burner coffee maker automatic	540.00
23 – 1 ea.	2 qt. Creamer	159.00
24 – 1 ea.	2'x4' Formica waitress station	265.00
25 – 1 ea.	Glass door refrigerator	1450.00
	Total for items 1 thru 25:	$ 27109.00

Thanking you for the opportunity of quoting you, we look forward to receiving your valued order.

Sincerely,

UNITED RESTAURANT EQUIPMENT CO.

Arthur Joyal
Sales

AJ: mmj

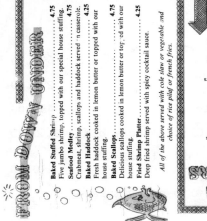

Welcome to THE WORKS

CHOOSE YOUR BOOZE

Rookies: If you came in here for a quick meal you are in the wrong place. ALL OUR FOOD IS Made to order. So relax, have a drink and prepare yourself for a unique experience.

Veterans: Congratulations on your discerning taste, good looks, charming personality and appreciation for the finer things in life.

ON DRAUGHT
(frosted mugs naturally).

Budweiser	.90
Bavarian Dark	.90
Miller Lite	.90
Pitchers of Beer	$4.50

BOTTLED BEER

Miller	1.10
Michelob	1.25
Molson	1.50
Heineken	1.75

INGLENOOK

Rose	1.15
Chablis	1.15
Burgundy	1.15
One Half Liter	2.90
Full Liter	4.95
Lambrusco	1.60

HOUSE RECOMMENDS

Roy's Martin 1.95
A martini man's martini.

Mallaghan's Manhattan 1.95
Named for two connoisseurs.

The Jungle Juice
All juice drinks are made with fresh squeezed juice. Sit at the bar and it's done before Your eyes.

Three varieties of Rum blended beautifully with the good Doctors secret concoction 2.20

Irish Coffee (Irish Whiskey)	2.20
Spanish Coffee (Kahlua)	2.20
Jamaican Coffee (Tia Maria)	2.20

FROM THE GARDEN

Chef Salad 3.10
A tasty combination of Turkey, Ham, Swiss Cheese on fresh crisp lettuce, garnished with hard boiled egg, red onion and tomato.

Spinach Salad 3.10
Fresh green spinach, mushrooms, bacon bits, olives and House Dressing.

Small Spinach Salad 1.60

Garden Salad .... .95
Crisp lettuce, tomato and red onion served with choice of dressing.

Vegetable Salad 3.10
Assortment of mixed vegetables topped with vinaigrette dressing.

Small Vegetable Salad 1.60

Hamburger 2.20
Choice beef, char-broiled to your liking served on a fresh bulkie.

Cheeseburger 2.30
Same as our hamburger, but with two thick slices of American cheese.

Baconcheeseburger 2.45
The elite of our burgers.

Mushroom Burger 2.45
Our choice beef topped with delicious hot mushrooms.

Cheddar Burger 2.35
Choice beef topped with thick slices of cheddar cheese.

The Works Burger 2.50
Choice beef, lettuce, tomato, russian dressing, cheese and raw onion char-broiled the way you like it!

Open Steak Sandwich 5.95
9oz choice sirloin, char-broiled, served on toast points with french fries, lettuce and tomato.

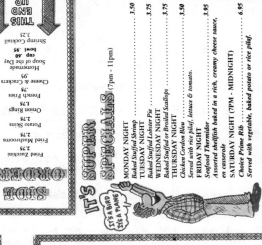

FROM DOWN UNDER

Baked Stuffed Shrimp 4.75
Five jumbo shrimp, topped with our special house stuffing.

Seafood Medley 4.75
Crabmeat, shrimp, scallops and haddock served in casserole.

Baked Haddock 4.25
Fresh haddock cooked in lemon butter or topped with our house stuffing.

Baked Scallops 4.75
Delicious scallops cooked in lemon butter or topped with our house stuffing.

Fried Shrimp Platter 4.25
Deep fried shrimp served with spicy cocktail sauce.

All of the above served with cole slaw or vegetable and choice of rice pilaf or french fries.

SIDE ORDERS

Fried Zucchini	2.75
Fried Mushrooms	2.75
Potato Skins	.75
Onion Rings	1.75
French Fries	.75
Cheese & Crackers	.95
Homemade Soup of the Day	cup .60 bowl .95
Shrimp Cocktail	3.25

THIS END UP

IT'S SUPER SPECIALS (7pm – 11pm)

MONDAY NIGHT	
Baked Stuffed Shrimp	3.50
TUESDAY NIGHT	
Baked Stuffed Lobster Pie	3.75
WEDNESDAY NIGHT	
Baked Stuffed or Broiled Scallops	3.75
THURSDAY NIGHT	
Chicken Cordon Bleu	3.50
Served with rice pilaf, lettuce & tomato.	
FRIDAY NIGHT	
Seafood Thermidor	3.95
Assorted shellfish baked in a rich, creamy cheese sauce, en casserole	
SATURDAY NIGHT (7PM - MIDNIGHT)	
Choice Prime Rib	6.95
Served with vegetable, baked potato or rice pilaf.	

I really shouldn't, but ...

Homemade Dessert of the Day	1.50
Ice Cream Puff	1.50
Cheesecake	1.60
w/ strawberries	

If you've read this far and you have not received your free popcorn yet, throw something at your waitress, she must be asleep.

AFTER 4 PM

French Dip 3.25
Thinly sliced roast beef served on a bulkie with hot Au Jus.

Reuben 2.95
Delicious corned beef, imported Sauerkraut, melted swiss cheese and russian dressing served on grilled rye.

Swiss Exchange 2.95
Sliced turkey, ham, russian dressing, tomato, melted swiss cheese served on grilled rye.

Lobster Salad Roll 3.95
Delicious Lobster Salad served open-faced on a fresh bulkie with french fries and garnish.

Pastrami Melt. 2.95
Hot sliced pastrami served on a fresh bulkie and topped with melted swiss cheese along with french fries.

Tuna Melt 1.95
Imported Tuna topped with melted american cheese served on a fresh bulkie.

Chicken di Saronno 3.75
Boneless chicken breast, breaded, topped with a delightful Amaretto sauce, with rice pilaf and vegetable.

Fried Chicken Wings .... 2.35   Large order 3.95
Finger licking good!

OUR REGULARS

Grilled Cheese, Bacon & Tomato 1.95
Two thick slices of american cheese topped with crisp bacon slices and fresh tomato, served on grilled rye.

Sliced Turkey 2.75
On rye, with mayonnaise, lettuce and tomato.

DAILY LUNCHEON SPECIALS

Check with your waitress for special of the day.

BUSINESS PLAN
NEBUR ENGINEERING CORP*

1.0 TABLE OF CONTENTS AND FIGURES

Chapter Headings

*Certain facts in this business plan have been disguised. However, the essence of the plan remains intact. It is presented not to demonstrate a good or bad business plan but to allow individuals preparing a business plan the insights into how others have prepared similar documents.

2.0 Executive Overview

Nebur Engineering Corporation will produce a computer system that is superior to competitive systems by significantly reducing the technical interface required between the man and the machine. The system will be priced competitively with other systems having similar storage and performance specifications.

The system will be focused on the retail industry, and provided with a complete set of packages for the following applications:

1. General Accounting
   Accounts Payable
   Accounts Receivable
   General Ledger
2. Retail/Point of Sale Applications
   —ECR Data Collection, Formatting, Reporting
   —POS Sales Audit and Reporting
   —Merchandise Control and Reporting
   —Order Entry
   —Purchasing

All of the application packages will be written in a specially developed proprietary language, for easy modification and augmentation. This high level language allows more direct user interaction with the system and greatly reduces the time and effort to develop a new program or modify an existing one.

The key to market penetration will be the distribution of the product through a unique channel—the independent cash register dealer. While many of these dealers have a low-budget, low technical skill image, a growing number have much to offer as a marketing channel to the retail industry:

1. They understand and are focused on the retail market. Further, they have credibility in that industry with their customer base.

2. They sell a sophisticated electronic product (Data Terminal Systems, Delta Systems, Sweda) and already have a level of programming and systems knowledge.
3. They provide service to their customer base with a two-hour response time, twenty-four hours a day, seven days a week.
4. They are beginning to meet IBM and NCR in the marketplace, and are facing a total system challenge—electronic cash registers plus computers.

The combination of Nebur Engineering Corporation and the electronic cash register dealer allows them to meet this challenge and to continue to sell their customer base, because:

1. We are focused strictly on this computer product.
2. We can offer a system interfacing to every major ECR manufacturer.

For independent dealers, the product's ease of use, high reliability, and focused application packages are suitable for distribution to their customers if sufficient support is provided by Nebur Engineering Corporation. Our support will take the form of:

Dealer Training—in installation and maintenance servicing, applications development and installation, and facilities planning.

Repair Depots—systems will be repaired in the field by the dealer, who will replace major subassemblies, and return them to Nebur Engineering Corporation for repair and eventual return to the dealer.

Hotline—Nebur Engineering will always be immediately available to answer the dealer's questions on service, applications, or sales techniques.

The total market for small computers during the period 1978–1987 will be over one million units sold, or over 20 billion dollars. Table 2–1 shows segmentation by average purchase price. Our product will sell for $35–50 thousand, so it will fit in Group II below.

TABLE 2–1 MARKET SEGMENT BY PURCHASE PRICE*

GROUP	AVERAGE PURCHASE PRICE	UNITS (000)	DOLLARS ($B)
I	$ 10,000	784	$ 7.3
II	65,000	187	10.5
III	140,000	36	4.4
		1,007	$22.2

The Retail Industry segment of Group II represents 88,000 units, or 4 billion dollars. (See Figure 2–2). According to Creative Strategies, Inc., a well-known market analyst, this market is only 5 percent penetrated today.

*Frost and Sullivan, "The Small Business Computer Market," 1979.

FIGURE 2–2 POTENTIAL USERS 1978–1987 BY INDUSTRY*

INDUSTRY	GROUP I	GROUP II	GROUP III
Manufacturing	168,000	37,000	24,000
Wholesale	179,000	57,000	31,000
Banking	3,500	6,600	5,700
Insurance Agents	25,000	11,000	4,000
Construction	219,000	20,000	4,800
Transportation	196,000	18,000	4,500
Retail	748,000	88,000	22,000
Services: Accounting	17,200	1,000	300
Legal	44,000	3,000	350

*Source: Frost and Sullivan, "The Small Business Computer Market" 1979.

Nebur Engineering Corporation's fiscal year covers the period November 1 through October 31. During our first full fiscal year, 1980, we will be in development phase with no sales. Dealers will be signed during FY80, and we expect to go into FY81 with a backlog exceeding $1 million. During FY81 we forecast sales of $8.3 million and small pre-tax profit. During FY82 we forecast sales of $18.8 million with a pre-tax profit of $5.6 million.

Achieving these sales figures through the development of a full-scale product, implementation of the distribution channel, with the necessary applications, training, and support services will require a peak investment of $6.5 million. Our initial financing is $2.4 million from employees' equity and a trust established by Steven A. Nebur. An infusion of significant venture capital will be required before the first prototypes are completed.

Managers are in place for the engineering, finance, marketing, and support areas. A manufacturing manager is currently being sought. In addition to the three year plan, detailed departmental plans and budgets are in place for all departments.

We have agreed in principal with the State Street Bank and Trust Company of Boston on conditions for short-term loans, and an objective of permanent financing based on revenue and corporate collateral. Our financial strategy includes the introduction of additional partners in our venture—venture capitalists to join our founder in bringing the product to the marketplace.

3.0 Background Information

Historically, there has been a "usability" gap between the computer and the user of computers. Major corporate users of computers have filled this gap with increasing numbers of data processing professionals who design systems, write programs, manage data bases, and operate the computer. These people are often separate from the corporate mainstream, speak their own language, and are responsive to a different set of criteria than the rest of the company. As more of the corporation has become aware of the need for data, the backlog of tasks has grown, resulting in longer lead times to get access to the corporate computer facilities.

This problem is amplified in smaller companies. First, the user in a small business is usually the manager of that business. He is concerned with a larger scope of problems, and has less resources to fill the information gap. His business typically cannot tolerate the existence of nonaligned staff people to manage his EDP facility, and he personally is consumed with the day-to-day problems of running his business. This problem has been masked by the relatively high cost of computer equipment, which made computers an academic issue for the small businessman. Today, however, the falling cost of computer hardware has driven the price of a "small business computer" down to as little as $500 and has generated an enormous interest in computers in the small business community.

TABLE 3–1 COMPUTER INDUSTRY PARAMETERS

	1955*	1965	1975	1985
Industry Size	1	20	80	320
Performance/Cost	1	10^2	10^4	10^6
Processing Power	1	2×10^3	8×10^5	32×10^7
Bits Stored/$	1	10^3	10^6	10^9
Programmer Productivity	1	2.4	5.6	13.3

*Base Year = 1

Note: Table 3–1 was presented at a seminar on distributed processing by James Martin. Using 1955 as a starting point, with an index of 1, the industry multiplied by 20 in the first decade, and is now quadrupling each decade. Computer performance per dollar has steadily increased by a factor of 100 each decade.

Thus, the computer of today is about 100 times more powerful than the same period computer of ten years ago (or the same computer hardware costs 100 times less). The computer industry has experienced large technical growth in all areas except programmer productivity. During a period of phenominal technology growth in hardware, programmers in 1985 will be about five times more productive than those of 1965! This will be the area of technology focus for Nebur Engineering.

Figure 3–2 is the result of a major Air Force study showing where it expected its DP dollar to be spent over time. This chart demonstrates the growing expenditure in software versus hardware, and further emphasizes the requirement for substantial increases in programmer productivity.

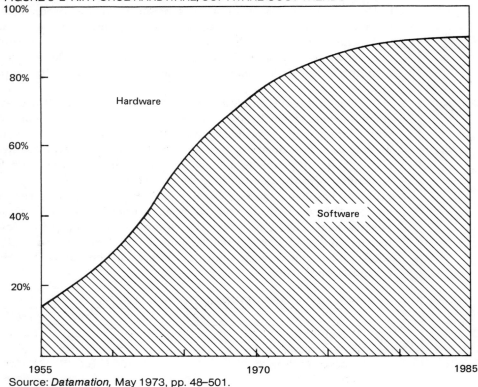

FIGURE 3–2 AIR FORCE HARDWARE/SOFTWARE COST TRENDS

Source: *Datamation*, May 1973, pp. 48–501.

Figure 3–3 shows a second amplifier of this requirement, presented by James Martin. In 1955 almost all users of computers had some knowledge of computers. By 1985, 75 percent of the labor force will be using computers, but less than 25 percent will have knowledge about these computers. This has resulted in a growing software backlog (today about 5 years in major corporations), and the need for nonprogrammers to access and program their computers. Clearly, the gap must either be filled with more and more people, or new techniques for interfacing man to machines must be developed.

The small businessman has several options available to him. The majority of them are not using computers, but are managing their businesses with paper systems, (and the incurred rising costs for personnel). Some are using time sharing or batch services from both major firms (such as ADP, SBC, National CSS, etc.) and local service bureaus.

A growing number are investigating their own small business computers, typically purchased from local suppliers or dealers. These dealers provide a micro or mini computer, a package of standard appli-

FIGURE 3-3 LABOR FORCE USING COMPUTERS

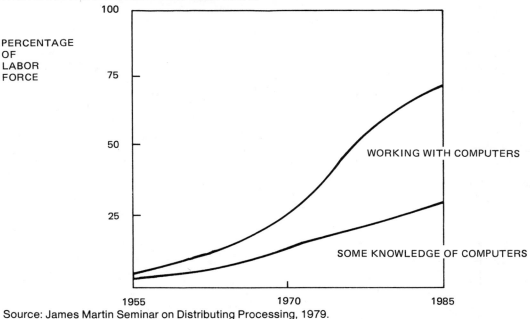

PERCENTAGE
OF
LABOR
FORCE

WORKING WITH COMPUTERS

SOME KNOWLEDGE OF COMPUTERS

Source: James Martin Seminar on Distributing Processing, 1979.

cations programs (General Ledger, Accounts Payable, Payroll, Accounts Receivable, Inventory, etc.), and the necessary skills to tailor these packages to the user's specific requirements. This supplier has the same problems of programmer productivity that the rest of the industry has. Unless the businessman can adapt his business to the package, the supplier is faced with high costs of the "special" software. Quite often, this problem does not become visible until the businessman has purchased the system, and is trying to use it.

Further, the businessman often finds that his supplier has not adequately considered service or reliability. When his system "breaks" (hardware or software), the supplier is not prepared to respond in a timely fashion, or to repair the problem when he gets there.

Nonetheless, market analysts Frost and Sullivan, in a report on "The Small Business Computer Market," published in February, 1979, predict that sales of small computers will grow from $1.3B in 1978 to about $2.8B in 1987. Figure 3–4 shows their estimate of growth.

Nebur Engineering Corporation was formed to address the gap between the small businessman and the computer. The following sections of this plan will address the products and services Nebur Engineering will produce to deal with this problem, and the business plans for achieving this goal.

267

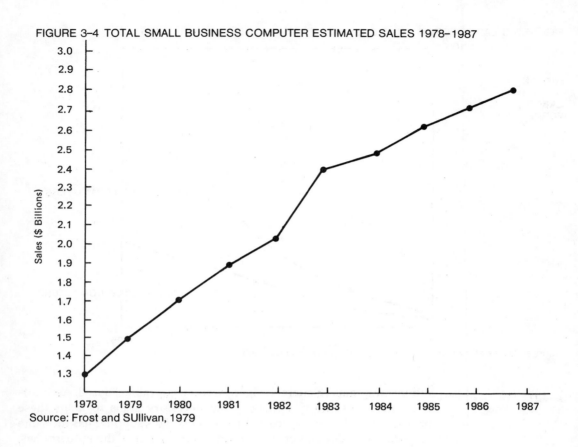

FIGURE 3–4 TOTAL SMALL BUSINESS COMPUTER ESTIMATED SALES 1978–1987

Source: Frost and SUllivan, 1979

4.0 Markets

4.1 MARKET SIZE AND SEGMENTATION

Frost and Sullivan reports, in a 1979 report entitled "The Small Business Computer Market," that the total shipments for the period 1978–1987 will be over one million units for a total price of over twenty billion dollars. They segment this market by price group, as follows:

GROUP	AVERAGE PURCHASE PRICE	UNITS	DOLLAR VOLUME ($M)
I	$ 10,000	784,000	$ 7,256
II	65,000	186,950	10,469
III	140,000	36,000	4,384
		1,006,950	$22,109

268

Nebur Engineering expects its average system price to be between $35,000 and $50,000 during this period. Therefore, we expect our market to be that defined as Group II with some potential in the high end of Group I.

Figure 4–1 shows the expected breakdown of units, average price, and total sales for this size segment.

Strategically, Nebur expects to focus on one vertical segment of this market, Retail, and will expand to other segments only when significant market share has been achieved. The reasons for this strategic approach are:

1. Steven Nebur the founder, has extensive experience and credibility in this market segment. As a co-founder of Data Terminal Systems, Inc., he brings a breadth of experience in the design of point-of-sale systems, electronic cash registers (ECR), and cash management systems.
2. Figure 4–2 shows that in Group II, the number of potential users in the retail industry exceeds all other industry areas. Further, Figure 4–3 shows that Retail has one of the lowest penetrations, making the field fertile for market penetration.
3. The independent cash register dealer is uniquely positioned to provide necessary sales, service, and system support functions to this segment, and is today looking for expansion into the small computer arena. By providing Nebur's unique features of ease of use and high reliability, by tailoring our applications packages to this market segment, and by providing a high level of training, it is expected that we will rapidly establish a unique channel of distribution to the retail segment.

FIGURE 4–1 GROUP II COMPUTER MARKET 1978–1987

	UNITS	AVERAGE SYSTEM PRICE	SALES $ (Million)
1978	9,350	65,000	608
1979	11,220	63,350	710
1980	13,090	61,700	807
1981	14,950	60,050	897
1982	16,820	58,400	982
1983	20,560	56,750	1,167
1984	22,430	55,100	1,236
1985	24,300	53,450	1,299
1986	26,180	51,800	1,356
1987	28,050	50,140	1,407
	186,950		10,469

Source: Frost and Sullivan Report "Small Business Computer Market," 1979.

FIGURE 4–2 APPROXIMATE NUMBER OF POTENTIAL USERS
FOR EACH TYPE OF SMALL BUSINESS COMPUTER GROUP

				POTENTIAL USERS
Manufacturing	168,000	37,000	24,000	229,000
Wholesale	179,000	57,000	31,000	267,000
Banking	3,500	6,600	5,700	15,800
Insurance Agents	25,0000	11,000	4,000	40,000
Insurance Companies	8,300	5,350	4,350	18,000
Construction	219,000	20,000	4,800	243,800
Transportation	196,000	18,000	4,500	218,500
Retail	748,000	88,000	22,000	858,000
Services: Accounting	17,200	1,000	300	18,500
Legal	44,000	3,000	350	47,350
Total Potential Users	1,608,000	246,950	101,000	1,955,950
Units Installed	40,000	60,000	65,000	165,000
Total Potential Purchasers	1,568,000	186,950	36,000	1,790,950
Estimated Number of Purchasers in Next 10 Years	784,000	186,950	36,000	1,006,950

Source: Frost and Sullivan Report, "Small Business Computer Market," 1979.

4. Figure 4–4 shows that 88,000 systems will be installed in this segment by 1987 resulting in sales of $4.9 billion. While IBM and NCR will take substantial portions of this market, the market is large enough to meet Nebur's goals of sales and growth.

4.2 COMPETITION

The small business computer market is a very competitive arena dominated by IBM with the System/38 and System/34. NCR is also a primary competitor in our marketplace because of its large installed base of electronic cash registers, which Nebur plans to interface to. Confusing the competitive marketplace are numerous other manufacturers, both large and small, that claim to have the most cost effective and easiest to use small business system. In addition to these competitors are electronic cash register manufacturers who now offer, or plan to offer, small business systems that interface to their cash registers to give the user a complete point-of-sale system. Nebur Engineering believes that it will succeed for the following reasons:

1. No other manufacturer offers a very high level language capability that allows the user to write and modify programs himself without hiring programming personnel or learning to program.

FIGURE 4–3 SMALL BUSINESS COMPUTER INSTALLATIONS BY INDUSTRY SECTOR

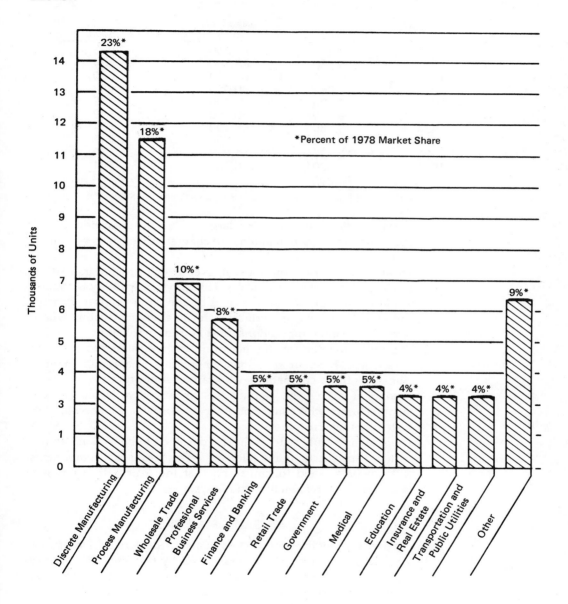

*Percent of 1978 Market Share

FIGURE 4–4 POTENTIAL RETAIL COMPUTER SALES:
GROUP II, 1978–1987

	UNITS	AVERAGE SYSTEM PRICE	SALES $ (Million)
1978	4,400	65,000	286
1979	5,280	63,350	334
1980	6,160	61,700	380
1981	7,040	60,050	422
1982	7,920	58,400	462
1983	9,680	56,750	549
1984	10,560	55,100	581
1985	11,440	53,450	611
1986	12,320	51,800	638
1987	13,200	50,150	661
	88,000		4,924

Source: Frost and Sullivan Report, "Small Business Computer Market," 1979.

This capacity offers the user a large savings in applications development and program maintenance charges as well as in personnel costs.

2. Through its distribution network, Nebur will provide immediate and superior service to all users. This service capability is already in place and can only be matched by the large vendors. Prompt and effective service is a critical factor in every installation where payroll and other applications must be run on schedule.

3. The ability to interface with electronic cash registers provides two advantages. First, in situations where this is a requirement it eliminates those competitors who cannot support this connection. Second, it makes the Nebur's system attractive to many ECR manufacturers who could not otherwise provide a complete POS system to their customers.

4. The system is truly state-of-the-art, designed to be well within the required specifications and tolerances. This means that components will not be pushed to limits and that the user will experience extremely high reliability with his system.

4.3 SALES FORECAST

Nebur expects to deliver its first systems to dealers in December, 1980. Our goal is to have 50 dealers signed by that time. We further expect that we will continue to add dealers at the rate of 5 per month through a three year period. Each dealer will take delivery on one system for his own use. The booking rate will increase from 6 to 12 per year based on the length of time a dealer has been selling the system as shown in Figure 4–5. The average dealer price of the system will be $20,900. Based on these assumptions, the three years forecast is present in Figure 4–6.

FIGURE 4–5 ANNUAL BOOKING ASSUMPTIONS—
NEBUR ENGINEERING

DEALER'S YEAR WITH NEBUR'S PRODUCT	ANNUAL BOOKING RATE
1	6 or .50/month
2	9 or .75/month
3	12 or 1.00/month

FIGURE 4–6 3 YEAR SALES FORECAST—NEBUR ENGINEERING

	BOOKINGS	AVAIL. ORDERS	SHIPMENTS		BACKLOG	
	Units	Units	Units	($000)	Units	$(000)
Nov. '80	28	28	10	209	28	585
Dec. '80	30	58	20	418	48	1003
Jan. '81	33	81	30	627	61	1275
Feb. '81	35	96	35	732	66	1379
Mar. '81	38	104	35	732	69	1442
Apr. '81	40	109	40	836	74	1547
May '81	43	117	40	836	77	1609
Jun. '81	45	122	45	940	82	1714
Jul. '81	48	130	45	940	85	1776
Aug. '81	50	139	50	1045	90	1881
Sept. '81	53	143	50	1045	93	1944
Oct. '81	55	148	400	$ 8360	98	2048
Nov. '81	73	171	55	1150	116	2424
Dec. '81	76	192	60	1254	132	2759
Jan. '82	80	212	65	1358	147	3072
Feb. '82	84	231	70	1463	161	3365
Mar. '82	88	249	70	1463	179	3741
Apr. '82	91	270	75	1568	195	4076
May '82	95	290	75	1568	215	4493
Jun. '82	99	314	80	1672	234	4891
Jul. '82	103	337	85	1777	252	5267
Aug. '82	106	358	85	1777	273	5706
Sept. '82	110	383	90	1881	293	6124
Oct. '82	114	407	90	1881	317	6625
			900	$18812		
Nov. '82	130	447	100	2090	347	7252
Dec. '82	135	482	110	2299	372	7775
Jan. '83	140	512	120	2508	392	8193
Feb. '83	145	537	125	2612	412	8611
Mar. '83	150	562	130	2717	432	9029
Apr. '83	155	587	135	2822	452	9447
May '83	160	612	140	2926	472	9864
Jun. '83	165	637	150	3135	487	10178
Jul. '83	170	657	160	3344	497	10387
Aug. '83	175	672	170	3553	502	10492
Sept. '83	180	682	175	3658	507	10596
Oct. '83	185	692	180	3762	512	10701
			1695	$35426		

5.0 PRODUCTS AND SERVICES

5.1 PRODUCT DESCRIPTION

Nebur Engineering Corporation's initial product is a computer system that can meet the full range of data handling and processing requirements for a small business. As a product, it is strongly differentiated from other small business computers because of:

1. Superior reliability and availability; and
2. extraordinary ease of use by individuals without specialized training in computers.

In addition, the product will be of a comparable cost to competitive products available with similar mass storage and throughput characteristics, and offer a variety of upgrade paths.

Superior Reliability and Availability. The product will be designed and packaged to provide both the appearance and reality of extreme reliability. The package will withstand extreme abuse (mechanical blows, temperature, coffee poured over it) while operating without damage.

The design will ensure that likely failure modes cannot destroy data on the disk in a nonrecoverable fashion, and the integrity of user data will be protected in the event of a power failure. Parity will be provided on RAM (random access memories), error detection and correction will be used with the tape and disk, and routine diagnostics will execute periodically to check the validity of ROM (read only data). The system is continually running diagnostic programs under a watchdog timer mechanism to assure that the hardware is operational.

A combination of package design and system resident diagnostics should provide mean time between failure, fault isolation capability, and mean time to repair, which is demonstrably superior to competing units. A total system MTBF (mean-time-between failure) of 3000 hours and MTBF of 10,000 hours (five years of normal use) for the electronic components are expected. It is a goal of the company to establish, by performance of the sysem, a reputation for reliability and service dramatically superior to competing products.

User-Friendliness. The system will provide an interface to the user that insulates him from the intricacies of its internal operation, and to a large extent de-emphasizes the fact that it is a computer. The image that the system presents to the user is that of an office assistant, performing routine tasks, manipulating information, and communicating in an informal, understandable manner.

This is accomplished by means of a unique high order language developed by Nebur Engineering that allows the user to communicate with the machine in normal English (actually a subset of the English language).

The user is led through his interaction by the use of special function keys, which present all feasible choices at each step; erroneous responses are thus limited to entry of names and data, and are answered with explanatory comments in English.

Because we follow a strict physical analogy to a real office, a system already familiar to the user, he can easily and correctly guess how the system will respond in any particular situation. The characteristics of the language, however, also permit him to implement procedures as complex and any that may exist on a computer system.

The user's primary task is to instruct his "Assistant" to give him (the user) what he needs. This can be as simple as requesting the "Assistant" to execute some well-known predefined procedure found in the "Assistant's" procedure book. To support this viewpoint, the "Assistant" is seen as operating in a work environment that is closely analogous to the environment found in a small business.

The data storage and retrieval system is derived directly from the typical paper handling system prevalent in most small businesses. All the data for a company is managed by a file clerk and is kept in file cabinet(s) (on-line) or in an archive (off-line). A file cabinet consists of an unspecified (but potentially large) number of drawers. Each drawer has a label and ID which together form a combined index (*e.g.* Personnel Drawer E, the Label is Personnel and the ID is E). Drawers are arranged alphanumerically in a file cabinet by Label and ID within Label.

Each file drawer can contain an unspecified (but potentially large) number of folders. Each folder is identified by its Type and ID (*e.g.* Employee Folder Smith, the Type is Employee, the ID is Smith). Folders are arranged within a drawer by Type and ID within Type.

The operation of the system can best be described in the following analogy. The "Assistant's" environment includes a desk, a work table, a blackboard, a copier, a printer, and a supply cabinet. On the "Assistant's" desk are the following: a pad, a clock, an appointment calendar, a mailbox, an in-box and out-box, a calculator, and a stamp wheel
The "Assistant" can be instructed to use these resources to carry out various tasks. When folders are pulled from a drawer by the file clerk and transmitted to the "Assistant," they are placed either on a pile on the desk or in some other pile on the work table. The "Assistant" can be instructed to go through each folder on a pile or through each document in a folder. The desk is the work area where data elements are operated on. The "Assistant" understands instructions to store and retrieve data, to manipulate it, perform logical and arithmetic operations,

format it for report output, take action contingent on logical conditions, and in general, perform any operations supported by a high-level computer language.

Editing is seen to take place at the desk. Information can be noted on pad temporarily. Any document can be copied by the copier. The clock can be used both to tell time and to notify the "Assistant" that some procedure should be executed. The appointment calendar is used to record and remind the user of appointments. Document transmission is accomplished via the in and out boxes and the mail box. These are serviced by a mail room, which picks up and distributes documents and mail. The "Assistant" uses the calculator on the desk to perform all the calculations needed in a procedure and to perform special functions such as mortgage payments and exchange rates.

In summary, the "Assistant" is designed so that every function that can be carried out has a direct analogy in the small business office.

5.2 HARDWARE DESIGN

Figure 5-1 provides an overview of the planned initial product. It consists of up to 8 CRT's and a main processing unit with Winchester disk storage, tape back up, and both serial and parallel printer interfaces. In addition, communications to selected brands of cash registers are provided. The principal components are described in more detail below.

CRT/Keyboard Assembly. A high quality, 6000 character CRT display will be provided with a detachable keyboard. The CRT will display a full page of text in either a vertical or horizontal orientation. If shipped with the display vertical it will provide a display 64×96 characters. If shipped in the horizontal orientation it will provide a display 128 characters across and 48 lines down. Two different character sets will be provided in order to differentiate "forms" displayed on the screen from material entered by the operator. As additional aids in user interfacing, the CRT will have the following features: half or full intensity, reverse video, underlining, blink, and the ability to draw boxes around the text.

Mass Storage. Twenty megabytes of on-line disk storage will be provided in a sealed Winchester disk drive package. As devices become available with higher capacity they will be provided with the system or as options. A tape cartridge will also be provided for back-up and archival storage, providing in excess of twenty megabytes storage.

FIGURE 5–1 SYSTEM OVERVIEW

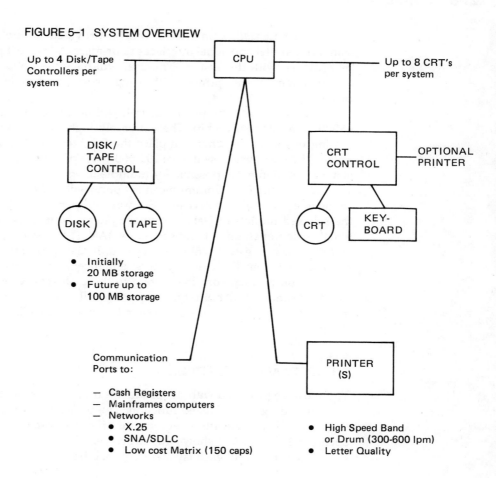

- Initially
  20 MB storage
- Future up to
  100 MB storage

Communication
Ports to:

- Cash Registers
- Mainframes computers
- Networks
  - X.25
  - SNA/SDLC
  - Low cost Matrix (150 caps)

- High Speed Band
  or Drum (300-600 lpm)
- Letter Quality

277

Printer Capability. Interfaces will be provided for both industry standard parallel and serial interfaces to printers. A low cost printer will be provided with the system. The user will have the option to substitute or augment this printer with a high speed and/or letter quality printer.

Processor Unit. The processor unit will be based on the Motorola 68000 computer on a chip. The extremely high throughput and processing power of this chip will place the CPU into the midi-computer range. The base system will have 192,000 bytes of memory, with expansion to a million bytes possible for multiple users.

Communications. Communications ports will be provided for interfacing to electronic cash registers. Software support will be provided for the selected models of Data Terminal Systems cash registers with the initial customer shipment. Subsequently, JAY, TEK, Sweda, NCR, Delta, and IBM cash registers will be supported. Initial capability will permit reading data from the cash registers; enhancements to allow sending prices or other data from the system to the cash register will be provided subsequently. Another future option will be network connections from system to system and from system to other manufacturing systems.

5.3 SOFTWARE DESCRIPTION

The software provided with the product is organized in modular layers, each providing a specialized function. The user interfaces to the outer layers, which present the image of the office "Assistant" described in Section 5.1. Figure 5–3 shows this structure.

The function of each layer is described below:

1. *Operating System Layer.* The operating system is a multi-tasking, multi-user operating system similar to that found in most time shared computers. It performs functions related to allocating and managing the machine's resources, the allocation of the processor to each user task, the allocation of memory to tasks and the allocation and sequencing of input and output.
2. *File System Layer.* The file system interfaces with the microprocessor based disk controller and provides management of files at the level of creating, deleting, and changing the data within them. Protection of private data for individual users in a multi-user situation is also enforced at this level.

FIGURE 5-3 THE VARIOUS LAYERS OF THE SOFTWARE

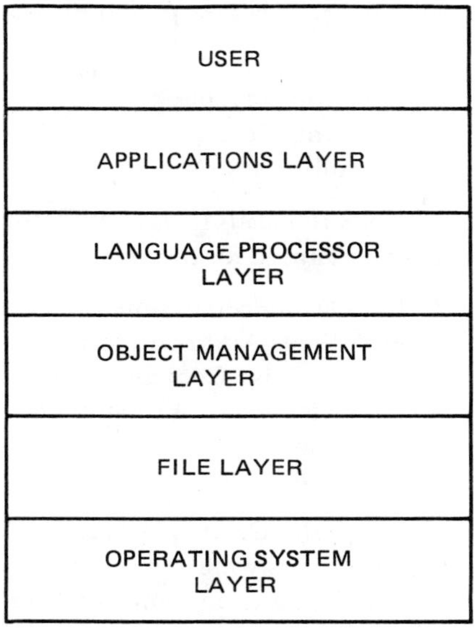

USER
APPLICATIONS LAYER
LANGUAGE PROCESSOR LAYER
OBJECT MANAGEMENT LAYER
FILE LAYER
OPERATING SYSTEM LAYER

3. *Object Manager Layer.* The object manager is a data base management system that is tailored to the Assistant model. It provides facilities for the manipulation of the various data organizations associated with that model, piles of papers or folders on the desk, the procedure book, etc.

4. *Language Processor Layer.* The language processor involves several major subfunctions: the editor for text, forms layout, and data entry that provide the actual interface to the user; a parser that converts entered programs to a format that can be processed by the machine; and the interpreter that performs the actual emulation of data movement and manipulation actions as called for in the language, and drives the object manager in the actual maintenance of data. This level performs the translation of data from electronic cash registers and other external communications devices.

5. *Applications Layer.* Applications programs are written in the high level language to allow easy preparation, modification, and expansion by either our users or dealers. These applications programs can be grouped into the following areas.

   Group I. General Accounting Packages This group encompasses what is considered to be the basic group of application programs, a group that is necessary when selling into the small business computer market. This group of applications packages includes:

1. General Ledger,
2. Accounts Payable,
3. Accounts Receivables,
4. Payroll

Group II. Retail Application Packages. This group encompasses programs planned for the retail market in which we will specialize.

1. POS Data Preparation and Formatting
2. POS Sales Audit and Reporting
3. Merchandise Control and Reporting
4. Financial Report Preparation
5. Order Entry
6. Purchasing

Group III. Dealer Application Packages. This group encompasses programs we are planning to supply to our dealer organization to aid them in running their business and to provide an excellent demonstration of the capability of the product.

Group IV. Utility Package. This group provides the user with commonly used procedures, such as:

1. Disk back-up and restore,
2. Utilization statistics,
3. Document preparation and printing,
4. Archival storage

In addition, the user or our dealers will write procedures at the applications layer to provide user-specific functions.

5.4 SERVICES

There are two providers of services, Nebur Engineering and our dealer organization. Nebur will supply dealer training, central repair depots, and rapid response spare parts to the dealer organization. Nebur will also provide applications seminars to the end-user as arranged for by the dealer. The dealer will provide end-user training, repair and installation services, and application program development and modification. Through the use of the high level language, the user will be able to develop his own application programs, or modify the supplied packages at a significantly lower cost and training than that required on competitive systems. The following is an expansion on this area.

Nebur Services

1. Dealer Training
   Sales
   Service and Installation procedures
   Use of system/language
   Applications packages
   Software installation
2. Repair Depot
   All repairs below major subassemblies
   Spare parts
3. Application Seminars
   Training to the customer in application areas
4. Hotline
   Service to the dealers for difficult HW/SW problems
   Applications questions

Dealer Services

1. Customer Training
   Use
   Applications
   Facilities planning
2. Repair and Installation
   Major subassembly replacement
   Systems installation
   Software update installation
   Upgrade installation
3. Applications
   Development
   Modification
   Upgrades

5.5 PRODUCT IMPACT

Section 3 of this document discusses the problems of programmer productivity and the "usability gap" experienced by the smaller business user of computers. The Nebur Engineering Corporation system addresses that problem in the following ways.

Increased Programmer Productivity

1. The availability of a business oriented high level language allows the programmer to concentrate on the system's specification rather than on programming.

2. By providing industry-specific application packages, the programmer is free to focus on either customization of those packages or customer-specific applications.
3. By using the general data base management capability, the entire data definition and specification process (a major portion of any COBOL-type program) is greatly reduced. Further, the applications programs are defined independent of that data definition, so changes to applications programs can be made much more rapidly.
4. The use of special function keys to create programs and procedures reduces the opportunity for input errors thereby reducing the time to get a new program operational.

Figure 5–4 shows the results of these benefits on both programmer productivity and the cost of maintenance of the programs already developed. These benefits are enjoyed by both the dealer organization and the end-user, but the principal benefit is reduced programming cost to those who develop and maintain the applications programs.

FIGURE 5–4 PROGRAMME PRODUCTIVITY

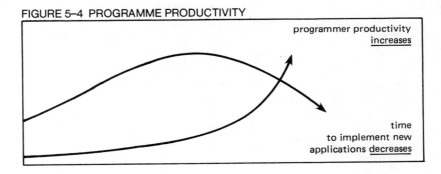

programmer productivity increases

time to implement new applications decreases

Decreased User Dependence on Programmers. The principal benefit to the end user is his reduction in dependence on computer specialists. For many users, the applications packages are complete solutions to business problems, and at most they want to upgrade their capability over time. However, the ability to access and process information will raise a new interest in management information for many of our customers. For them, the system becomes a new tool for helping them manage their businesses—their original goal for getting a computer in the first place!

FIGURE 5–5 USER DEPENDENCE ON PROGRAMMERS

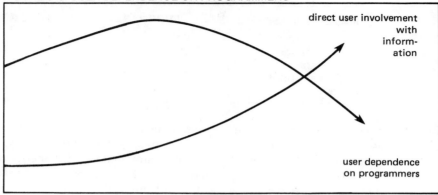

direct user involvement
with
inform-
ation

user dependence
on programmers

6.0 Manufacturing

Nebur Engineering Corporation will purchase major components and integrated circuits, and will assemble them to produce the system hardware. It will test that hardware extensively in several stages to achieve the reliability goals outlined in the product section. The hardware is classified according to the following major subassemblies.

FIGURE 6–1 ASSEMBLY LISTING

MAJOR SUBASSEMBLIES	PURCHASE	ASSEMBLED
Mainframe Assembly		
CPU Board		X
Memory Board		X
I/O Control Board		X
Power Supply Assembly		X
Board		X
Battery	X	X
Disk/Tape Assembly		X
Control Board		X
Disk Drive	X	
Tape Drive	X	
Mechanical		
Cabinet	X	
Cables		X
Front Panel	X	
CRT Assembly		
CRT Tube	X	
Control Board		
Keyboard Assembly		
Keyboard	X	
Controller		X
Cable		

FIGURE 6-1   ASSEMBLING LISTING (*Cont.*)

MAJOR SUBASSEMBLIES	PURCHASE	ASSEMBLED
Mechanical		X
Package	X	
Cable		X
Power Supply		
Printer	X	X

Initially, a minimal amount of assembly will be done in-house. Chip testing, board soldering, and cable-making will be done by subcontractors. All printed circuit boards and major components (disk, tape, CRT, printer) will be purchased. Circuit testing of I/C's will also be subcontracted. Internally, we will insert the tested components, test at the board level, assemble the system, and test the final system.

The manufacturing organization will consist of the following major areas and responsibilities:

FIGURE 6–2 MANUFACTURING AREAS AND RESPONSIBILITIES

AREA	RESPONSIBILITIES
1. Manufacturing Administration	Planning and Control Personnel Cost Accounting Facilities Management
2. Production	Production Control Assembly Work in Process Inventory Inspection Final Assembly and Test Final Inspection Finished Goods Inventory
3. Material Control	Purchasing Incoming Inspection Part Inventory Kitting
4. Manufacturing Engineering	Manufacturability Test Equipment Cost Reduction Process Definition

As we gain experience in the production of the product, more of the assembly process will be moved in-house as justified by a return on investment and cost basis. As volumes increase, it will be cost justifiable to purchase a wave solder machine, component testers, environment chambers, and automate component insertion, possibly starting in 1982.

The facility at 60 Aberdeen Avenue has the following options for expansion:

		Expansion	Total Avail.
Initial Space	10/79	—	11,600 ft²
First Expansion	4/81	3,000 ft²	14,600 ft²
Second Expansion	12/82	7,400 ft²	22,000 ft²

Beyond that we will expand outside of that facility, presumably in the Cambridge area. Our expectation is that no outside space will be necessary before the end of 1982, except perhaps for storage of raw material inventory and systems in the final test/burn-in stage.

7.0 Financial

This section will discuss our financial resources, requirements, milestones, strategy, and the controls we will put in place to manage them.

7.1 FINANCIAL RESOURCES

Nebur Engineering Corporation purchased the Nebur proprietorship on August 7, 1979. At that time, approximately $214,000 had been spent by the proprietorship to establish the product concept, to explore the engineering feasibility, and to recruit the core of the management and engineering group. At the time of our incorporation, Steven Nebur, our founder, established a trust for the benefit of the corporation. Monies from the trust, principally from the sale of Data Terminal Systems stock, are available to the corporation on a scheduled basis.

The total funding for the corporation is approximately $2.5 million based on the following schedule:

```
$  250,000  Founder's Equity
     20,000  Employee's Equity (including options)
  1,950,000  Long-Term Loan
 $2,450,000
```

The employee's equity consists of stock purchased plus options exercisable over five years. Employee stock purchases and options will be paid for over a six year period. The long-term loan from Steven Nebur is payable after the initial development period depending upon corporate profitability and cash flow. Interest is accrued on the long-term loan to Steven Nebur at a rate of 12 percent per year.

As of October 31, 1979, our year-end, $661,000 has been invested in the business, including $4,487 of accrued interest payable.

Purchase of Proprietorship	$203,000
Fixed Assets and Leasehold Improvements	221,000
Salaries and Operating Expenses	237,000
	$661,000

We have agreed in principle with the State Street Bank and Trust Company of Boston on the following Corporate objectives:

1. a line of credit for credit reference,
2. liquidity for the Trust based on Data Terminal Systems stock or other collateral,
3. permanent financing based on revenue and corporate collateral.

Loans to the corporation based on collateral provided by the Trust or by the corporation will incur interest on the first $1 million of borrowings at prime less ½ percent; after 1 million the entire loan would revert to prime plus ½ percent. To date, no monies have been borrowed from the bank.

In addition, the corporation maintains a combination checking/savings account with the New England Merchants National Bank of Boston (with balances in the low five figures), and a payroll account with the Newton/Waltham Bay Bank.

7.2 FINANCIAL REQUIREMENTS

Our financial requirements for the start-up and first three years of operations can be summarized as follows:

(ALL IN MILLIONS)	OPERATING EXPENSES	INVENTORY PURCHASES	FIXED ASSETS	TOTAL EXPENSES	COLLECTED REVENUES	CASH REQUIRE. CURRENT	CUM
Start-up	$ .3	$ —	$ .2	$ .5	$ —	$ .5	$ .5
FY80	2.7	.2	.4	3.3	—	3.3	3.8
FY 81	4.7	3.6	.2	8.5	6.2	2.3	6.1
FY82	6.4	7.1	.5	14.0	17.2	(3.2)	2.9

The calculation of cash requirements is based on sunk costs incurred during the start-up; detailed departmental budgets for the first full year of operation; and a detailed forecast, product cost breakdown, and the extension of trends for the second and third full years of operation.

Key assumptions in the cash requirements include an estimate of average collections (60 days), the payment of personnel and related costs (immediate), and the average payment to major supplies (45 days).

The calculation of cash requirements is based on sunk costs incurred during the start-up; detailed departmental budgets for the first full year of operation; and a detailed forecast, product cost breakdown, and the extension of trends for the second and third full years of operation.

Key assumptions in the cash requirements include an estimate of average collections (60 days), the payment of personnel and related costs (immediate), and the average payment to major suppliers (45 days).

There are no cash reserves built into the current schedule or the budgets. We expect to negotiate reserves as part of our search for additional capital. No credit is given for employee contributions which will constitute a maximum of $42,000 per year.

Complete details of the cash requirements are presented in Figure 7–1 "Cash Requirements" and in Figure 7–3 "Financial Model-Assumptions and Methods".

Sales and profitability for the start-up and first three years can be summarized as follows:

(ALL IN MILLIONS)	REVENUES	COST OF SALES	GROSS PROFIT	OPERATING EXPENSES	INTEREST	NET BEFORE TAXES
Start-up	—	—	—	($ .3)	—	($ .3)
FY 80	—	—	—	(2.3)	(.2)	(2.5)
FY 81	$ 8.4	(3.8)	4.6	(3.2)	(.7)	.7
FY 82	18.8	(8.1)	10.7	(4.5)	(.6)	5.6

The calculations of projected income are based on the previously described forecasts, product costs, and budgets. The key assumptions in the projected income statement are the dealer's ability to increase his rate of sales from 6 to 12 systems per year over 3 years, and our ability to build and ship the systems on time. We have examined product cost from the engineering viewpoint, the manufacturing viewpoint, and as an industry average. We are confident that the gross margin levels can be achieved.

Complete details of the projected income statements are presented in Figure 7–3 "Financial Model-Assumptions and Methods."

FIGURE 7–1 CASH REQUIREMENTS FISCAL YEAR 1980

	NOV	DEC	JAN	FEB	MAR	APR	MAY	JUNE	JULY	AUG	SEPT	OCT	TOT
Sold Units—Memo	—	—	—	—	—	—	—	—	—	—	—	—	
Collections	—	—	—	—	—	—	—	—	—	—	—	—	
Other Revenue	—	—	—	—	—	—	—	—	—	—	—	—	
Total Inflow	—	—	—	—	—	—	—	—	—	—	—	—	—
Build Units	—	—	—	—	—	—	—	—	—	5	5	5	15
Inventory													
Bulk	—	—	—	—	—	—	—	—	25	25	—	88	138
Components	—	—	—	—	—	—	—	—	—	—	25	25	50
Total Inv. Reg.	—	—	—	—	—	—	—	—	25	25	25	113	188
Salaries and Expenses													
DL	—	—	—	—	—	—	—	—	—	3	3	3	9
Mfg. D/H	—	—	6	10	13	15	15	15	15	18	24	25	156
Marketing	5	7	20	12	13	20	15	15	38	31	47	43	266
Support	7	12	21	27	30	32	34	38	38	42	46	48	375
Engineering	71	108	105	131	120	125	104	78	83	84	84	89	1,182
Finance and Admin.	10	16	10	16	10	10	10	10	10	11	11	12	136
Corp. and Genl.	22	22	32	22	22	22	32	26	26	26	32	26	310
Total Sal. and Exp.	115	165	194	218	208	224	210	182	210	215	247	246	2,434
Fixed Assets	35	35	35	35	35	35	35	35	35	35	35	35	420
Interest Exp.	—	6	8	11	13	16	19	21	24	27	30	33	208
Total Outflow	150	206	237	264	256	275	264	238	294	302	337	427	3,250
Net Flow	(150)	(206)	(237)	(264)	(256)	(275)	(264)	(238)	(294)	(302)	(337)	(427)	(3,250)
Cumulative Flow	(625)	(831)	(1,068)	(1,332)	(1,588)	(1,863)	(2,127)	(2,365)	(2,659)	(2,961)	(3,298)	(3,725)	—

FIGURE 7–1 CASH REQUIREMENTS FISCAL YEAR 1981

	NOV	DEC	JAN	FEB	MAR	APR	MAY	JUNE	JULY	AUG	SEPT	OCT	TOTAL
Sold Units—Memo	—	10	20	25	30	35	40	40	45	50	50	55	400
Collections	—	—	70	209	383	522	627	732	802	872	941	1,010	6,168
Other Revenue	—	—	—	—	—	—	—	—	—	—	—	—	—
Total Inflow	—	—	70	209	383	522	627	732	802	872	941	1,010	6,168
Build Units	10	20	25	30	35	40	40	45	50	50	55	60	460
Inventory													
Bulk	44	22	210	84	42	270	108	54	309	124	62	356	1,685
Components	25	49	96	120	144	168	192	192	216	240	240	248	1,930
Total Inv. Reg.	69	71	306	204	186	438	300	246	525	364	302	604	3,615
Salaries and Expenses													
DL	11	20	25	30	35	40	40	45	50	50	44	48	438
Mfg. O/H	25	28	28	29	30	33	33	33	36	37	37	40	389
Marketing	44	44	50	53	58	61	69	71	73	74	82	83	762
Support	44	52	53	53	57	57	58	62	62	66	67	68	704
Engineering	90	91	92	94	95	96	97	98	99	100	101	103	1,156
Finance and Admin.	12	12	15	15	15	15	16	16	18	19	19	19	191
Corp. and Genl.	26	27	27	28	28	32	33	33	33	34	34	35	370
Total Sal. and Exp.	257	274	290	302	318	334	346	358	371	380	384	396	4,010
Fixed Assets	20	20	20	20	20	20	20	20	20	20	20	20	240
Interest Exp.	37	41	45	51	55	57	60	61	60	62	62	60	651
Total Outflow	383	406	661	577	579	849	726	685	976	826	768	1,080	8,516
Net Flow	(383)	(406)	(591)	(369)	(196)	(327)	(99)	47	(174)	46	173	(70)	(2,348)
Cumulative Flow	(4,108)	(4,514)	(5,105)	(5,473)	(5,669)	(5,996)	(6,095)	(6,048)	(6,222)	(6,176)	(6,003)	(6,073)	—

FIGURE 7–1 CASH REQUIREMENTS FISCAL YEAR 1982

	NOV	DEC	JAN	FEB	MAR	APR	MAY	JUNE	JULY	AUG	SEPT	OCT	TOTAL
Sold Units—Memo	60	60	60	70	70	70	80	80	80	90	90	90	900
Collections	1,079	1,149	1,219	1,254	1,324	1,394	1,464	1,533	1,602	1,671	1,741	1,811	17,241
Other Revenue	—	—	—	—	—	—	—	—	—	—	—	—	—
Total Inflow	1,079	1,149	1,219	1,254	1,324	1,394	1,464	1,533	1,602	1,671	1,741	1,811	17,241
Build Units	60	60	70	70	70	80	80	80	90	90	90	100	940
Inventory													
Bulk	143	71	413	165	83	469	188	94	525	210	105	581	3,047
Components	270	270	270	315	315	315	360	360	360	405	405	405	4,050
Total Inv. Reg.	413	341	683	480	398	784	548	454	885	615	510	986	7,097
Salaries and Expenses													
DL	48	48	56	56	56	64	64	64	72	72	72	80	752
Mfg. D/H	40	44	45	48	49	52	53	54	57	58	62	62	624
Marketing	86	93	94	101	103	111	113	121	123	130	133	141	1,349
Support	69	73	74	78	79	83	84	88	89	94	95	96	1,002
Engineering	104	105	106	108	109	110	112	113	114	115	117	118	1,331
Finance and Admin.	19	22	22	23	23	26	26	27	27	30	31	31	307
Corp. and Genl.	35	36	36	37	42	42	43	43	44	44	45	46	493
Total Sal. and Exp.	401	421	433	451	461	488	495	510	526	543	555	574	5,858
Fixed Assets	42	42	42	42	42	42	42	42	42	42	42	42	504
Interest Exp.	61	59	56	56	54	50	50	47	42	41	37	31	584
Total Outflow	917	863	1,214	1,029	955	1,364	1,135	1,053	1,495	1,241	1,144	1,633	14,043
Net Flow	162	286	5	225	369	30	329	480	107	430	597	178	3,198
Cumulative Flow	(5,911)	(5,625)	(5,620)	(5,395)	(5,026)	(4,996)	(4,667)	(4,187)	(4,080)	(3,650)	(3,053)	(2,875)	

FIGURE 7-2 PROJECTED INCOME STATEMENT FISCAL YEAR 1980

	NOV	DEC	JAN	FEB	MAR	APR	MAY	JUNE	JULY	AUG	SEPT	OCT	TOTAL
Units—Memo	—	—	—	—	—	—	—	—	—	—	—	—	—
Revenue	—	—	—	—	—	—	—	—	—	—	—	—	266
Cost of Sales	—	—	—	—	—	—	—	—	—	—	—	—	375
Gross Profit	—	—	—	—	—	—	—	—	—	—	—	—	—
Operating Expenses													
Marketing	5	7	20	12	13	20	15	15	38	31	47	43	266
Support	7	12	21	27	30	32	34	38	38	42	46	48	375
Engineering	71	108	105	131	120	125	104	78	83	84	84	89	1,182
Finance and Admin.	10	16	10	16	10	10	10	10	10	11	11	12	136
Corp. and Genl.	22	22	32	22	22	22	32	26	26	26	32	26	310
Depreciation	9	9	9	9	9	9	9	9	9	9	9	9	108
Total Operating Exp.	115	165	188	208	195	209	195	167	195	194	220	218	2,269
Net Before Intr. and Taxes	(115)	(165)	(186)	(208)	(195)	(209)	(195)	(167)	(195)	(194)	(220)	(218)	(2,269)
Interest	—	6	8	11	13	16	19	21	24	27	30	33	208
Net Before Taxes	(115)	(171)	(196)	(219)	(208)	(225)	(214)	(188)	(219)	(221)	(250)	(251)	(2,447)

FIGURE 7–2 PROJECTED INCOME STATEMENT FISCAL YEAR 1981

	NOV	DEC	JAN	FEB	MAR	APR	MAY	JUNE	JULY	AUG	SEPT	OCT	TOTAL
Units—Memo	—	10	20	25	30	35	40	40	45	50	50	55	400
Revenue	—	209	418	523	627	732	836	836	941	1,045	1,045	1,150	8,362
Cost of Sales	—	100	200	238	285	333	380	380	428	475	475	523	3,817
Gross Profit	—	109	218	285	342	399	456	456	513	570	570	627	4,545
Operating Expenses													
Marketing	44	44	50	53	58	61	69	71	73	74	82	83	762
Support	49	52	53	53	57	57	58	62	62	66	67	68	704
Engineering	90	91	92	94	95	96	97	98	99	100	101	103	1,156
Finance and Admin.	12	12	15	15	15	15	16	16	18	19	19	19	191
Corp. and Genl.	26	27	27	28	28	32	33	33	33	34	34	35	370
Depreciation	14	14	14	14	14	14	14	14	14	14	14	14	168
Total Operating Exp.	221	226	237	243	253	261	273	280	285	293	303	308	3,183
Net Before Intr. and Taxes	(221)	(117)	(19)	42	89	136	183	176	228	277	267	319	1,362
Interest	37	41	45	51	55	57	60	61	60	62	62	60	651
Net Before Taxes	(258)	(158)	(64)	(9)	34	81	123	115	168	215	205	259	711

FIGURE 7-2 PROJECTED INCOME STATEMENT FISCAL YEAR 1982

	NOV	DEC	JAN	FEB	MAR	APR	MAY	JUNE	JULY	AUG	SEPT	OCT	TOTAL
Units—Memo	60	60	60	70	70	70	80	80	80	90	90	90	900
Revenue	1,254	1,254	1,254	1,463	1,463	1,463	1,672	1,672	1,672	1,881	1,881	1,881	18,810
Cost of Sales	540	540	540	630	630	630	720	720	720	810	810	810	8,100
Gross Profit	714	714	714	833	833	833	952	952	952	1,071	1,071	1,071	10,710
Operating Expenses													
Marketing	86	93	94	101	103	111	113	121	123	130	133	141	1,349
Support	69	73	74	78	79	83	84	88	89	94	95	96	1,002
Engineering	104	105	106	108	109	110	112	113	114	115	117	118	1,331
Finance and Admin.	19	22	22	23	23	26	26	27	27	30	31	31	307
Corp. and Genl.	35	36	36	37	42	42	43	43	44	44	45	46	493
Depreciation	26	26	26	26	26	26	26	26	26	26	26	26	312
Total Operating Exp.	313	329	332	347	356	372	378	392	397	413	421	432	4,482
Net Before Intr. and Taxes	401	385	382	486	477	461	574	560	555	658	650	639	6,228
Interest	61	59	56	56	54	50	50	57	42	41	37	31	584
Net Before Taxes	340	326	326	430	423	411	524	513	513	617	613	608	5,644

FIGURE 7–3 FINANCIAL MODEL—ASSUMPTIONS AND METHODS

Average Dealer Price = $20,900
Average End User Price = $34,500

Cost of Goods Sold	Systems 1–39	40–400	> 400
	Cost $10,000	$ 9,500	$ $9,000

Commission = 2% of collections (paid when collected)

Parts Cost

Category	1–39	40–400	> 400
Components	$4,900	$4,800	$4,500
Bulk	3,300	3,200	3,000
Total	$8,200	$8,000	$7,500

Payment Terms
 –Dealers pay us ⅓ in 30 days, ⅓ in 60 days, ⅓ in 90 days (average 60 days).
 –We pay our suppliers ⅝ in 30 days, ¼ in 60 days, ⅛ in 90 days.

Inventory Planning
 –To ship units in month n, they are built and tested in month n–1
 –For units *built* in month n–1, purchase components in month n–2
 –Buy bulk items quarterly for future requirements as follows:

buy in	*for build requirements in*
Dec.	Feb.–Apr.
Mar.	May–June
June	Aug.–Oct.
Sept.	Nov.–Jan.

Manpower Budgets
 –FY80 data is from departmental operating budgets for headcount, personnel costs, and other expenses.
 –FY81 is calculated as follows:

1. Direct Labor: first 39 units $1,100/unit built
                      40–40 units $1,060/unit built
                      >400 units $1,000/unit built

 but not less than Direct Labor in October of FY80.
 To calculate *headcount* from these $ figures:

   a. Allow Personnel cost perman (CPM) to increase by 15% annually for inflation (1.25%/mo.) from October FY80.
   b. Headcount = $\frac{(Direct Labor)}{CPM}$, but not less than October FY80.

2. All other departments: increase CPM by inflation factor (1.25% mo.). Increase headcount by following growth factors:

MFG O/H Labor	1.67%/mo.	(40%)
Marketing	8.3%/mo.	(100%)
Support	1.67%/mo.	(30%)
Engineering	.4%/mo.	(0%)
Fin + Admin.	4.2%/mo.	(50%)
Corp. + Gen.	1.67%/mo.	(20%)

PERSONNEL COSTS = CPM × HEADCOUNT

3. Increase Corp. + Gen. other expenses by 25% to cover variable compensation for executives and floor space growth. For all other departments other expenses increase 15% beyond FY80.

–FY82 calculated as above using October FY81 figures as basis

Capital Equipment
Budgets are projected for annual requirements and then spread evenly over 12 months for cash flow. Depreciation is straight line over 4 years.
Manufacturing

	1980	1981	1982
Plant	0	30	60
Equip.	120	120	360
	120	150	420

Interest Rate
Assumed 1%/mo. of total cash requirements

Debt
Assumed all cash requirements resolved by debt financing at above interest rate. Initial debt (going into FY80) is $475,000.

7.3 FINANCIAL MILESTONES

Initial Financing (August, 1979). The beginnings of the operation date back to November, 1978 when the proprietorship was started. As of August 7, 1979 the initial investment was formalized by the formation of the corporation and the establishment of the trust for the benefit of the corporation.

Venture Capital (May, 1980). Entry into the computer market with a full-scale product, delivered to end-users, supported by multiple applications will require an infusion of significant capital before the first prototypes are completed and sold.

First Prototype (July, 1980). The first working prototypes are due in July of 1980. At this point we can fully demonstrate the viability of our product to a customer, supplier, banker, or any other potential investor.

First Revenue (December, 1980). We are essentially a research and development company until the first sale is made. Significant debt financing from a bank will be available after we have earned revenue and quality receivables.

First Profitable Quarter (April, 1981). By holding support costs to a minimum, the calculated gross profit margin will enable us to show a profitable quarter as early as April of 1981.

Net Cash Inflow (August, 1981). The total investment requirement will continue to grow until our monthly cash outflow for all expenses is less than our monthly cash inflow from revenue collections. At this point, we would have demonstrated the financial viability of our company.

First Million of Surplus Cash (November, 1981). Before payback provisions for bank borrowings and venture capital, the operation should have available a cumulative capital surplus of $1 million by November, 1981.

New Investment Plans (May, 1982) . By continuing to borrow on assets and by generating a major cash surplus, our company will be in a position to consider a variety of new investment options by the middle of our third full year of operations. These investments can take the form of new products, better production facilities, or entirely new ventures.

7.4 FINANCIAL STRATEGY

Our financial strategy includes the introduction to venture capitalists who are willing to join our founder in a major new venture. At the point the venture capitalists are introduced, our founder will have invested more than $2 million in the research and development of the product, and in the management required to make the project successful. The total venture capital requirement, prior to reserves, is $2.5 million. (see Figure 7–4)

Bank financing continually increases from the point of first revenue to a peak of $4.3 million after three years. The actual schedule of bank borrowings is based on the following.

Asset	Borrowing Capacity
Receivables	75%
Material Inventory	33⅓%
Work in Process	—0—
Finished Goods	—0—
Fixed Assets	25%

We are not prepared to speculate on payback provisions, convertibles, warrants or other forms of financing until we have concrete proposals. Consequently, we have identified the potential cash inflow as Capital Surplus for purposes of planning and negotiation.

7.5 FINANCIAL CONTROLS

Budgets. One of our primary means of financial control is monthly budgets by department for personnel, expenses, and capital requirements. At the present time we have budgets for each department, and the total budget for the corporation for the first fiscal year ending October 31, 1980.

FIGURE 7–4 FINANCIAL MILESTONES AND INVESTMENT DOLLARS (Cumulative)

1980

	Prior	Nov.	Dec.	Jan.	Feb.	Mar.	Apr.	May.	Jun.	Jul.	Aug.	Sept.	Oct.	1980 Total
Total Cash Req.	.5	.6	.8	1.1	1.3	1.6	1.9	2.1	2.4	2.7	3.0	3.3	3.8	3.8
Trust Invst.		.6	.8	1.1	1.3	1.6	1.9	2.0	2.0	2.0	2.0	2.0	2.0	
Bank Loan Base		—	—	—	—	—	—	—	—	—	.1	.2	.2	
Venture Cap Req.								.1	.4	.7	.9	1.1	1.6	

Milestones: △ Initial Financing (Nov.) · △ Venture Capital (May.) · △ First Prototypes (Jul.)

1981

	Prior	Nov.	Dec.	Jan.	Feb.	Mar.	Apr.	May.	Jun.	Jul.	Aug.	Sept.	Oct.	1981 Total
Total Cash Req.	4.1	4.5	5.1	5.5	5.7	6.0	6.1	6.1	6.0	6.2	6.2	6.0	6.1	6.1
Trust Invst.	2.0	2.0	2.0	2.0	2.0	2.0	2.0	2.0	2.0	2.0	2.0	2.0	2.0	
Bank Loan Base	.2	.5	.8	1.0	1.3	1.5	1.6	1.8	1.9	1.9	1.9	2.2	2.3	
Venture Cap Req.	1.9	2.0	2.3	2.5	2.5	2.5	2.5	2.5	2.5	2.5	2.5	2.5	2.5	
(Capital Surplus)									(.3)	(.2)	(.2)	(.7)	(.7)	

Milestones: △ First Revenue (Dec.) · △ First Profitable Quarter (Apr.) · △ Net Cash Inflow (Aug.)

1982

	Prior	Nov.	Dec.	Jan.	Feb.	Mar.	Apr.	May.	Jun.	Jul.	Aug.	Sept.	Oct.	1982 Total
Total Cash Req	5.9	5.6	5.6	5.4	5.0	5.0	4.7	4.2	4.1	3.7	3.1	2.9	2.9	
Trust Invst.	2.0	2.0	2.0	2.0	2.0	2.0	2.0	2.0	2.0	2.0	2.0	2.0	2.0	
Bank Loan Base	2.4	2.7	2.7	2.9	3.2	3.2	3.4	3.7	3.8	3.9	4.3	4.3	4.3	
Venture Cap Req.	2.5	2.5	2.5	2.5	2.5	2.5	2.5	2.5	2.5	2.5	2.5	2.5	2.5	
(Capital Surplus)	(1.0)	(1.6)	(1.6)	(1.6)	(2.0)	(2.7)	(2.7)	(3.2)	(4.0)	(4.2)	(4.7)	(5.7)	(5.9)	

Milestones: △ First Million of Surplus Cash (Nov.) · △ New Investment Plans (Jun.)

Reporting against budget will be done through computer processing on an outside service bureau in conjunction with the automated general ledger. Conversion to computer processing is due by the end of December.

In addition to the operating budget, we have prepared a Corporate Cash budget which schedules cash requirements by month to control both total spending and the rate of spending.

Monthly Financial Statements. We have prepared statements (Balance Sheet and Operating Statement) for each month since August, 1979. These statements must be considered preliminary until the audit of the October year-end statements. During this process, we will establish, together with our auditors, methods of accounting to be used on future statements.

Audit. We have engaged Coopers & Lybrand as our certified public accountants for the initial year ending October 31, 1979, and for the first full year ending October 31, 1980. Independent audits will be a requirement for large-scale bank financing, for the public sale of stock, and possibly for other investment transactions, as well as for our internal control. The first audit report should be completed by January, 1980.

Financial Model. We have created a financial model on a national time-sharing service. The model allows us to project our financial assumptions over three years in terms of income statements and cash requirements. The model allows us to see the results of changes in assumptions, or to input additional facts as they become known.

The financial model continues to be our most important planning and control device. Successive iterations of the model have highlighted poor assumptions or omissions which we have subsequently corrected. Major update to the plan, and actuals compared against the plan, will be issued to the directors on a continuing basis.

8.0 Ownership Distribution

Nebur Engineering Corporation is totally owned today by the employees. Currently there are fifteen stockholders. Table 8–1 shows the status of the stock today. The 3,500 shares from the original issue, shown as "available" in Table 8–1, are planned for future key employees and as incentives for current employees. It is expected that this stock will be diluted for future equity offerings.

Table 8–2 shows the distribution of ownership by management levels, and Table 8–3 shows the distribution by function.

TABLE 8–1 OWNERSHIP STATUS

TOTAL ISSUES SHARES		50,000
Purchases	31,863	
Options	14,637	
TOTAL	46,500	46,500
Available		3,500

TABLE 8–2 OWNERSHIP DISTRIBUTION BY MANAGEMENT LEVEL

	OWN	*OPTIONS*	*TOTAL*
Steven Nebur	25,050	0	25,050
Top Management Team	3,832	7,668	11,500
2nd Level Management	2,332	6,168	8,500
Other Key Personnel	649	801	1,450
TOTAL	31,863	14,637	46,500

TABLE 8–3 OWNERSHIP DISTRIBUTION BY FUNCTION

	OWN	*OPTIONS*	*TOTAL*
General	26,050	2,000	28,050
Engineering	3,647	6,803	10,450
Support	833	1,667	2,500
Finance	883	1,667	2,500
Marketing	500	2,500	3,000
TOTAL	31,863	14,637	46,500

**THE CENTER FOR
ENTREPRENEURIAL
MANAGEMENT**
83 Spring Street
New York, N.Y. 10012
(212) 925-7304

Joseph R. Mancuso, President

Dear Reader:

For an analysis of how each of these three businesses fared in real life, write to:

> Dr. Joseph Mancuso
> The Center for Entrepreneurial Management, Inc.
> 83 Spring Street
> New York, New York 10012
> (212-925-7304)

and I will send you a free one-page summary of how well they actually performed. The plans are presented not to be judged as good or bad, but to show how business plans are prepared.

Looking forward to hearing from you.

Sincerely,

Joseph R. Mancuso

APPENDIX I

Overhead Slides Used in Mancuso's Seminar

Joseph Mancuso, the founder and president of the New York-based Center for Entrepreneurial Management, Inc., is a frequent speaker. One of his most popular seminars is entitled, "How to Develop a Business Plan That Rates an Eleven (on a scale of 1 to 10)." Consequently, we judged it useful to include the text of the overhead slides that he uses in this book. While of course these overheads need Dr. Mancuso's verbal explanations to be totally complete, many of them are self-explanatory. We have also included a description of the seminar, which will help the reader better understand the overheads.

HOW TO WRITE A BUSINESS PLAN THAT RATES AN ELEVEN (ON A SCALE OF 1 to 10)

Why Prepare A Plan?

The business plan is the heart of the heart of the raising capital process. If a lender or investor discovers you don't have one, they'll say something like, "Your deal looks pretty good but come back when you can show me your business plan."

No company ever raises money without this foundation document, and well managed companies who don't need capital prepare them for internal use. "If you don't know where you're going, any road will take you there." Trips go better when you rely on a roadmap and use road signs for secondary (not primary) direction.

What's Unique About This Seminar?

Joe Mancuso tells you how venture capitalists analyze business plans and avoids talking about how to bring the plan from a one to a nine, rather he concentrates on adding the right touches to take it from a nine to an eleven. Dr. Mancuso concentrates on the last five percent which will enable you to put the frosting on the cake. Remember, venture capitalists only invest in so-called "tens," all other plans are the brides-maids, never the brides.

Background

The material for the course is based on Mancuso's, and CEM's, two best sellers: *How to Start, Finance, and Manage Your Own Small Business,* and *How to Read and Write a Business Plan.*

Technique

You'll learn by doing, not only by listening. This program is action-oriented and you will analyze five different business plans and make your own investment decisions. Then you'll learn how investors analyze plans based upon your own experience. The five plans you will be analyzing are:

> BRIOX Technologies (Medical Equipment)
> BLT (Car Wash/Gas Station chain)
> American Laser, Inc. (an employee spin-off)
> InLine Technology (a custom machine builder)
> Perspective (a new magazine)

Who Should Attend

Established entrepreneurs, would-be entrepreneurs, managers of small business, bankers, lawyers, accountants, venture capitalists . . . This is the course that also attracts many "internal" entrepreneurial managers, those who work in someone else's garden—many of our graduates are training in some of the largest companies. (They tell us they need miracles just to break even!)

Course Highlights

This is a building-block program for entrepreneurs, and especially for established entrepreneurs on the brink of their first major expansion. In one of the most profitable sessions you'll ever spend, you learn the proven ways to get your venture off the ground; that's why it's our most repeated course!

Who is the entrepreneur? What makes him or her tick? If you're already established, how can you expand your present business? If you're thinking of becoming an entrepreneur, do you really have what it takes to be your own boss?

This is a unique forum designed to help you determine your own entrepreneurial potential. It includes a personal assessment of an individual entrepreneur's traits and how they compare to the traits of other entrepreneurs.

The entrepreneur's traits are combined with the business plan to determine the viability of a venture. And that's how miracles happen.

Key Topics

- How to determine your entrepreneurial potential.
- How to name a business.
- How to develop and read a business plan.
- How to approach sources of capital.
- How and when to employ professionals.
- Sources of help for entrepreneurs.

What to Learn

A Learn about the theory of the "Hockey Stick."
B Learn why investors use only five minutes to read your plan, even if it took you three years to write it.
C Learn to tailor your plan by following these 6 steps:
    1—The characteristics of the company and the industry
    2—The terms of the deal
    3—Reading the latest balance sheet
    4—Sizing up the people and the team
    5—How to put sizzle in the deal
    6—The plan's "once-over-lightly" treatment
D Learn how a "good" plan raises money—but how money alone does not ensure a profitable enterprise.
E Learn why investors bet on the management team and not the product or service
F Learn the appeal of an "answer sheet."

TAX SHELTERS

A) Traditional/Agressive
B) Recourse/Non-Recourse
C) Bottom Line/Top Line
D) Front-End Costs, 6 months: $25k–$50k
E) Bad movies up to 1976, MESBIC after 1977
F) Traditional
   Distribution
   Subscription
G) R & D
H) Lawyers
I) Abusive (Attorney General)

DEAL FLOW

1) SBA
2) National Bankruptcy Reporter (lawyers)
3) Merger and Acquisition Broker
4) WSJ
5) Venture Resources, Victor Nederhoffer,
   Business Brokers
6) First list of the First National Bank of Maryland
7) Connecticut State BAnk
8) Direct Mail:
   (a) Banks (b) Lawyers (c) Accountants

CUSTOMER FINANCING

A) Franchising — (Buy Back) WSJ (Thursday)
B) Direct Response
C) Facilities Management

H. Ross Perot— E.D.S.
IBM Salesman

3rd Year: $36M Sales
            9M Profit
            115 P/E

$20,000 himself
  5,000 mother

Eagles, Turkeys, Push-ups

SOURCES OF CAPITAL

1) Commercial Banks
    1a) SBA
2) Private & Corporate Venture Funds
3) S.B.I.C.s
4) M.E.S.B.I.C.s
5) Tax Shelters— R & D/Marketing/Other (Newsletter)
6) Grants (R&D)
7) Foreign Governments
8) Business Development Corporation
9) E.D.A.
10) FmHA
11) I.R.B.s & 502 Loans
12) Public Offerings
13) Asset-Based Lenders
14) Customer & Suppliers
15) Franchising
16) Pension Funds
17) Hidden Sources of Capital
    1) License
    2) Tax Refund

S.B.A.

1) Don't Pay Consultants
2) Seven (7) Year Loans
3) D/E = 1:3
4) Don't Bail Out Bad Loans
5) Direct/Bank
6) Politicians
7) Guarantees vs. Direct ($100M)
8) Small Business Prime
9) SBA Banks
10) Moratoriums
11) Direct Loans/Handicaps/Minority

WHAT'S HAPPENING

1) Raising Capital is the Art of Reducing RISK.
2) Raising Capital is the Art of Increasing CONFIDENCE.
3) Raising Capital is the Art of Reaching AGREEMENT.
4) While Raising Capital an Entrepreneur is Selling STOCK and Buying MONEY.
5) A Venture Capitalist is Selling MONEY and Buying STOCK.

Partial List of Questions to Ask a Venture Capitalist

1) List of past investments
2) Names & addresses of entrepreneurs
3) Most successful investment
4) Most unsuccessful investment
5) Nature of venture capital funds
   (A) SBIC   (B) non-SBIC
6) Length of partnership maturity
7) Length of time in business
8) Depth of pockets
9) Venture firms you like to team up with
10) Decision-making process within firm
11) Help in:
    (1) Public Offering
    (2) Overseas
    (3) Marketing
    (4) Personnel
    (5) Banks
12) Ability to access the limited partner
13) Why should we do the deal with you?
14) Type of investor:
    — passive,
    — active,
    — leader, or
    — follower

DESAT PROPOSALS RECEIVED AND WINNERS		
State	No of Proposals Received	Selected Winners
AL	18	1
AZ	10	0
CA	230	17
CO	23	2
CT	28	3
DC	10	1
FL	31	0
IL	12	1
MD	77	8
MA	142	21
ME	6	3
MI	29	2
MN	19	1
MO	10	1
MT	5	1
NH	7	1
NJ	51	3
NM	19	2
NY	81	2
NC	10	0
OH	47	6
PA	39	5
TX	24	3
UT	11	0
VA	63	10
WA	18	4
All Other States	83	0
Total	1103	98

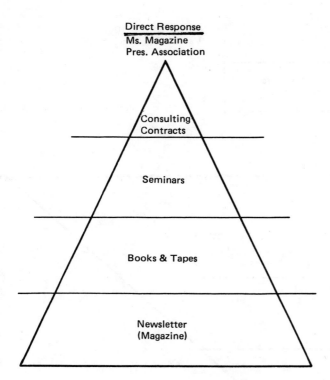

Direct Response
Ms. Magazine
Pres. Association

Consulting
Contracts

Seminars

Books & Tapes

Newsletter
(Magazine)

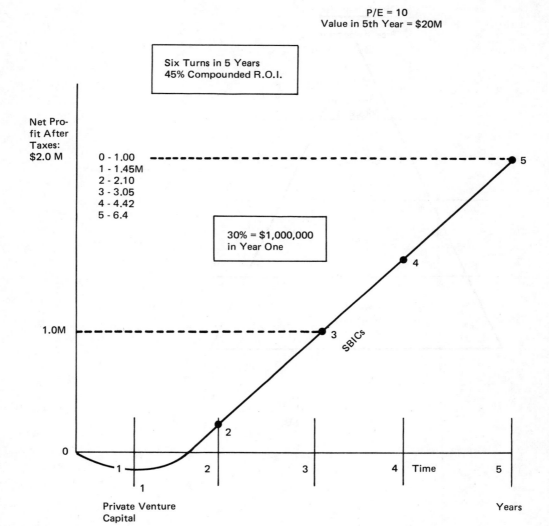

P/E = 10
Value in 5th Year = $20M

Six Turns in 5 Years
45% Compounded R.O.I.

Net Pro-
fit After
Taxes:
$2.0 M

0 - 1.00
1 - 1.45M
2 - 2.10
3 - 3.05
4 - 4.42
5 - 6.4

30% = $1,000,000
in Year One

1.0M

3

SBICs

4

5

2

0

1

2

3

4   Time   5

1

Private Venture
Capital

Years

Leveraged Buyout

Assets

Accounts Receivable	$ 800,000
Inventory	1,200,000
Fixed Assets	2,000,000
	$4,000,000

Accounts Payable	$ 600,000
Long-Term Debt	1,400,000
Total Debt	$2,000,000

Profit After Taxes $500,000

Selling Price: $3.5 M (1:1-1/2 book) or 7 x earnings)

Asset-Based Lender	Percentage	Traditional	Aggressive
Accounts Receivable	75%	600,000	800,000
Inventory	40%	300,000	600,000
Fixed Assets	75%	$ 1,500,000	$ 1,800,000
		$ 2,400,000	$ 3,200,000

Net Debt of $3.2 M @ 20% =	$640,000
	500,000
Annual Short Fall	$140,000

U.D.A.C.

A) $700 Million

B)   H.H.S.

C)   Mayor

D)   No Equipment or Working Capital

E)   30 Years — 3%

PUBLIC OFFERINGS

A) Public Shells —
           OTC Net
           W.S.J.
B) Penny Market (Denver)
C) Dime Market —
        First Jersey
        First Ohio
        First Albany
D) Dollar Market — Wall Street

Best Method of Discovering Growth Industries

    A) Newsletters

What to Do When the Venture Capitalist Turns You Down

1) <u>Confirm</u>: That means you don't want to participate in this round at this time?

2) <u>Sell for Future</u>: Can we count you in after we complete this financing for consideration of a second round of financing?

3) <u>Why Rejected</u>: Why were we declined at this time (timing, fit, all filled-up, etc.)

4) <u>Advice</u>: What would you do if you were me?

5) <u>Who</u>: Can you suggest a source who does these kinds of deals?

6) <u>Name</u>: Who should I see?

7) <u>Why</u>: Why do you suggest them?

8) <u>Introduction</u>: Who should introduce me?

9) <u>Excuse</u>: Can I tell him about your decision to turn us down because of _____.

10) <u>Referral</u>: What will you tell him when he calls?

A — What is the single most attractive financial packaging technique available to an entrepreneur to close a venture capital deal?

"You get all YOUR money back first."

---

1) Please list the single most important element in a business plan.
   A)   MANAGEMENT.

2) Please list the six-step process for presenting a business plan.

   1. Prospecting   4. Presenting the Plan
   2. Approach   5. Handling Objections
   3. Hot Button   6. Gaining Committment

3) What two elements bring a business plan from a range of 7 to 9, on a scale of 1 to 10, to an eleven?
   1. Answer the Negatives
   2. Answer Sheet
      2a) It's just like . . .
      2b) If it goes bad,
      2c) The other guys have deep pockets

4) Please list the six questions a venture source needs an answer to:
   1) What business are you in?
   2) How Much Money?
   3) For what percentage of the business? (Company Valuation)
   4) Who is in the deal?
   5) What's unique about this deal?

5) How Is a Business Plan Read?
   A) Determine the characteristics of company & industry
   B) Terms of the Deal
   C) Read Balance Sheet
   D) Caliber of People
   E) Find U.S.P.
   F) Once Over Lightly

6) Please Rank the Best Source of Linkage People to Introduce Your Deal to Venture Capital Sources.
   1) Entrepreneur in the Venture Portfolio _____
   2) Another Venture Capitalist _____
   3) Account Familiar with Venture Source _____
   4) Lawyer Familiar with Venture Source _____
   5) Banker Familiar with Venture Source _____
   6) Social Friend of Venture Source _____
   7) Blind Letter Sent to Venture Source _____
   8) Customer of Company Familiar with Venture Source _____
   9) Investor in Venture Capitalists' Portfolio _____
   10) Phone Source to Solicit Interest _____

7) Identify the Entrepreneurial Team
   (1) Partners (2) Lawyers (3) Accountants
   (4) Advertising Agencies (5) Consultants (6) Bankers
   (7) Board of Directors (8) Manufacturers' Agents (9) Controller

8) Summary Page Outline
   1) Percentage of Company Being Sold
   2) Price/Share—vs. last Price/Share
   3) Minimum Investment (Number of Investors)
   4) Total Valuation (after placement)
   5) Terms of Placement

8 1A) Common Stock
8 1B) Preferred Stock
8 1C) Debt with Warrants
8 1D) Convertible Debentures
8 1E) Subordinated Convertible Debt
8 1F) Straight Debt

Reading a Balance Sheet

   (1) Determine Liquidity
   (2) D/E Ratio
   (3) Net Worth
   (4) Examine Assets and Liabilities

INDEX

315